How to Organise and Operate a Small Business in Australia

You have an idea for a business, but you're not sure where to begin. Or perhaps you have made a start, but you're not sure what to do next. It's a common dilemma shared by everyone who has been down the same path. Where can I go for help? What are my legal obligations? How do I start making sales? How can I use digital marketing? How do I organise my operations? What's involved in employing staff? How do I handle my finances?

How to Organise and Operate a Small Business in Australia is your hands-on guide to running your own business. This new 12th edition contains information, skills, and ideas that are up to date, easy to understand, and simple to use. It reflects fundamental changes that have taken place as a result of the pandemic and the surge in small business digital technology. A feature of this new edition is a series of reflective exercises designed to help you evaluate your business ideas for their commercial potential.

Used by tens of thousands of Australians to become self-employed, this new 12th edition is the most comprehensive small business handbook in Australia. An essential read for anyone who wants to have a business of their own.

John English brings together a lifetime of business insight as an accountant, entrepreneur, and associate professor in entrepreneurship at the University of Tasmania. The simplicity and clarity of this book is a reflection of the author's ability to blend his academic expertise with years of practical first-hand business experience.

JOHN ENGLISH

How to Organise and Operate a Small Business in Australia

Turning Ideas into Success

12th Edition

Routledge
Taylor & Francis Group

LONDON AND NEW YORK

Designed cover image: © Getty Images

Twelfth edition published 2024
by Routledge
4 Park Square, Milton Park, Abingdon, Oxon, OX14 4RN

and by Routledge
605 Third Avenue, New York, NY 10158

Routledge is an imprint of the Taylor & Francis Group, an informa business

© 2024 John English

First edition published by Allen & Unwin 1981
Eleventh edition published by Routledge 2012

British Library Cataloguing-in-Publication Data
A catalogue record for this book is available from the British Library

ISBN: 978-1-032-67660-9 (hbk)
ISBN: 978-1-032-67659-3 (pbk)
ISBN: 978-1-032-67661-6 (ebk)

DOI: 10.4324/9781032676616

Typeset in Baskerville
by MPS Limited, Dehradun

Contents

Disclaimer   *ix*

Introduction   **1**

Part A   Preparing for Self-Employment

One   **The Self-Employment Decision**   **5**

The Power of Being Small • Diversity of Small
Businesses • Pros and Cons of Self-
Employment • Personal Characteristics and
Success • Management Skills and Experience
• Taking the Plunge • Risk of Failure
• Summary

Two   **Information and Assistance**   **20**

Choosing an Accountant • Choosing a Solicitor
• Finding a Mentor • Business Enterprise
Centre • Trade Association • Australian
Institute of Company Directors • Networking
• State and Territory Small Business Agencies
• Commonwealth Government • Training
Programs • Summary

Reflective Exercise: Why Do I Want to Be Self-Employed?   32

Part B Getting Started

Three Pathways into Business   51

Parallel Opportunities • New Market
Opportunities • New Product and New Service
Opportunities • Buying a Business • Buying a
Franchise • Starting from Scratch • Summary

Four Start-Up Nuts and Bolts   66

Legal Structure • What's in a Name? • Business
Registration Service • Licenses and Permits
• Insurance • Summary

Five Business Plan   79

Myths and Reality of Planning • Putting Your
Plan on Paper • Sample Business Plan
• Adapting to Change • Summary

Reflective Exercise: Evaluating the Risks   96

Part C Marketing Plan

Six Marketing Strategy   105

Understanding Your Customers • Customer
Information • Positioning Your Business
• Products and Services • Distribution
• Promotion • Pricing • Marketing Mix
• Summary

Seven   Traditional Marketing   119

Direct Marketing • Media Advertising • Writing
Advertising Copy • Publicity • Sponsorship
• Personal Selling • Summary

Eight   Digital Marketing   134

What Is Digital Marketing? • Do I Need a
Website? • Search Engines and Directories
• Email Marketing • Online Promotion • Social
Media • Mobile Marketing • Getting Help
• Summary

Reflective Exercise: Capturing the Target Market   149

Part D   Operations Plan

Nine   Operating Practices   159

Service Operations • Retail Operations •
Online Operations • Manufacturing Operations
• Summary

Ten   Location and Layout   173

Temporary Premises • Home-Based Business
• Retail Premises • Service Businesses
• Manufacturing Premises • Local Government
Regulations • Negotiating a Lease • Summary

Eleven   Employing Staff   189

Legal Framework • Designing a Job • Hiring
New Staff • Motivation and Performance • Staff
Turnover • Summary

Reflective Exercise: Creating a Smooth Operation   **202**

Part E   Financial Plan

Twelve   **Financial Information**   **209**

Paper Trail • Accounting System • Balance
Sheet • Income Statement • Financial Ratios
• Monitoring Performance • Summary

Thirteen   **Managing Liquidity**   **227**

Operating Cycle • Managing Accounts
Receivable • Managing Inventory • Managing
Accounts Payable • Managing Cash Flow
• Overcoming Problems • Summary

Fourteen   **Managing Profitability**   **243**

Cost Structure • Contribution Margin • Break-
Even Point • Product and Service Profitability
• Customer Profitability • Market Channel
Profitability • Monitoring Costs • Summary

Fifteen   **Financing and Taxation**   **255**

Borrowing Money • Leasing • Equity Capital
• Government Grants • Australian Taxation
System • Summary

Reflective Exercise: Financial Forecasts   **269**

Appendix: Assessing Commercial Potential   *272*
Index   *286*

Disclaimer

The information contained in this book is to the best of the author's knowledge true and correct. Every effort has been made to ensure its accuracy. The author does not accept any liability for any loss, injury, or damage caused to any person acting as a result of information in this book nor for any errors or omissions.

Introduction

A business is classified as a *small* business if it has fewer than 20 employees. In addition, a small business is typically financed, operated, and controlled by the owner. The Australian Bureau of Statistics reports there are over 2.5 million small businesses in Australia. About 2.3 million are classified as *micro* businesses with fewer than five employees. In fact, 1.6 million micro businesses have no employees at all. These figures not only demonstrate that the majority of small businesses are very small indeed but also that a huge number of Australians choose to be self-employed.

The small business sector has felt the impact of the pandemic for some time. It created shifts in consumer behaviour that represent risks for some businesses and opportunities for others. The surge in self-employment and the shift toward working remotely has revitalised interest in home-based businesses. New small business registrations are rising at an unprecedented rate. Small business operators are becoming younger, there are more females, and there are more from diverse cultural backgrounds.

How to Organise and Operate a Small Business in Australia is focused on readers who are contemplating having their own business and are looking for ideas and guidance. It provides a framework for helping you to decide if you want to be self-employed and how to find the information and assistance you need to get started. It is not just a book about going into business and getting paid for what you do; it also symbolises a set of values about how you want to live and how you want to be sustained by the work you do. The book is divided into five parts:

- Part A is about preparing for self-employment. It describes what is special about being small and the diversity of small businesses. The

DOI: 10.4324/9781032676616-1

pros and cons of going into business, the kinds of management skills and experience that you may need, and the sources of information and assistance are explained. A reflective exercise at the end of Part A offers some insights into why you may want to be self-employed.

- Part B is about the taking the initial steps to get into business. It explains how to look for business opportunities, the different pathways that lead into business, the nuts and bolts of getting established, and how to put together a business plan. A reflective exercise at the end of Part B helps you to evaluate the risks.
- Part C is about developing your marketing plan. It outlines a framework for establishing a marketing strategy, how to use traditional advertising and promotion methods, and how to engage in digital marketing. At the end of Part C is a reflective exercise to help you evaluate if you can capture your target market.
- Part D is about developing your operations plan. It examines operating practices in service operations, retail operations, online operations, and manufacturing operations. It also includes chapters on establishing premises and employing staff. At the end of Part D is a reflective exercise to help you evaluate what it will take to create a smooth operation.
- Part E is about developing your financial plan. It explains financial information and how it is used, how to manage liquidity, how to manage profitability, sources of capital, and how the taxation system works. At the end of Part E is a reflective exercise in which you can construct and evaluate your own financial forecasts.
- The end of the book contains an appendix. It draws together the results of the reflective exercises to help you assess the commercial potential of your business idea.

How to Organise and Operate a Small Business in Australia is dedicated to the reader who wants practical, commonsense information that is easy to understand and simple to use. Written in plain language, it emphasises the how-to techniques for navigating your way into a business of your own.

Part A
Preparing for Self-Employment

People get into a small business for a variety of reasons. Some are weary of being a cog in a large organisation and long for some freedom and independence. Others are looking for a way to make a living out of doing something they enjoy. A lot of people take the plunge in the hope of improving their financial circumstances. Part A focuses on how to go about making the decision to become self-employed and the sources of information and assistance that can help you along the way. It concludes with a reflective exercise that offers some personal insight into self-employment as a career choice.

DOI: 10.4324/9781032676616-2

One
The Self-Employment Decision

The individual who decides to become self-employed stands on the threshold of an exciting and rewarding part of life. It is a time to make decisions that will not only have an impact on the success of the business but also on the quality of the owner's life. The purpose of this first chapter is to help you decide if you want to become self-employed. We begin by explaining the power of being small and the kinds of choices that can be found in service businesses, online businesses, retail businesses, and manufacturing businesses. The pros and cons of self-employment, the personal characteristics that are associated with success, and key management skills and experience are fundamental considerations in making the decision to become self-employed. The reasons that finally lead individuals to take the plunge are as diverse as the businesses themselves. The chapter concludes with a frank discussion about the risk of failure.

THE POWER OF BEING SMALL

There are advantages to being small that big businesses cannot match. Customers want a genuine relationship with a local business and not some call centre in another country. Having a close relationship with your customers builds loyalty and trust. You have greater flexibility to make decisions and take action. It enables you to respond quickly to correct problems or respond to new opportunities. Although big businesses do have their strengths, a small business can use timeliness, flexibility, and personal attention more effectively than larger organisations.

DOI: 10.4324/9781032676616-3

Consumers

Consumers are the end users of products and services. Some consumer market segments represent attractive opportunities for a small business. Here are a few examples:

- Products and services that big business cannot afford to offer are great opportunities for a small business. These are generally businesses with limited economies of scale such as making products to order, offering a short delivery time, or frequent product and service modifications.
- Products and services that encounter significant fluctuations in demand such as seasonal variations, tourism, or sporting services. Small businesses can be more flexible than larger businesses in coping with high and low periods of activity.
- Products and services that provoke a great deal of customer loyalty and are effectively promoted by word-of-mouth recommendations. These include segments that have a strong group identity such as an ethnic group, religious affiliation, or special interest group.
- Products and services that place a very high value on specialist expertise. Inasmuch as specialist expertise is closely identified with the individual who provides it, this is fertile ground for small business opportunities.
- Products that include a very high proportion of services. Inasmuch as both technical services and personal services are difficult to mass produce or to mass market, products with a high service content make ideal small business opportunities.
- Products and services that are effectively promoted by personal selling rather than mass marketing and paid advertising represent opportunities for a small business.

Business and Government

There are opportunities in business and government that lend themselves to a small business. A big lift in sales and profits is the reward for a small business that can sign up just one major corporate customer or government department. Too many small business operators think this market is unreachable because they are small. The reality is just the opposite.

- Do you cost less? A small business has the advantage of low overheads and low operating costs. If you can provide a product or service for a better price, why wouldn't institutional customers be interested in saving money?
- Are you more flexible? A small business can adapt its product or service to fit the unique needs of business and government customers without the bureaucratic inflexibility of larger competitors.
- Do you have a specialised niche? A small business operator can be a highly sought-after expert in a speciality or niche market that cannot be duplicated by larger competitors.
- Are you always available? Your advantage over your competitors may be proximity. The best institutional clients to approach are the ones that are close by because you can have quick response times and low travel costs.
- Do they know you want the business? You can provide the customer service and personal attention they cannot get from larger suppliers. Why wouldn't a corporate or government client want to give you their business?

DIVERSITY OF SMALL BUSINESSES

The way in which you go about organising and operating a small business depends on whether the business you choose is a service business, an online business, a retail business, or a manufacturing business.

Service Business

A service business performs a task for the customer. The task generally requires specialised training, experience, or equipment. Service businesses are typically small because they only require a modest initial investment and depend largely on the skills of the owner. The services sector is an inexhaustible source of small business opportunities. Here are some examples:

- Personal services such as a hairdresser, photographer, tutor, pet groomer, wedding planner, fitness trainer, or music teacher.
- Maintenance services such as home or office cleaning, garden maintenance, appliance repairs, house painting, or pool maintenance.
- Professional services such as a pharmacist, architect, solicitor, insurance broker, veterinarian, or financial planner.
- Business services such as bookkeeping, consulting, training, advertising, graphic design, information technology support, or public relations.
- Counselling services such as weight loss, marriage counselling, career planning, or life coaching.
- Transport services such as a taxi, truck, bus, limousine, or car rental.
- Hospitality services such as a restaurant, cafe, caterer, takeaway, pub, hotel, motel, or bed and breakfast.
- Family services such as childcare, residential care, elder care, or health and wellbeing.
- Recreational services such as travel agent, miniature golf, tour guide, ski instructor, or dive instructor.

Service businesses tend to be local, so they do not have to contend with the national and international competitors that are common in retail and manufacturing. The recent growth in the small business sector has largely been the result of new service businesses.

Online Business

There are many advantages to starting an online business such as low start-up costs, the ability to scale up quickly, and the potential for global reach. Online technology has transformed the small business sector by offering new opportunities for traditional businesses as well as new businesses that are conducted entirely online. Online opportunities can be based on products, services, software, or information.

Practically any physical *product* can be sold online ranging from home and kitchen products, apparel, health and beauty care products, handicrafts, and more. They can be sold on your own website, in one of the popular online marketplaces such as eBay or Amazon, or through social media that are aligned with your business. You can also combine all three channels to sell your products online.

There are unlimited opportunities for an individual with skills to sell their *services* online. Examples include copywriting, content creation, website design, programming, advertising services, and graphic design. You are essentially selling your time and you can charge by the hour, by the day, by the completed project, or on whatever basis you and your client agree. Find a Freelancer at *fiverr.com* is a way to offer services online.

If you have the technical knowledge to create *software* products and web-based solutions, then these can be sold either as a complete package or on a subscription basis. Examples include software packages, mobile apps, games, and other downloadable software. The objective is to design and build the software once and keep selling it to many users. You can sell software products on your own website or through third-party platforms such as the Apple App Store or the Google Play Store.

Knowledge can be sold by packaging it in the form of an *information* product. Online courses, blogging, podcasts, eBooks, and webinars are examples. You can also create offerings by outsourcing the content using other experts in their fields. Online information businesses are the easiest to set up and the most cost-effective entry point for an online business. The key to success is quality and well-timed content.

Retail Business

A retailer buys goods from manufacturers, wholesalers, and importers and resells them to their customers. The retail sector has been going through tremendous changes both before and during the pandemic. Success for small retailers depends on finding a unique market niche and providing genuine value for customers.

Retailers have traditionally represented the final link in the distribution system for consumer goods including convenience stores, specialty stores, food stores, and consumer durables stores. Here are some examples:

- A *convenience store* is generally a small store with a limited number of product lines that are bought regularly. Examples include a newsagent, tobacconist, bottle shop, coffee bar, souvenir shop, confectionary, and the well-known corner store.
- A *speciality store* concentrates on a relatively narrow product line in which it focuses on depth of choice. Examples include florists, sporting goods, men's wear, women's wear and accessories, children's clothing, bookstore, pharmacy, garden shop, musical instruments, sewing supplies, party supplies, jewellery, shoes, gifts, baby supplies, office supplies, toy store, art supplies, butcher shop, and fishing supplies.
- A *food store* generally occupies a niche that is not catered for by the major supermarkets. Examples include a neighbourhood grocery store, organic food store, greengrocer, bakery, and ethnic food stores.
- A *consumer durables store* is focused on higher priced products that are not bought frequently such as household appliances and electronics. Household appliances include products like vacuum cleaners, dishwashers, air conditioning, washing machines and dryers, and furniture. Electronics products include music systems, televisions, cameras, computers, and mobile phones.

Not all retailers do business out of a shop. There are a variety of other retail channels including catalogues, mail order, the internet, vending machines, market stalls, and kiosks.

Manufacturing Business

A manufacturer either makes a product that is sold to consumers or a product that is sold to other businesses. Small manufacturers generally depend on a specialised market niche to prosper. They may choose to specialise in custom manufacturing, batch manufacturing, or continuous manufacturing. Here are some examples:

- In *custom manufacturing*, products are made to order for each customer. A single skilled individual or a small group of workers produce individual high-value products by hand or with specialised tooling. Examples include a boat builder, house builder, monument mason, or sail maker.
- *Batch manufacturing* generally consists of a single production line with the flexibility to make different products. It is also ideal for making products with fluctuating demand. The production line can be reconfigured between batches. Examples include a joinery, garment maker, furniture maker, cheesemaker, microbrewer, or a winery.
- A *continuous manufacturing* business is designed for high-volume production of a single product. Semiskilled workers complete each stage along a production line. Because of the high up-front investment, continuous manufacturing is generally associated with larger businesses.

PROS AND CONS OF SELF-EMPLOYMENT

Competition is an essential ingredient in the Australian business environment. It encourages businesses to be efficient. Customers will patronise efficient businesses rather than their inefficient rivals. The efficient firms flourish, and the inefficient ones do not. In this way, competition results in success and prosperity going to those firms that best serve their customers.

Engaging in competition means you must honestly face the fact that the operation of a small business is not an easy way to make a living. Before you make the decision to become self-employed, you should think seriously about some of the advantages and disadvantages of organising and operating a small business.

Advantages
- You can be your own boss, you can be independent, and you can exercise your own talents and capabilities.
- You will have the chance to make money, maybe even a great deal of money, and you will not be dependent on a fixed wage or salary.

- You will have the opportunity to achieve a feeling of personal worth, accomplishment, and recognition.
- You can develop your own ideas, products, and services.
- You will be able to work at something you enjoy by doing personally satisfying work and perhaps succeeding where others have not.
- You may achieve economic security for yourself and your family.
- You may be able to provide something of value to your community.

Disadvantages

- You can fail and lose your money as well as the money your friends or relatives may have invested in your business.
- Many small business operators work long hours, which means finding time for family and friends can be difficult.
- Your income may be uncertain, and sometimes it could fluctuate enormously as a result of factors you cannot control.
- You may face the unrelenting pressure of having to make decisions and solve problems when you are not sure what to do.
- You will still have a boss; in fact, you will have many bosses including customers, suppliers, government agencies, and your banker.
- You may eventually hate your business in the same way that other people hate their job, and you may find it difficult to get out of business without incurring a big loss.

PERSONAL CHARACTERISTICS AND SUCCESS

Small businesses are frequently in the hands of men and women who are the rebels of the business world. They have a highly developed sense of independence, or at least a strong desire to be independent. They have a strong sense of enterprise, or at least a desire to put their own ideas and capabilities to good use. And they often have a strong dislike of conformity and routine. Is there something about successful small business operators that makes them different from other people?

Research studies from all over the world have attempted to identify the personal characteristics that result in a successful small business operator. Although certain personal characteristics are found more frequently than others, it is simply not possible to predict future success based on them. Here are some of the personal characteristics that have been found to be associated with successful small business operators:

Drive and energy	Self-confidence
Long-term involvement	Persistence
Goal-setting	Sense of time
Moderate risk-taking	Dealing with failure
Using feedback	Initiative
Tolerating uncertainty	Using outside resources
Innovation	Assertiveness
Opportunity recognition	Ambition
Competitiveness	Independence
Resourcefulness	Determination
Task orientation	Optimism

There is tremendous diversity in the types of small businesses and even greater diversity in the characteristics and motives of the people who own and operate them. What really matters is how you feel about yourself and whether you think your personality is suited to the particular business you want to operate. The reflective exercise at the end of Part A will help you gain more insight into your personal characteristics and your motivation for becoming self-employed.

MANAGEMENT SKILLS AND EXPERIENCE

To be a successful small business operator, you need to wear many hats. A good knowledge of just one or two elements of business management is simply not enough. What you need before you can realistically contemplate organising and operating your own business is well-rounded management skills together with some hands-on experience in the line of business you want to enter. Management skills fall into three categories: marketing, operations, and finance. Within each category, the emphasis on particular skills depends on the nature of the business.

Marketing skills

Business location

Competitor evaluation

Market research

Marketing strategy

Product positioning

Store layout

Pricing and discounts

Credit terms

Sales forecasting

Product life cycle

Merchandising

Customer service

Distribution channels

Packaging and presentation

Personal selling

Advertising and promotion

Online marketing

Export marketing

Operating skills

Purchasing

Stock control

Service delivery

Plant and equipment

Recruitment and selection

Regulations and awards

Staff training

Supervising

Productivity

Quality control

Scheduling and workflow

Transport and freight

Computer systems

Negotiating

Problem-solving

Decision-making

Financial skills

Budgeting

Cash flow

Breakeven analysis

Banking relationship

Bookkeeping

Borrowing money

Leasing

Equity capital

Using an accountant

Financial statements

Ratio analysis

Debtor control

Creditor control

Cost control

Payroll

Goods and services tax

Income tax

Pay-as-you-go procedures

The best time to get management training is before launching into business. The best way to get experience is to work in the type of business in which you intend to become self-employed. A thorough preparation for self-employment is just as important as any other form of apprenticeship.

If you are already in business and some of your management skills are weak, you need to do something about closing the gap before it is too late. Finding the time to attend a training program may not be easy, and getting hands-on experience in another firm may not be practical. More expedient and effective alternatives may include employing people with complementary skills, taking on a partner with complementary skills, engaging an outside consultant or adviser, or seeking assistance from a Business Enterprise Centre or your state small business agency. Chapter 2 shows you where to look for sources of information and assistance.

TAKING THE PLUNGE

Individuals who are inspired to have their own business are usually looking for a lifestyle that enables them to have interesting, stimulating, and challenging work. They want control over their time, including the flexibility to take time off when they wish. Many prefer to work part time without the responsibility and stress of a full-time job. The reasons that finally lead people into their own business are as diverse as the businesses they enter. Do you see yourself in any of these examples?

- **Lifestyle choice.** Are you looking for a way to gain greater control over your work-life balance? Do you want to be autonomous, operate by your own rules, and have the freedom to decide when and where you will work?
- **Career change.** Do you have a distaste for wage slavery in a large company or public sector organisation? Do you yearn for something smaller, simpler, and more personally gratifying?
- **Home business.** Home businesses are popular among individuals who want to earn an income while staying close to home. Your reasons might range from needing to care for other family members to the convenience of not having to commute for work.
- **Retirement business.** A growing number of retirees are going into business. Most are baby boomers who want to continue to pursue a creative and productive way of life.

- **Intentional entrepreneur.** Are you the dreamer and the free spirit who has always wanted to have your own business? When you find the right business opportunity, you can test it by starting out on a small scale.
- **Accidental entrepreneur.** Have you been cast adrift in mid-career as a result of corporate or public sector restructuring? Are you looking for a way to use your talents, skills, and experience to set up your own business? Perhaps you were lucky enough to exit with a redundancy package to help you get started.
- **Limited job prospects.** Have you found yourself in a dead-end job with little chance of improvement? Some individuals consider starting a business out of necessity because their employment prospects are limited.

You will be ready make the self-employment decision when you are confident that you are doing it for the right reasons, you are motivated to give it your energy and attention, it is compatible with your personal circumstances, you have found the right business opportunity, and you have a sound plan for going into business.

RISK OF FAILURE

New evidence suggests that small business failure rates are not as high as once thought. In the past, all businesses that ceased operating were regarded as failures. However, it is becoming clear that only a few of these alleged business failures actually resulted in bankruptcy. The vast majority of discontinued businesses simply did not measure up to the owner's expectations and were either sold or closed.

Small business ventures that result in bankruptcy generally do so because they run out of money and stop paying their bills. Eventually, the creditors are forced to take action to protect the debts owed to them. The business is closed, the assets are liquidated, and the proceeds are used to satisfy some of the debts.

Small businesses that do not meet the owner's profit expectations are not strictly failures. These businesses simply lack the degree of success that justifies their continued operation. Nevertheless, they are weak businesses that could become failures if the owners do not cut their losses and abandon them. A number of studies have revealed that some businesses falter because the owner's motives are misguided.

- Some underestimate the commitment that a small business requires and the impact this commitment will have on their lifestyle.
- Some do not realise that along with the opportunity for financial independence is the risk of losing everything they own.
- Some dislike working with others, and it affects how they get on with their customers, employees, and suppliers.
- Some dislike bureaucracy and paperwork, but they find out it is a big part of their life as a small business operator.
- Some simply have a desire for creative freedom, but they learn that doing their own 'thing' doesn't always pay the bills.

There are other reasons why some small businesses eventually fall short of the owner's expectations and are abandoned.

- Some do not succeed because the owner relies on the advice of family and friends. The advice is generally offered with the best of intentions, but it can be coloured by a close personal relationship. Someone close to you does not want to tell you that your product is not up to scratch, your service is inferior, or your prices are too high. Family and friends are not likely to offer the kind of hard-nosed business advice you need.
- Some do not succeed because the owner gets worn out. It takes a serious commitment to working long hours to give a small business a good chance for success.
- Some do not succeed because they exert too much pressure on the owner's family. There can be a conflict between what is best for the family and what is best for the business. The two most sensitive issues are time and money, and there is never enough of either. To give both the business and the family the best opportunity to prosper, a small business operator needs to strike a mature balance between work and life pressures.
- Some do not succeed because the owner does not fully understand the nature of the marketplace. They may overestimate the

number of potential customers or underestimate the size and strength of the competition. Even when a good market exists, it is necessary to thoroughly understand what customers want to gain their patronage.

• Some do not succeed because the owner does not appreciate the importance of timely and accurate financial information. Financial information is the scorecard that tells us how well we are doing. This information is important for every business, but it is crucial for a new business.

Perhaps there is some comfort in knowing that the risk of small business failure is not as daunting as was once thought. Nevertheless, the risk of failure is real, and the evidence tells us that it is greatest during the first year or two of operation. We also know that there are many reasons for small business failures, but it is clear that the vast majority are caused by the owner's limitations rather than by outside influences. There is also an element of luck, which means that success can elude you no matter how carefully you do your homework.

You should carefully consider the consequences of failure before you decide to become self-employed. If you fail, you will lose some money, maybe even all of your money. You may feel bad because your self-esteem will be bruised. There may even be some lingering ill will on the part of former partners, suppliers, employees, or customers. Nevertheless, the independent small business operator is respected for what he or she is working to achieve. The individual who tries and fails is not finished. People learn from their mistakes and make a go of it the next time around.

SUMMARY

The purpose of this first chapter is to help you decide if you want to become self-employed. The power of being small is explained together with the kinds of opportunities that are found in service businesses, online businesses, retail businesses, and manufacturing businesses. A small business is not an easy way to earn a living, so the pros and cons of self-employment are considered. A great deal of research has been undertaken on what makes a successful small business operator, and some of the findings about the personal characteristics and key management skills associated with success are summarised. The reasons that finally lead people to take the plunge turn out to be as varied as the businesses they enter. The chapter concludes with a frank discussion about the risk of failure.

Two
Information and Assistance

Small business operators are often surprised to discover how much information and assistance is available. At the local level, these include choosing an accountant, choosing a solicitor, finding a mentor, and contacting your local Business Enterprise Centre. Other organisations that offer help include your trade association and the Australian Institute of Company Directors. State, territory, and commonwealth governments offer a variety of small business programs, and there is a central website where you can see what is available. To find information and assistance, you need to know where to look. The purpose of this chapter is to show you where to look.

CHOOSING AN ACCOUNTANT

An accountant can play an indispensable role in your business. Running a business is a big enough challenge without having to keep up with the constant changes in accounting, finance, and taxation. Most small businesses cannot afford to employ their own accountant, so they typically engage the services of an outside accounting firm. There are a variety of ways in which an accountant can help your business:

- Start-up advice about your business structure, help with your business plan, and getting your business registered with various agencies.
- Advice about setting up your accounting system including manual versus computerised accounting, cash versus accrual accounting, and establishing your chart of accounts.
- Preparing periodic financial statements including your income statements, balance sheets, and audit reports.
- Help with analysing your financial statements to identify problem areas and ways to improve your business.

DOI: 10.4324/9781032676616-4

- Preparing your tax returns and planning for pay-as-you-go, income tax, goods and services tax, fringe benefits tax, and capital gains tax obligations.
- Help with setting up management information systems for budgeting, cash flow forecasting, profit planning, credit control, and inventory control.
- Identifying sources of finance, assisting with loan applications, introductions to lenders and investors, and helping to present your case.
- Advice about buying or selling a business including valuation, due diligence investigations, and assisting with the negotiations.
- Personal financial advice for matters such as mortgages, income tax planning, and superannuation.

Finding an accountant with whom you can work comfortably and effectively may take a little digging. You are not just looking for someone to do your tax returns and statutory reports; you want someone who is prepared to be a key adviser to your business. Determine the scope of the services you want your accountant to deliver and then ask around for some recommendations.

- Ask your business friends and contacts what accounting services they have used and would they recommend their own accountant.
- Ask professionals who work with accountants like your solicitor and your trade association who they recommend.
- Ask small business support agencies such as your local Business Enterprise Centre or state small business agency for recommendations.

Draw up a shortlist of two or three candidates and arrange for appointments. Talking with more than one firm increases your chances of finding the one that suits your requirements and you will be better informed to negotiate the level of service you require and the fees you will pay. Ask what services they provide, how much experience they have with businesses like yours, and if you can talk with a couple of their other clients. Be sure you are dealing with a chartered accountant

(CA), a certified practising accountant (CPA), or a member of the Institute of Public Accountants (IPA). Compared with large international accounting firms, smaller accounting firms tend to specialise in small business clients, charge less for their time, and are more likely to give you direct access to an experienced partner when you need it.

You will be charged different hourly rates for work done by various staff in the firm depending on their seniority. Always ask for a written estimate of the cost before you sign up. Enquire if they offer a basic package of services for a fixed fee. This is usually the most cost-effective arrangement, especially if it includes provision for periodic reviews and advice. If your accounting system is compatible with the accounting firm's software, there is less work for them to do and so the fees should be lower. Periodically compare the fees you are paying and the services you are receiving with what other small business operators are getting.

When you find the right accountant, make maximum use of this major source of information and assistance. Be sure to see your accountant before you start or buy a business. Meet with your accountant personally and as frequently as you require. You can save time and money if you prepare for meetings by drawing up an agenda of the matters on which you need advice.

CHOOSING A SOLICITOR

Ask around for recommendations and make a note when the same name keeps cropping up. The solicitor you engage should be able to deliver a range of legal services including the following:

- Registration procedures
- Leases
- Legal structure
- Partnership agreements
- Contracts
- Employment agreements

- Conveyancing
- Warranties
- Litigation
- Liabilities and insurance
- Winding up

Be sure you are dealing with a solicitor who has training and experience in commercial law and is familiar with the problems of small business operators. Smaller legal practices often specialise in small business clients, charge less for their time, and you are more likely to see an experienced partner when you need it.

A solicitor should anticipate your legal needs, but they cannot do this unless you take them into your confidence and keep them informed about anything with potential legal implications. It is also important for your solicitor and your accountant to work together, so be sure to ask for a recommendation from your accountant.

FINDING A MENTOR

A mentor is someone with experience and knowledge who can advise and guide you on a range of business matters. Business mentors are coaches, not consultants; they do not take the place of your accountant or your solicitor. Instead, it's a relationship between you and a trusted individual with business experience who can guide you through making decisions, point out ways of improving your operation, ask you the tough questions, and encourage you to achieve your goals.

A business mentor is typically motivated by a desire to foster the development of individuals who want to go into business. They generally do so voluntarily. There are no risks in working with a business mentor. No one is going to tell you what to do or how to run your business. The objective of working with a business mentor is to gain fresh insights into your business through impartial, objective discussion and feedback. There are various ways in which you can benefit by working with a business mentor:

- Exploring options becomes easier when you have the counsel of someone who understands and shares your concerns.
- Having a business mentor motivates you and helps you concentrate your attention on the things that matter most.
- By focusing your time and energy, you may be able to achieve your goals more quickly.
- A business mentor may be able to point out business opportunities that you have missed.

- A business mentor can help you identify your strengths, weaknesses, opportunities, and threats.
- A growing business brings new challenges such as hiring staff, raising capital, and entering new markets. A business mentor can offer advice about best practice, caution against potential pitfalls, and help you to have confidence in your plans.
- The key role of a business mentor is to listen, stimulate, and challenge your thinking. This will help you develop ideas and arrive at solutions more quickly than doing it on your own.
- A business mentor can help you establish a business network by introducing you to people within your industry as well as other professionals.

Locating a business mentor will take some effort. Do you know anyone with the right skills and experience that you could ask to be your mentor? Your state or territory small business agency and your nearest Business Enterprise Centre have mentor matching programs. Your accountant and solicitor may also be able to help. There are some consulting firms that offer what they describe as 'mentoring' on a fee-for-service basis.

BUSINESS ENTERPRISE CENTRE

A Business Enterprise Centre (BEC) is a community-based, not-for-profit, small business assistance organisation. Through their partnership with commonwealth and state governments, private enterprise, and local communities across Australia, BECs provide low-cost, practical, confidential business facilitation services. They have offices in every state and territory. BEC services vary from one location to another, so it is wise to check with your local office to determine what services are available. The kinds of services they offer include the following:

- Literature and publications on a variety of topics including commonwealth, state, and local legislation that may affect your business

- Business analysis such as feasibility analysis, business planning, or advice on purchasing a business
- Training programs including starting a business, financial management, recordkeeping, marketing, business planning, customer service, and social media for business
- Business referrals for local accountants, solicitors, marketing consultants, insurers, tax consultants, and financial planners
- Government grants and assistance including state, territory, and commonwealth programs
- Business networking in which local businesses meet with each other at workshops and other events to share experiences, develop alliances, and establish local connections
- Mentoring support for start-ups as well as established small businesses

A BEC understands local issues, so they are capable of providing the kind of assistance that is relevant to your local community. If the expertise you need is not available at your local BEC, they can call on colleagues in other BECs for help. Most BECs produce a regular newsletter that keeps you up to date with business news and events in the local business area. To learn more about your local BEC, visit their website at *becaustralia.org.au*.

TRADE ASSOCIATION

A trade association consists of people who are engaged in the same or similar types of business. These organisations tend to be the best source of industry-specific information and assistance. There are hundreds of trade associations in Australia. To locate one for your line of business, do an internet search or ask your state small business agency. When you find the right trade association, join it and take advantage of all the information and assistance that it provides. Most trade associations hold regular meetings where you can meet with others in the trade to discuss matters of common interest.

Don't be intimidated when you discover that your competitors are also members of the same trade association. Getting to know who they are can be useful. Also, most of them won't be direct competitors because they are operating in other locations. They are facing the same types of problems that you face and they are likely to share what they have learned. Membership of a trade association also helps you make other contacts. For example, suppliers usually advertise and promote themselves through trade association publications and they often attend trade association events.

AUSTRALIAN INSTITUTE OF COMPANY DIRECTORS

The Australian Institute of Company Directors (AICD) is the professional organisation for company directors in Australia. It provides leadership on company director issues, promotes excellence in corporate governance, and provides company director education and development programs. The AICD runs the *Company Directors Course* and publishes *Company Director* magazine. You can visit their website at ***aicd.com.au***. The national office is in Sydney and there are offices in each state and territory capital city. If you intend to be a company director, then joining the AICD will help you prepare for the role.

NETWORKING

Networking is the process of developing personal contacts through professional associations and other organisations such as Rotary, Kiwanis, or Lions clubs. It can be time well spent, but it takes time out of your schedule and money out of your pocket, so you want to be selective about which organisations you join. When you do decide to join one, you will get more out of it by being an active member rather than just reading the newsletter.

Prepare for networking meetings by having a brief, succinct description about what you do. It's a bit like speed dating in the sense that you typically have only a minute or two to get someone's attention and to explain what it is you do. Make sure you always have a supply of business cards. You also need to listen to learn about the other person's business and what they do. A network of personal contacts will eventually prove to be enormously valuable, not only in terms of information and assistance but also as a source of potential sales.

STATE AND TERRITORY SMALL BUSINESS AGENCIES

Small business agencies operate in all states and territories. Their activities have drifted away from providing direct counselling and advice and more toward online portals, publications, and referrals to other government departments and related organisations such as a BEC. There are not many grants available for starting a business. The grants that are offered are generally competitive and they may only be available for specific purposes. Visit the website for your state or territory to see what help and assistance they offer.

Australian Capital Territory	***act.gov.au/business***
New South Wales	***smallbusiness.nsw.gov.au***
Northern Territory	***nt.gov.au/industry***
Queensland	***business.qld.gov.au***
South Australia	***business.sa.gov.au***
Tasmania	***business.tas.gov.au***
Victoria	***business.vic.gov.au***
Western Australia	***smallbusiness.wa.gov.au***

COMMONWEALTH GOVERNMENT

There are scores of commonwealth government programs for small business operators including information, advice, counselling, subsidies, loans, and grants. Some government agencies are mainly concerned with regulation and compliance, so their assistance is usually aimed at helping you to follow their rules. It is incredibly difficult to keep tabs on all of the commonwealth government programs as they ebb and flow with the political and economic tide. One way of finding your way around the labyrinth of government agencies is to use the information service they have put into place that helps you find the right contact. The website ***business.gov.au*** makes it easy to find and contact all levels of government including commonwealth government agencies, state and territory government agencies, and other organisations of interest to small business operators. Here are the websites for some of the commonwealth government programs that you may find useful:

- The Advisor Finder website at ***business.gov.au/expertise-and-advice*** is a search tool that helps you find advisers and experts according to your interests and location. You enter your postcode and select the type of advice you are looking for, and the search tool will list all of the local providers that meet your criteria with their contact details.
- The Australian Business Licence and Information Service (ABLIS) website at ***ablis.business.gov.au*** provides a one-stop service for licences, permits, approvals, and registrations from all three tiers of government. The ABLIS website not only identifies what you require but also enables you to download forms and other information. This is an enormous help in complying with the red tape involved in obtaining licenses, permits, approvals, and registrations. However, you may want to seek advice before you complete and submit some of the forms.
- The Australian Small Business and Family Enterprise Ombudsman website at ***asbfeo.gov.au*** has many useful resources, tools, and sources of information to assist and support small businesses and family enterprises. They also help small businesses and family enterprises to resolve disputes involving other businesses or commonwealth government agencies.
- The Workforce Australia website at ***workforceaustralia.gov.au*** has a self-employment assistance program for new starters and existing businesses. It offers workshops, business plan development, small business training, advice, and small business coaching. You may be eligible for financial support as part of small business coaching.
- The AusIndustry Outreach Network website at ***business.gov.au/expertise-and-advice/ausindustry-outreach-network*** provides a number of assistance programs to help Australian businesses to become more successful and internationally competitive. They have offices in all the capital cities and some regional areas with

local experts who can work with you to provide targeted support and guidance.

- The Online website at **_business.gov.au/online_** features tools to help you learn about the benefits of going digital, setting up a website, buying and selling online, social media for business, and cybersecurity. The Digital Solutions program through the Australian Small Business Advisory Services offers advice specific to your business such as how digital tools can help your business, websites and selling online, social media and digital marketing, using small business software, and online security and data privacy.
- The AusTender website at **_tenders.gov.au_** contains commonwealth government business opportunities and annual procurement plans. By registering your area of interest in your AusTender profile, you will receive automatic notification via email of the latest opportunities. Each state and territory government also has their own website that lists available tenders.
- GrantConnect is a website that makes it easy to find commonwealth, state, and territory government grants for individuals, businesses, and community projects. The GrantConnect website at **_grants.gov.au_** lists scores of grant programs under several headings including business and industry.
- The Australian Competition and Consumer Commission (ACCC) website at **_accc.gov.au_** provides information about franchising, advertising and selling, country-of-origin requirements, anti-competitive practices, unconscionable conduct, consumer protection, product safety and liability, and collective bargaining. There are also consumer affairs agencies in each state and territory.
- The Fair Work Ombudsman website at **_fairwork.gov.au_** provides up-to-date information about employment matters such as rates of pay, awards, conditions, leave, termination, complaints, and other employment issues.
- The Safe Work Australia website at **_safeworkaustralia.gov.au_** has information about health and safety and workers compensation arrangements. State and territory agencies are also responsible for promoting and enforcing state legislation for workers compensation and occupational health and safety.

- The Australian Taxation Office (ATO) website at **ato.gov.au** covers a wide range of topics including income tax, goods and service tax, capital gains tax, and fringe benefits tax. There is a special section to help small business operators comply with the tax law. Each state and territory also has their own revenue office that is responsible for collecting state taxes such as stamp duty and payroll tax.

- In addition to AusIndustry, there are two government agencies that provide information and assistance for importers and exporters. The Australian Trade Commission (Austrade) website at **austrade.gov.au** covers a range of services to help Australian businesses win overseas business. The Australian Border Force website at **abf.gov.au** has a section that is mostly concerned with regulation and compliance for clearing goods for import or export and for collecting customs duties and excise taxes.

- The Australian Bureau of Statistics (ABS) is Australia's official statistical organisation. On the ABS website at **abs.gov.au**, you can find out what is available and how to download or order reports and other services. Much of the ABS information can be downloaded for free. Each capital city office has an information service to answer inquiries about what information is available and how it can be accessed.

- The Australian Securities and Investments Commission (ASIC) regulates companies and financial services providers in Australia to protect consumers, investors, and creditors. The ASIC website at **asic.gov.au** provides information about director's duties, company registrations, records of company office holders, and consumer protection for financial products and services.

- IP Australia is the commonwealth government agency that administers intellectual property rights including patents, trademarks, design registration, and plant breeder's rights. In addition to direct services, the IP Australia website at **ipaustralia.gov.au** also has information to help you learn about intellectual property and how to use it.

TRAINING PROGRAMS

There are a variety of small business education and training programs throughout Australia. They include informal discussion groups, one-day workshops, part-time courses, and formal full-time courses. Some programs can be undertaken through home study or online. Your state small business agency or local BEC can tell you about small business programs in your local area. If you are a new starter, you may want to look for a basic course that covers all of the important aspects of small business management. If you are already in business, you may prefer to look for short seminars on topics that currently concern you. Visit *training.com.au* for the range of vocational education and training information, products, and services in Australia. It is a gateway to many other websites and services. If you are interested in more formal training, visit *training.gov.au*, which is the register of the Vocational Education and Training (VET) sector for nationally recognised training packages and the organisations approved to deliver them.

SUMMARY

This chapter explains where to look for small business information and assistance. At the local level, these include choosing an accountant, choosing a solicitor, finding a mentor, and contacting the nearest Business Enterprise Centre. Other organisations that can help are your trade association and the Australian Institute of Company Directors. Networking is part of being in business and it can be enormously valuable in terms of information and a source of potential sales. There are numerous small business information and assistance programs offered by state, territory, and commonwealth governments and the website at *business.gov.au* can help you sort through what is available. Small business education and training programs are offered throughout Australia ranging from short seminars and workshops to more formal training.

Reflective Exercise: Why Do I Want to Be Self-Employed?

The purpose of this reflective exercise is to enable you to gain an insight into self-employment as a potential career choice. Achieving success in business is much easier for some people than it is for others. This exercise will help you reflect on your personality and reach your own conclusions about self-employment. If you are not clear about your strengths or what direction to pursue, then using this tool will help you take a fresh look at your natural capabilities and how they might be used to pursue a small business opportunity.

Exercises like this are always subject to some degree of uncertainty. If you feel strongly that this one has incorrectly assessed some aspect of your personality, then you are probably right. Nevertheless, what these questions can do is help you discover things about yourself that you may not have previously recognised. Use the answer sheet on page 42 to record your answers. Each question has two responses. Tick the box for the response that best reflects your feelings. When you are finished with the questions, turn to the feedback on the results.

1. Do you
   a. usually offer your unsolicited opinions?
   b. only offer your opinion if asked?
2. Would you prefer the atmosphere in your business to be
   a. one big, happy family?
   b. strictly business?
3. Are you inclined to
   a. get involved in too many projects at once?
   b. make sure that you do not get overextended?

DOI: 10.4324/9781032676616-5

4. Do you find yourself using your imagination
   a. occasionally?
   b. often?
5. Are you usually
   a. comfortable with making plans?
   b. impatient with making plans?
6. Are you more likely to
   a. keep the promises you make to yourself?
   b. not keep the promises you make to yourself?
7. Is being able to live in a particular community
   a. very important to you?
   b. not important to you?
8. Is competing and winning
   a. not very important to you?
   b. important to you?
9. Is building your business around a specific skill or technical area
   a. not important to you?
   b. very important to you?
10. Would you be more likely to
    a. risk your lifestyle to start a promising venture?
    b. pass up a promising venture to protect your lifestyle?
11. Do you tend to find yourself doing most of the
    a. talking?
    b. listening?
12. Would you be best described as a
    a. sentimental person?
    b. calculating person?
13. Do you tend to
    a. leave things unresolved for a while?
    b. look for quick resolution of issues?
14. Do you think that you would run your business in a more
    a. conventional manner?
    b. unconventional manner?

15. When you go into business, will you have a
    a. detailed plan for getting started?
    b. a rough plan for getting started?
16. Do you tend to
    a. find it easy to finish the things that you begin?
    b. have some difficulty in finishing some things?
17. Is work that is free from organisational restrictions
    a. moderately important to you?
    b. very important to you?
18. Has the real challenge in your life been to
    a. develop an overall lifestyle?
    b. confront and solve problems?
19. Is becoming a business manager
    a. your main career goal?
    b. only a means to becoming self-employed?
20. Have events in your life been mostly determined by
    a. yourself?
    b. forces outside your control?
21. Do you tend to
    a. mix easily in a group?
    b. not mix easily in a group?
22. In making business decisions, would you take
    a. people into account most?
    b. facts into account most?
23. Would you tend to run your business with a
    a. flexible approach?
    b. decisive approach?
24. Would you be more likely to run your business
    a. in a tried or proven manner?
    b. in an untried or experimental manner?
25. Are you a person who
    a. plans in advance?
    b. waits until the last minute?

26. Do you think you are
    a. very motivated?
    b. moderately motivated?
27. Is a business that provides you with complete financial security
    a. extremely important to you?
    b. moderately important to you?
28. Is a successful business worthwhile
    a. only if it enables you to lead your life in your own way?
    b. even if you have to make some changes to your lifestyle?
29. Is pursuing your particular trade or specialty
    a. not as important to you as general management?
    b. more important to you than general management?
30. Are you more likely to
    a. do whatever it may take to finish a job?
    b. apply only a reasonable amount of effort to finish a job?
31. In a group, do you tend to be more of
    a. an organiser?
    b. a participator?
32. Would you prefer your staff to have personalities that are
    a. warm and gentle?
    b. formal and businesslike?
33. Would you prefer to run your business in a
    a. flexible and spontaneous manner?
    b. planned and controlled manner?
34. Would you consider yourself to be more
    a. practical?
    b. creative?
35. If you wanted to buy a used car, would you talk it over with a
    a. motor mechanic?
    b. a few of your friends?
36. Have you
    a. made some progress toward achieving your goals?
    b. not yet made much progress toward achieving your goals?

37. Is a business that will give you long-term job stability
    a. very important to you?
    b. only moderately important to you?
38. Is choosing and maintaining a certain lifestyle
    a. more important than success in business?
    b. less important than success in business?
39. Is a management role in which you can supervise other people
    a. very important to you?
    b. not important to you?
40. In running your business, would you place more emphasis on
    a. looking for new business opportunities?
    b. developing existing business opportunities?
41. Are you a person with a
    a. considerable amount of social charm?
    b. modest amount of social charm?
42. Would you be best described as
    a. emotional?
    b. logical?
43. Would you prefer to run your business with a
    a. spontaneous approach, keeping your options open?
    b. predictable and controlled approach?
44. When you perform a task, do you like to
    a. do it in the usual way?
    b. try to find another way?
45. When you begin a project, do you
    a. plan it out first?
    b. work it out as you go along?
46. Do you
    a. usually complete things on time?
    b. often run out of time?
47. Is work that permits you to have complete freedom
    a. moderately important to you?
    b. very important to you?

48. Is working on tough problems
    a. not usually enjoyable for you?
    b. almost always enjoyable for you?
49. Is working in your trade or specialty for your entire career
    a. not important to you?
    b. very important to you?
50. Do you have a
    a. considerable amount of self-confidence?
    b. moderate amount of self-confidence?
51. Would you describe yourself as more
    a. outgoing?
    b. reserved?
52. When you make decisions, do you tend to use
    a. your feelings?
    b. facts and logic?
53. Does your thinking tend to be more
    a. unstructured and free?
    b. structured and focused?
54. Is the most important quality that you will bring to your business
    a. practical experience?
    b. a vision of the future?
55. If you had to plan an office party, would it be
    a. enjoyable?
    b. a burden?
56. Do you consider yourself a
    a. person who gets things done?
    b. bit of a procrastinator?
57. In your working life, have you been mostly concerned about
    a. security and stability?
    b. your own sense of freedom?
58. Is giving equal weight to your family life and your business life
    a. very important to you?
    b. moderately important to you?

59. Is being a business manager
    a. more important than your trade or specialty?
    b. less important than your trade or specialty?
60. Is having friends and business associates
    a. very important to you?
    b. only moderately important to you?
61. Are you
    a. always willing to try something new?
    b. reluctant to try something new until you understand it first?
62. Are you more inclined to be a
    a. warm and understanding person?
    b. firm but fair person?
63. Are you usually
    a. open to the views of others?
    b. not easily influenced by others?
64. When you were in school, did you do better at
    a. practical subjects?
    b. theoretical subjects?
65. Does success in business depend mostly on
    a. planning?
    b. a lucky break?
66. Are you a person with a bit
    a. more than average initiative?
    b. less than average initiative?
67. Is a business that provides you with lifetime employment
    a. very important to you?
    b. not important to you?
68. Is competing and winning
    a. not an important part of your life?
    b. the most exciting part of your life?
69. Do you want to be a manager
    a. as soon as you possibly can?
    b. only if it is in your area of expertise?

70. Do you think that you would be best at
    a. developing new products or services?
    b. refining existing products or services?
71. Are you more likely to
    a. act spontaneously?
    b. think about something before acting?
72. As a boss, would you tend to
    a. get upset by disagreements?
    b. not get upset by disagreements?
73. Do you like to work in
    a. an environment that is constantly changing?
    b. a more predictable environment?
74. When you think about the future, do you rely mostly on
    a. known facts?
    b. your intuition?
75. Do you usually
    a. plan your day in advance?
    b. wait to see what happens first?
76. If it was late at night and you were tired, would you be more likely to finish a job
    a. that night?
    b. the next day?
77. Is living in one particular place and not having to move
    a. very important to you?
    b. not important to you?
78. Is a business that permits you to pursue your own lifestyle
    a. very important to you?
    b. only moderately important to you?
79. Is being in charge of a business organisation
    a. very important to you?
    b. not important to you?
80. Do you usually
    a. feel comfortable taking moderate risks?
    b. avoid situations in which you have to take risks?

81. Do you have a tendency to react
    a. quickly according to your 'gut' reaction?
    b. only after you know all of the details?
82. In making business decisions, is it more important to
    a. consider the feelings of everyone concerned?
    b. make logical and objective decisions that are not influenced by other people's feelings?
83. Do you
    a. feel comfortable when you are involved in many projects at once?
    b. prefer to finish one project before starting another?
84. Would you describe yourself as more
    a. practical?
    b. imaginative?
85. When you have to do several things, do you
    a. make a list first and then do them one at a time?
    b. attack them all simultaneously or in no particular order?
86. Do you
    a. like to get things done ahead of time?
    b. usually put things off until they have to be done?
87. The thing you care about most in your working life is
    a. security?
    b. freedom?
88. Does being constantly confronted by problems or competitive situations
    a. depress you?
    b. excite you?
89. If you had less time for your specialty and you were forced to spend more time in general management, would you
    a. be just as happy?
    b. possibly sell your business?
90. Would you prefer a business venture with
    a. higher risk and greater possible rewards?
    b. lower risk and smaller guaranteed rewards?

91. Are you the sort of person who
    a. is easy to get to know?
    b. reveals yourself slowly to others?
92. Do you think that you would be a
    a. sympathetic boss who gets involved with your staff?
    b. firm boss who does not get involved with your staff?
93. Would you describe yourself as more
    a. flexible?
    b. firm?
94. Do you like doing things in
    a. tried and proven ways?
    b. new and different ways?
95. Have you
    a. established your goals for the next five years?
    b. focused mainly on the initial steps toward establishing your goals?
96. Do you
    a. like to set your own deadlines?
    b. dislike deadlines, even if you set them yourself?
97. Is the need to plan and organise your own work
    a. moderately important to you?
    b. very important to you?
98. In getting your business off the ground, would you
    a. not be prepared to spend much time away from your family?
    b. be prepared to spend time away from your family?
99. Is the process of supervising and managing people
    a. very important to you?
    b. not important to you?
100. Would you prefer to
    a. be your own boss with no guarantee of success?
    b. have a guaranteed career as a manager in a big company?

ANSWER SHEET

	1	2	3	4	5	6	7	8	9	10
a	□	□	□	□	□	□	□	□	□	□
b	□	□	□	□	□	□	□	□	□	□

	11	12	13	14	15	16	17	18	19	20
a	□	□	□	□	□	□	□	□	□	□
b	□	□	□	□	□	□	□	□	□	□

	21	22	23	24	25	26	27	28	29	30
a	□	□	□	□	□	□	□	□	□	□
b	□	□	□	□	□	□	□	□	□	□

	31	32	33	34	35	36	37	38	39	40
a	□	□	□	□	□	□	□	□	□	□
b	□	□	□	□	□	□	□	□	□	□

	41	42	43	44	45	46	47	48	49	50
a	□	□	□	□	□	□	□	□	□	□
b	□	□	□	□	□	□	□	□	□	□

	51	52	53	54	55	56	57	58	59	60
a	□	□	□	□	□	□	□	□	□	□
b	□	□	□	□	□	□	□	□	□	□

	61	62	63	64	65	66	67	68	69	70
a	□	□	□	□	□	□	□	□	□	□
b	□	□	□	□	□	□	□	□	□	□

	71	72	73	74	75	76	77	78	79	80
a	□	□	□	□	□	□	□	□	□	□
b	□	□	□	□	□	□	□	□	□	□

	81	82	83	84	85	86	87	88	89	90
a	□	□	□	□	□	□	□	□	□	□
b	□	□	□	□	□	□	□	□	□	□

	91	92	93	94	95	96	97	98	99	100
a	□	□	□	□	□	□	□	□	□	□
b	□	□	□	□	□	□	□	□	□	□

FEEDBACK

The questions in this exercise are designed to help you reflect on self-employment as a career choice. They provide a snapshot across ten dimensions of your personality.

Extroversion

Count the number of 'a' boxes that you ticked in the column beginning with question 1 on the answer sheet. A score of 7–10 indicates that you have an *extroverted* personality. A score of 0–3 indicates that you have an *introverted* personality. A score of 4–6 indicates no clear tendency between extroversion and introversion.

Success in organising and operating a business is highly correlated with an individual's tendency toward extroversion. Extroverted individuals are sociable, active, occasionally impulsive, and enjoy working with people. They draw their energy from others, and their charm and charisma help them gain support from customers, staff, and suppliers. Introverted individuals are territorial, reflective, hesitant and prefer to work alone. They find it difficult to develop the kind of interpersonal relationships that attract customers, motivate staff, and encourage suppliers to look after them.

Decision-Making

Count the number of 'b' boxes that you ticked in the column beginning with question 2 on the answer sheet. A score of 7–10 indicates that you are a *rationalist* decision-maker. A score of 0–3 indicates that you are a *humanist* decision-maker. A score of 4–6 indicates no clear tendency one way or the other.

To achieve success in a business of your own, you need to be able to make rational decisions. Rational decision-makers generally make logical decisions based on the facts rather than the feelings of other people. Humanists usually consider people first when they make decisions. They are very sensitive about other people's feelings, and they tend to approach business decisions with a great deal of compassion. The analytical, logical, and somewhat impersonal rationalist has been shown to be associated with survival and success in business.

The sensitive and compassionate humanist tends to struggle with making the hard decisions.

Flexibility

Count the number of 'a' boxes that you ticked in the column beginning with question 3 on the answer sheet. A score of 7–10 indicates that you are *flexible*. A score of 0–3 indicates that you are *inflexible*. A score of 4–6 indicates no clear tendency one way or the other.

Flexible individuals accept change as natural. They may have many projects under way at the same time. Sometimes they even appear to be indecisive because they like to keep their options open. Inflexible individuals like a planned, predetermined way of life. They have a tendency to resist change and they like to finish one project before beginning the next. Having made a decision, inflexible individuals are not likely to change their mind.

Successful business operators are flexible. This flexibility is related to the ability to deal with risk spontaneously and for having a special tolerance for ambiguous and uncertain situations. Flexibility is not the indecision that it may appear to be because it actually consists of a series of revised decisions that reflect new information as it appears.

Creativity

Count the number of 'b' boxes that you ticked in the column beginning with question 4 on the answer sheet. A score of 7–10 indicates that you have a *high capacity for creativity*. A score of 0–3 indicates that you have a *low capacity for creativity*. A score of 4–6 indicates that you have average creativity.

Success in business is directly related to an individual's capacity for creativity. Creative individuals are idea generators while non-creative individuals tend to use the ideas of others. If you are creative, then your inventiveness and intuition will enable you to visualise how you will react in new situations. Your creative intuition also plays an important role in reducing risk by substituting itself for a lack of information. If you are not creative, then it will probably reflect itself in your business.

Planning

Count the number of 'a' boxes that you ticked in the column beginning with question 5 on the answer sheet. A score of 7–10 indicates that you are an *effective planner*. A score of 0–3 indicates that you are an *ineffective planner*. A score of 4–6 indicates that you are an average planner.

A number of research studies have shown that successful business operators set realistic goals and plan how they are going to achieve them. If you are an effective planner, then you will be at ease with formulating and implementing a plan for your business. If you are an ineffective planner, then you may not only have problems establishing your business but also with its ongoing operation.

Initiative

Count the number of 'a' boxes that you ticked in the column beginning with question 6 on the answer sheet. A score of 7–10 indicates that you have a *high degree of initiative*. A score of 0–3 indicates that you have a *low degree of initiative*. A score of 4–6 indicates average initiative.

Many individuals who intend to become self-employed simply never end up in business. They include the procrastinators, those who lack self-confidence, and those who see too many hurdles to overcome. For these individuals, the missing ingredient is initiative. There is considerable agreement among researchers that successful business operators actively seek and take the initiative. They willingly put themselves in situations where they are personally responsible for success or failure. Successful business operators are doers; they are goal-oriented and action-oriented.

Independence

Successful small business operators have been shown to have a strong sense of independence. This sense of independence, however, stems from one of two needs. The first is the need to achieve autonomy in one's life, while the second is the need to achieve security and stability. Count the number of 'b' boxes that you ticked in the column beginning with question 7 on the answer sheet. A score of 7–10 indicates that your sense of independence is based on the need for *autonomy*. A score of

0–3 indicates that your sense of independence is based on the need for *security and stability*. A score of 4–6 indicates that your sense of independence is balanced between these two needs.

Autonomy is important to individuals who do not wish to be bound by the constraints of large organisations. They have an overriding need to do things their own way, at their own pace, and according to their own standards. Therefore, they tend to be pulled towards work situations in which they can satisfy their need for autonomy. Security and stability are important to individuals who want their future to be certain. Not every small business operator wants or needs unlimited growth. If they can achieve the security and stability they seek, then these individuals are content. People are different and want different things out of life, so it is important to recognise these differences and to take them into account when contemplating the type of business that is best for you.

Goal

Why do you want to be self-employed? Are you drawn by the challenge of starting and managing your own business? Or will self-employment enable you to achieve a certain lifestyle? Count the 'b' boxes that you ticked in the column beginning with question 8 on the answer sheet. A score of 7–10 indicates that your goal for going into business is based on the need for *challenge*. A score of 0–3 indicates that your goal for going into business is based on the need for an integrated *lifestyle*. A score of 4–6 indicates a balance between challenge and lifestyle.

Some individuals look on self-employment in terms of the pure challenge of organising and operating their own business. They define success in terms of overcoming obstacles, solving problems, and winning against competition. The type of business they choose and the way they operate it provides an ongoing opportunity for challenges. Other individuals look on self-employment as a way to integrate and balance their family, career, and personal development. This is not independence; it is the need for a balanced way of life in which career decisions do not have to dominate. It places a premium on things like where to live, the amount of time spent working, and the whole family-versus-business relationship.

Role

What emphasis will you place on your role as a small business operator? Do you see yourself as a general manager, or are you more inclined to pursue a particular technical or functional specialty? Count the number of 'a' boxes that you ticked in the column beginning with question 9 on the answer sheet. A score of 7–10 indicates an emphasis on *general management*. A score of 0–3 indicates an emphasis on a *technical or functional specialty*. A score of 4–6 indicates an equal emphasis on both roles.

Some individuals want a business in which their overall managerial efforts are what matters. They want to exercise their capacity to identify and solve problems, to influence and control other people, and to be stimulated by crises. Other individuals have strong talents in a particular functional or technical specialty. They build their sense of identity around the content of their work and they see themselves as a specialist. These individuals find the work itself intrinsically meaningful and satisfying. They look forward to their own business in terms of that specialty. They tend to shun management responsibilities and usually prefer a smaller operation.

Determination

Determination is much more than initiative. It is a well thought-out, assertive action plan driven by a deep desire to succeed in your own business. Count the number of 'a' boxes that you ticked in the column beginning with question 10 on the answer sheet. A score of 7–10 indicates *strong determination*. A score of 0–3 indicates *weak determination*. A score of 4–6 indicates average determination.

Determination generally makes the difference between actually starting a business and just talking about it. Being goal-oriented is not enough; what you also need is the determination to make it happen. Successful business operators tend to believe strongly in themselves and their ability to achieve the goals that they set. They believe that events in their life are mainly self-determined and that they have a major influence on their personal destiny. They possess an intense level of commitment to overcoming hurdles, solving problems, and completing the job.

Part B
Getting Started

When an individual first decides to get into business, they are usually not aware of what is involved or where to begin. The purpose of Part B is to provide some guidance. The first step is to identify a genuine business opportunity. It may be a parallel opportunity, a new market opportunity, a new product opportunity, or a new service opportunity. It may lend itself to buying an existing business, buying a franchise, or starting a new business from scratch. The second step is to work through the nuts and bolts of getting established. There are important questions to be considered, decisions to make, and lots of paperwork to complete. The third step is to develop a business plan. Doing a business plan enables you to explore opportunities, identify and evaluate your options, and arrive at the way you are going to achieve tangible results.

DOI: 10.4324/9781032676616-6

Three
Pathways into Business

Most individuals get their business idea from previous work experience, their education or training, hobbies, a personal interest, or by recognising an unmet need. The pathway into business begins by searching for a business opportunity. It might be a parallel opportunity, a new market opportunity, a new product opportunity, or a new service opportunity. Each represents a different proposition in terms of the nature of the opportunity, the risks involved, and the strategies that might be used to exploit it. Having identified an opportunity with promising commercial potential, the next step is to consider the alternatives for turning it into a business. These include buying a business, buying a franchise, or starting from scratch. The purpose of this chapter is to describe how to search for an opportunity and consider the choices for organising a business to exploit it.

PARALLEL OPPORTUNITIES

Parallel opportunities exist when there is a potential for existing products or services to be sold in competition with one or more existing businesses. A new hairdressing salon in an area that already has a salon is a parallel opportunity. The majority of new business opportunities compete in parallel with other businesses by selling similar products and services to the same sorts of customers. These are the most straightforward types of business opportunities because there is already a lot of information about them.

A parallel start-up makes sense when existing firms are unable to meet demand or if you can offer better value to customers. In some cases, existing businesses have had it too good for too long and have grown complacent. In other cases, existing operators with poor quality, high prices, or poor service enable you to gain a foothold

DOI: 10.4324/9781032676616-7

because you are more competent and determined. Parallel opportunities in the services sector are particularly attractive when the capital required is low and specialist know-how is not too important. The key to parallel opportunities is to position the business in a way that distinguishes it from the competition. Examples of pathways in which parallel opportunities can be exploited include buying a business, copying a business, import replacement, and becoming an agent or distributor.

If you buy an existing business, you get a going concern including the location, premises, equipment, stock, customers, staff, and goodwill that have been established by the seller. If you choose to buy one that is not doing so well, then you need to be sure that you have the knowledge and skills to turn it around. To find businesses for sale, look at newspaper advertisements, make enquiries with commercial real estate agents, and talk to people in the trade. Ask your accountant and solicitor if they know of any suitable businesses for sale. Keep an eye out for owners who may want to retire or sell out for other reasons like loss of interest, divorce, or poor health.

Copying another business makes sense if the market has expanded and is not adequately served, or if the existing operators are clearly failing to meet the needs of customers. There are advantages to starting a new business over buying an existing one. You can choose your own target market, select the right mix of products and services, design your own promotional strategy, and decide on your own location and facilities.

Replacing imports means producing a product or service in Australia that is currently being imported from overseas. Do you know of an imported item that you could produce locally? Can you match its quality at the same price? Can you get a cost advantage by eliminating shipping costs or tariffs? To find out what is imported into Australia, check with Austrade and subscribe to import publications and importers' catalogues. Contact purchasing agents and ask them what they are importing. Examine the products where you shop to find out where they are made. Talk to potential customers and ask them if they would be prepared to switch to a locally made item.

Agents and distributors sell the products and services of other businesses. Some businesses do not have their own distribution channels and they look for ways to fulfil this role. Some businesses simply prefer to concentrate on what they do best and outsource distribution. An *agent* contracts with a producer to sell their products or services for a fee or a commission. A *distributor* buys the producer's products or services and resells them to consumers or wholesales them to other businesses. What products or services could you sell as an agent or a distributor? What producers need the services of an agent or a distributor in your area?

NEW MARKET OPPORTUNITIES

New market opportunities are existing products or services that are introduced into a new market. A new domestic version of an existing industrial product is a new market opportunity. New market opportunities may be customers in new geographical areas or customers that are attracted by new distribution channels, new merchandising methods, or new advertising media. Since there is already some experience with existing products or services, new market opportunities usually involve only medium risk. Examples of pathways in which new market opportunities can be exploited include transferring an idea, buying a franchise, going online, and importing and exporting.

If you see a successful business concept in another place, consider the possibility of transferring the same idea into your own market. Have you seen any successful products or services that are not available where you live? Keep your eyes open for products or services in other locations that you can expand into your area. Buy a few overseas newspapers and read through the advertising and the stories about their local businesses.

Franchising has been responsible for the spectacular growth in new market opportunities. The franchisor not only provides the product, service, and trademark but also the entire business format consisting of a marketing plan and support, operating methods and manuals, training, quality control, and ongoing backup services. In the retail sector, examples include auto parts, apparel, paint and hardware, electrical appliances, and fast food. Franchising can also be found in services such as motels, income tax services, gardening services, and business and professional services. Keep an eye out for successful franchise operations in other locations. Talk to some of the franchisees and ask them what they think about the franchise system they operate.

The internet is a tremendous source of new market opportunities. If your prospective customers buy products or get information via the internet, then you should be online. The role of a website in creating new market opportunities varies. Some businesses have a website that is designed simply to create a marketing presence as part of an overall advertising and promotion strategy. Other businesses have a website that goes further by offering an online catalogue and contact details for handling orders and enquiries. A complete website includes online ordering and credit card approval. Fully featured websites are also capable of tracking a customer's preferences and transaction history as part of a strategy for cross-promotion and on-selling. The opportunities for entering new markets online is greater than most other pathways.

Importing is a source of new market opportunities in Australia. An importer brings existing products and services into Australia from other countries for resale. Many foreign producers are looking for local agents or distributors. The embassies of foreign countries are an excellent source of information about agency and distribution opportunities. Exporting is a source of new market opportunities in other countries. Most Australian exporters concentrate their efforts on the countries that make up the Asia-Pacific Economic Cooperation region, the United States, and Europe. Do you have contacts in other countries that might become distributors? Do you know of any Australian producers who need help to export their products and services? Importing and exporting are highly specialised activities. You need to be aware of your legal obligations in both the country of origin and the destination including quarantine laws, tariffs, quotas, duties, and other restrictions.

NEW PRODUCT AND NEW SERVICE OPPORTUNITIES

A new product or a new service opportunity consists of modifying an existing one or developing a new one. Organic and environmentally friendly versions of well-known household products are examples of modified products. Nanny software aimed at protecting children from inappropriate internet content is an entirely new service that was developed to provide a solution to a new problem.

To the extent that you have little previous experience with a new product or service, the risks become greater. Product and service opportunities that are totally new are very rare indeed. Instead, look for products and services that are already working in the marketplace that you can improve or expand by

- Upgrading quality or service
- Broadening or narrowing the range of products or services
- Increasing usability, performance, or safety
- Changing the delivery method, packaging, or unit size
- Adding new features, accessories, or extensions
- Making them more convenient
- Simplifying repair, maintenance, replacement, or cleaning
- Increasing mobility, access, portability, or disposability
- Changing colour, material, or shape
- Making them larger/smaller, lighter/heavier, or faster/slower

In addition to improving or expanding existing products or services, other pathways in which new product and service opportunities can be exploited include making new combinations, piggybacking on growth, inventing something new, or buying a licence to make and sell something that someone else invented.

Sometimes it is possible to combine existing products and services to create a new business opportunity. One example is a beauty salon that combined with a cosmetic therapy centre to offer an expanded range of beauty and cosmetic treatment services in one location. Another example is combining the skills of several tradespeople to offer a comprehensive home maintenance and repair service. The objective is to combine products, services, people, businesses, and assets to create a new combination of products or services that is more attractive than its separate parts.

Piggybacking on the growth of another product or service consists of offering additional related products or services. For example, there has been a long-term trend toward personal fitness and health. Businesses offering fitness monitoring equipment, health foods, and apparel designed for specific activities such as yoga are piggybacking on this trend. Look for growth trends by running an internet search for 'trend spotters' and see what you get. What products or services could you provide that fit into these trends?

What customer needs could be met by a new invention? Do you already have an idea that you could develop into a new procedure, product, or service? Is there a market for it? Look through magazines and research reports devoted to consumer topics and search through the IP Australia website at *ipaustralia.gov.au* and the Google Patent Search website at *google.com.au/patents* to see what has already been registered. IP Australia can also provide you with information about how to apply for a patent over your own invention. Once a patent is granted, you have an exclusive right to produce and sell it including the right to sell a license to someone else who may want to produce and sell it.

The flip side of selling patent rights is to buy a licence to produce and market an invention patented by someone else. Is there an interesting patent for a product or service with genuine market potential that has never been produced, or has it been produced but was not successfully exploited? Some patents are available under licence, and there are many old patents that have expired and no longer require a licence. Even very old patents may have been ahead of their time and represent opportunities that are marketable today.

BUYING A BUSINESS

One way to get into business is to buy one. You are buying the location, premises, equipment, stock, customers, staff, and goodwill that have been established by the seller. That can make it much easier to get started, or you could be buying a big mistake if the seller's original decision to start the business was not justified or badly executed.

Advantages and Disadvantages

Buying a going concern has the initial advantage that you will not only receive immediate income from sales to existing customers, but you will also save the time and effort needed to equip and stock the business yourself. A successful business will have a proven location, established relationships with suppliers and creditors, and existing employees. Buying a going concern as a package may turn out to be cheaper than trying to assemble all the bits and pieces yourself. It is also simpler to finance a single purchase transaction, and a proven track record will be a significant advantage in persuading a financial backer to support you. When you purchase a business, the risk of failure is significantly less than if you tried to start the same business from scratch.

There are also potential disadvantages. Initially, you are stuck with the previous owner's bad decisions. For example, the inventory may be unsaleable, the choice of equipment and fixtures may be outmoded, some of the staff may not be suitable, or the location may be poor. You could pay too much for the business if you misjudge its value, and there could be unexpected expenses if the business turns out to be run-down. If the previous owner had a bad reputation, then you are likely to inherit ill will among customers and poor morale among staff. Visit the business a few times before you identify yourself as a potential buyer to check out the operation under normal trading conditions.

Purchase Price

When you buy a business, the price is usually based on its ability to earn a profit over and above your own salary. The first step is to ask your accountant to analyse past financial statements and income tax records. Have sales and profits been increasing or decreasing? What will be the return on your investment? You can use the financial information described in Chapter 12 to help you with an analysis of the seller's financial statements.

There are two basic methods used to determine the value of a business. The first method is based on expectations of future profit and return on investment. It is called the *capitalised value* method. The second method consists of valuing the business on the basis of the *appraised value* of the assets.

Capitalised value is the amount of money you would need to invest at your required rate of return to earn an income equal to the profit potential of the business. The required rate of return is called the *capitalisation rate.* Capitalised value is found by dividing the annual projected profit by the capitalisation rate. For example, suppose a business is capable of earning $50,000 per year after paying all of its expenses including your own salary. If the investment in this business is as safe as a bank deposit, you could use the fixed deposit rate of about 5 percent to capitalise the profits and arrive at a value for the business of $50,000 / 5% = $1,000,000. No small business, however, is as safe as a bank deposit. Capitalisation rates ranging from 20 percent to 50 percent more realistically recognise the risks in a small business. If we use a capitalisation rate of 25 percent for this business, then its capitalised value is $200,000. If there is any chance that the profits may not be sustained over the long term, then you should increase the capitalisation rate to compensate for this risk.

Some small businesses are purchased on the basis of the net value of the assets to be transferred. The process consists of establishing what assets are going to be transferred and appraising their current market value such as inventory, fixtures, and equipment. If the business sells on credit, you need to consider whether you want to take over the accounts receivable. Since none of the assets are likely to be new, take their remaining useful life into consideration when you value them. It is important to be sure that fixtures and equipment are serviceable, inventory is saleable, and accounts receivable are collectable.

If the asking price is greater than the value of the assets, the difference is an intangible asset called *goodwill*. Goodwill represents the ability of the business to earn greater profits than if you started the same business from scratch. The value of goodwill should not be any greater than the difference between the capitalised value of the business and the value of the assets. Agents and vendors are always quick to claim that a business's goodwill justifies a higher price. However, few small businesses that are put up for sale are genuinely producing extraordinary profits, so the problem of valuing goodwill is not usually a pressing one.

Negotiation

The aim of the negotiation process is to agree on the terms of a formal contract covering the details of the purchase. There are a number of matters over which you and the seller may have differences. For example, the seller is interested in the best price, getting paid as quickly as possible, favourable tax treatment on capital gains from the sale, avoiding any continuing liabilities associated with the business, and avoiding any contract terms that are not in their interest. You are looking for the lowest price, extended payment terms, a favourable tax basis for resale and depreciation, and warranties or guarantees from the seller that give you extra protection.

The central negotiating issue is usually price. What is actually paid for a business can be quite different from what it is worth. In other words, price and value are not the same thing. The price paid reflects the negotiating positions of the parties. If the seller's desire to sell is stronger than your desire to buy, then the value you receive may be greater than the price you pay. This situation might occur if the seller needs to exit the business quickly because of age, health, or financial reasons. On the other hand, if you are unable to raise enough money to purchase the business, the seller may offer to accept deferred payment if you agree to a higher price. In this case, you are paying a price that is greater than the value of the business in order to get vendor finance.

Have your solicitor check to be sure there are no mortgages, back taxes, or other creditor claims against the assets you are buying. It is not usually a good idea to assume any of the seller's liabilities such as outstanding loans. Occasionally, however, these can represent a source of finance for you. If you do assume any of the seller's liabilities, the amount must be subtracted from the asking price to arrive at a net price for the business.

A number of new problems will emerge when you ask your solicitor to exchange contracts. At this point, you and the seller will probably have reached agreement on price, assumption of liabilities, and terms of payment. To protect your interests, however, your solicitor will advise you to include a number of other matters in the contract. What if the seller's financial statements turn out to be inaccurate or false? What if the seller has undisclosed liabilities that have not been taken into account in arriving at the price? What if some of the assets you are purchasing do not actually belong to the seller? What if substantial changes occur to the business between the exchange of contracts and settlement? What if the seller decides to open a competing business nearby? These questions reflect the uncertainty of your position as a buyer. It is important to get the protection you need formally written into the contract. It is also important to make sure you are registered for goods and services tax (GST) before you buy a business. If it turns out you are liable for GST on the purchase price, then you can claim it back.

BUYING A FRANCHISE

Franchising is changing the way many Australian small businesses are organised and operated. Franchising is a method of getting into business for yourself but not by yourself. Franchising may appeal to you if you are unable to find a suitable business opportunity or you consider the risks of going it alone too great. Franchising consists of a relationship between a parent company (called the *franchisor*) and an individual operator (called the *franchisee*) in which the franchisor's knowledge, market position, and operating techniques are made available to the franchisee. In other words, a franchise is a pre-packaged business that you can operate under an agreement with a franchisor.

There are four types of franchises. The *business-format franchise* is the most common type with a brand name, training, and detailed blue-print for running the business. Fast food outlets are an example. In a *product franchise*, the franchisee sells the franchisor's products. Branded tyre outlets are an example. In a *service franchise*, the franchisee is licensed to provide services in the name of the franchisor. Home care services and tax preparation services are examples. In a *manufacturing franchise*, the franchisee manufactures the products and distributes them using the manufacturer's brand name.

Advantages of a Franchise

A number of research studies suggest that franchises have a better survival rate than other small businesses. Franchising cannot save someone from incompetence, but it does act as a safety net for individuals who are otherwise capable but need some assistance in getting started. In particular, franchises reduce the scope for making the types of mistakes that lead to business closure because they are total business systems that have already been proven.

Another appeal of franchising is that it enables people with limited business experience to become self-employed. You can take advantage of the franchisor's knowledge and experience that you would otherwise have to build up over a long time through trial and error. By having access to the managerial resources of a franchisor, you are able to reduce the uncertainty associated with starting a new business from scratch.

As a franchisee, you get an established business concept with proven products and services. Your business has instant pulling power. To develop this pulling power on your own might take years of promotion and considerable expense. You get the benefit of regional and national advertising and promotion, ongoing market research, and the goodwill of the franchisor's name, product, and service.

You can expect to be trained in the mechanics of the franchisor's business and guided in its day-to-day operation until you are proficient at the job. Management services and quality control monitoring are usually provided by the franchisor on a continuing basis. You are able to benefit from the franchisor's centralised purchasing of products, equipment, supplies, advertising materials, and other business needs.

You can also expect to get competently designed facilities, floor layout, displays, and fixtures. The franchisor has usually designed very efficient facilities based on their experience with many franchisees and they can help you avoid functionally or aesthetically poor facilities. The franchisor can also help you to maximise customer traffic with site selection.

The franchisor may give you financial assistance by making it possible for you to start out with less than the full amount of the upfront costs. Financial assistance could be provided in the form of trade credit, low-interest loans, or loan guarantees. With the name of a well-known successful franchisor behind you, your ability to negotiate with financial institutions will be strengthened.

Disadvantages of a Franchise

It could be more costly to become a franchisee than to set up your own business. You will have to pay an up-front franchise fee, which may be substantial, as well as continuing royalty fees that may range between 5 and 15 percent of gross sales. You may also find yourself paying management fees and advertising levies. You may even be required to buy merchandise, supplies, or equipment from the franchisor that you can get cheaper elsewhere. The big question is whether all of these extra costs can be justified in terms of higher profits and lower risk as a franchisee.

Contrary to the 'be your own boss' lures in franchise advertisements, you will not actually be your own boss. To ensure uniformity, franchisors control how franchisees conduct their business. These controls significantly restrict your ability to exercise your own business judgement. Here are some examples:

- Site approval—The franchisor will usually want to approve the site for your franchise. This may increase the likelihood that your franchise will attract customers, but it may not be the site you want.
- Design or appearance standards—The franchisor may impose design or appearance standards to ensure uniformity of appearance. Some franchisors require periodic renovations or seasonal design changes that may increase your costs.
- Restrictions on goods and services offered for sale—The franchisor may restrict the goods and services offered for sale. For example, as a restaurant franchise owner, you may not be able to add your own dishes to the menu or delete some that are unpopular.
- Restrictions on the method of operation—The franchisor may require you to operate during certain hours and use only approved signs, employee uniforms, and advertisements. These restrictions may prevent you from operating your outlet in the way you wish.
- Competitive restrictions—You may not have the freedom to meet local competition in the ways you think are most appropriate. For example, under a franchise arrangement, you will be restricted in the way you set prices or offer customer incentives.

The franchise contract is usually written to the advantage of the franchisor. Clauses in some franchise contracts call for unreasonably high sales quotas or mandatory opening hours. Most franchise agreements expire at some time in the future and there may not be a guarantee they can be renewed. Even if renewal is guaranteed, the terms may not be favourable. Contracts also specify conditions for the cancellation or termination of the franchise by the franchisor and restrictions on a franchisee selling their franchise or otherwise re-covering their investment.

When you establish an independent small business, most of the risk is in how you operate it. When you become a franchisee, most of the risk is in your choice of franchisor. Although franchising has a better record of survival than independent small businesses, there have been and there will continue to be failures. Not every franchise system is the same. Not every franchise product or service will succeed. If the franchisor fails, then the franchisees also risk failure.

Evaluating a Franchise

To evaluate a franchise, you need to evaluate both the business opportunity and the franchise organisation. Under the Franchising Code of Conduct, all prospective franchisees and existing franchisees that are renewing their franchise must be given a Disclosure Document. As a further protection, a prospective franchisee is entitled to a cooling-off period after signing the franchise agreement. The Franchising Code of Conduct is administered by the Australian Competition and Consumer Commission (ACCC). If a franchisor has not been consci-entious in complying with the code, the ACCC may take action on your behalf. The ACCC website, *accc.gov.au*, is where you can access the Franchising Code of Conduct and a free online course titled *Is Franchising for Me?*

The written franchise agreement constitutes the legal relationship between you and the franchisor. Make sure that every aspect of the franchise agreement is spelled out in detail. What rights does the franchisor grant to you? What obligations does the franchisor un-dertake to fulfil? What obligations does the agreement impose on you? Be sure the agreement contains everything that was discussed during the negotiations. Have your solicitor, your accountant, and an independent specialist franchise adviser review the terms and conditions of the franchise agreement and explain them to you. Do not depend on the people who represent the franchisor for advice. Do not sign an agreement unless you are completely satisfied that it represents a viable working relationship with the franchisor.

The Franchise Council of Australia (FCA) is the franchising industry association. It concerns itself with lobbying government, ethics in franchising, member education, industry development, and the promotion of franchising. FCA members not only include franchisors and franchisees but also others with an interest in franchising such as solicitors, accountants, bankers, and industry consultants. *Franchising* magazine is published bimonthly and distributed through newsagents. You can visit the FCA's website at ***franchise.org.au***.

STARTING FROM SCRATCH

Starting from scratch involves higher risks compared with buying an existing business or buying a franchise. Errors of judgement can be costly, especially if the business is organised around a new product or service. On the other hand, a new business may be able fill a gap in the marketplace with exceptional rewards for the adventurous small business operator.

There are a number of advantages to starting a business from scratch. You can match the business to your own goals. It is easier to innovate when you have the flexibility to select your target market, product and service strategy, competitive strategy, location, and facilities. You can design the business around the policies and procedures that you select, and you can train staff your own way. You also avoid the goodwill expense of buying an existing business along with the possibility of unknown or contingent liabilities. Moreover, you will not inherit any pre-existing ill will from disgruntled customers, suppliers, creditors, or employees.

Starting a new business from scratch also has disadvantages. It carries the highest risk of failure because there is less certainty about its ability to generate sales revenue. It takes time and energy to create an image, build patronage, work the bugs out of new systems and procedures, and reach a break-even level of sales. Meanwhile, staff must be found, contacts developed with suppliers, and a marketing strategy put into practice. There are the added risks that investment capital may be difficult to find, unexpected competition may emerge, or potential customers are more difficult to attract than you anticipate. New businesses always run a significant risk that the time lag between the initial investment and positive cash flow turns out to be too long.

There is clearly more involved in starting from scratch than there is in buying a business or a franchise. There are more ways in which to make mistakes, and it takes longer to plan, organise, and launch a new business. If you get it right, however, the rewards may also be much greater. Starting from scratch can be the most exciting pathway into business. It offers a unique opportunity to create something that is not only personally satisfying, but it also offers the possibility of creating considerable wealth. For these reasons, this book is mainly focused on starting from scratch.

SUMMARY

This chapter describes how to search for a business opportunity and outlines the ways in which a business can be organised to exploit it. The pathway into business begins by searching for a business opportunity. It may be a parallel opportunity, a new market opportunity, a new product opportunity, or a new service opportunity. Each represents a different profile in terms of the nature of opportunity itself, the risks involved, and the strategies that might be used to exploit it. Having identified an opportunity with promising commercial potential, the next step is to consider the options for turning it into a business. Buying a business that is already in place makes it easier to get established provided the business is a genuine going concern. Buying a franchise is another alternative if you are unable to find a suitable business opportunity or you consider the risks of going it alone too great. Starting from scratch is a higher risk option because errors of judgement can be costly, especially if it is organised around a new product or service. Nevertheless, there are a number of advantages to starting from scratch with exceptional rewards for those who are successful.

Four
Start-Up Nuts and Bolts

Getting into business doesn't just happen. There are important questions that need to be considered, decisions that need to be made, and paperwork that needs to be completed. What is the right legal structure for your business? What should the business be called? How do you register a business name? What is required to form a company? What is involved in applying for an Australian Business Number, a Tax File Number, and GST registration? What other licences and permits are needed? The purpose of this chapter is to explain the nuts and bolts involved in getting started.

LEGAL STRUCTURE

One of the important decisions you will make is whether to set up your business as a sole proprietorship, a partnership, a proprietary company, or a trust. When you do select a legal structure, the decision is never really final because legal, financial, and taxation changes may modify the characteristics and relative advantages of the various legal structures. When changes do occur, your solicitor and your accountant may need to re-examine the structure that best suits your business.

Sole Proprietorship

A sole proprietorship is the easiest, simplest, and least expensive legal structure in which to organise a business. As the proprietor, you are the sole owner of the business and you have complete control over it. You are also personally liable for business debts and responsible for negligent acts committed within the scope of the business. A sole proprietorship is automatically terminated by the death or incapacity

DOI: 10.4324/9781032676616-8

of the owner. Here are some of the advantages and disadvantages of a sole proprietorship:

Advantages	Disadvantages
Ease of formation	Unlimited personal liability
Low start-up costs	Narrow management base
More freedom from regulation	Lack of continuity
You are in direct control	Difficulty in raising capital
All the profits are yours	Higher tax rates at higher profits
Maximum privacy	
Easy to change legal structure	
Lower tax rates at modest profits	

Partnership

A partnership is a business conducted by yourself and one or more other people all of whom have the status and authority of owners or principals. Most partnerships are based on an agreement or contract among the co-owners. A carefully prepared written agreement spelling out the rights and duties of the partners is highly recommended. Nevertheless, a formal contract is not essential, and a partnership can be created by two or more people running a business together for profit. When partners do enter into a written agreement, it is a private agreement and they are free to include almost any details they wish.

Although people often think of a partnership as distinct from the individuals who are the partners and although it is treated that way for accounting purposes, the law does not regard the partnership itself as a separate legal entity. The assets of the business are viewed as belonging to the partners and each partner is personally responsible for the full amount of any partnership debts. Members of a partnership have equal rights in the firm's management and in the conduct of its business unless otherwise agreed. People dealing with the business are not affected by agreements among the partners that limit the authority of some partners, at least if the outsiders do not know of these agreements. Each partner is an agent of the firm and of the partners. Therefore, even a partner who is not particularly experienced or skilled in business affairs has the power to enter into contracts or other transactions that will be binding on the other partners. Here are some of the advantages and disadvantages of a partnership:

Advantages	Disadvantages
Ease of formation	Unlimited personal liability
Low start-up costs	Lack of continuity
More sources of capital	Divided authority
Broader management base	Friction between partners
Privacy of affairs	Limitations on size
Limited outside regulation	Limited flexibility in
Easy to change legal structure	transferring ownership

There are also provisions for a *limited partnership* that enables some partners to contribute capital while retaining limited liability for the debts and obligations of the partnership. Limited partners do not usually take part in the management of the business. Ask your solicitor for advice.

Proprietary Company

A company is an association of individuals that is recognised in law as having an existence separate and apart from the individuals (shareholders) who own it. The company holds property, enters into contracts, transfers property, and conducts legal matters in a capacity separate and distinct from its shareholders. The separateness of the company is also recognised for tax purposes.

The requirements for forming and operating a company are set down in the Corporations Act, which provides for the regulation of companies by the Australian Securities and Investments Commission (ASIC). You can find information about forming and operating a company on the ASIC's website at ***asic.gov.au***.

Advantages of a Company

• Your liability as a shareholder for debts and other business obligations of the company, and therefore your risk, is limited to the amount you paid for your shares.

- The management of a company can be centralised in a board of directors, thereby permitting selection of experts as managers of the business whether they are shareholders.
- A company has a continuous existence, which means that it is not dissolved by the death, incapacity, or withdrawal of a shareholder.
- Ownership in a company, represented by shares, can be bought or sold, thus permitting a shareholder to withdraw from the company without jeopardising its continuity.
- Capital can usually be attracted in larger amounts and more readily than a sole proprietorship or a partnership.
- A shareholder in a company can also be an employee.
- There is greater tax flexibility between profits, salaries, and dividends.

Disadvantages of a Company
- Closer regulation by government and the courts.
- More expensive to organise and maintain.
- Activities may be restricted by the Corporations Act.
- Extra reporting requirements and more recordkeeping.
- Less privacy regarding financial and other affairs.
- Director's duties are a serious responsibility.

A proprietary company is usually formed to obtain the advantage of limited liability for individuals who might otherwise conduct business as a sole proprietorship or a partnership. The name of the company must contain the words *Proprietary Limited* or *Pty Ltd*. The chief limitations are restrictions on the right to transfer shares to new shareholders, a ceiling on the number of shareholders, and a prohibition on inviting members of the public to subscribe for shares. A 'single-person company' only needs to have one director and one shareholder who can be the same individual. A proprietary company must also have a company secretary who may also be a director and shareholder.

The duties of a company director are complex and you should be aware of your personal responsibilities. Any breach of your duties may lead to a civil suit against you by the company's other shareholders, by creditors, or any other persons with whom your company has dealt. If your company is insolvent and you continue to trade, you may find yourself personally liable for its debts. Ask your solicitor to explain what is involved. Consider joining the Australian Institute of Company Directors. They offer a number of services designed to inform and educate company directors. You can visit their website at *aicd.com.au*.

Trust

Some small businesses are organised as a *discretionary trust*. A trust is not a legal entity; it simply holds property in trust for the beneficiaries. The trustee administers the trust according to the trust deed, which may include discretionary powers over the distribution of trust income and capital. This is often done to minimise tax.

Many of the advantages of a company can be maintained by having a company act as the trustee. For example, this enables the members of a family business to retain control over the trust by becoming directors of the trustee company as well as beneficiaries of the trust. Here are some of the main advantages and disadvantages of a discretionary trust:

Advantages	Disadvantages
Flexibility	Costly to set up and run
Continuity can be preserved	More complicated to administer
Limited liability possible	Limited life of the trust deed
More privacy than a company	Trustee subject to the Trustee Act

An alternative arrangement is a *unit trust* in which the beneficial ownership of the trust property is divided into units. Unit trusts differ from discretionary trusts because trust property is divided on a predetermined basis according to the number of units held. There is no discretion to vary the proportional distribution of income and capital. Beneficiaries of a unit trust may act as the trustees and the units may be bought and sold, making it possible for individuals to withdraw from the business by selling their units.

WHAT'S IN A NAME?

Choosing a name for your business is not only important commercially but also legally. There are different kinds of names and it is important to distinguish between them because a name can be a business name, a company name, and a domain name. Even registering a name does not give you proprietary or ownership rights to the name because that is only possible in Australia through trademark registration. When you choose a name, check that the name is available in each category before you pay any fees to register it.

The law requires anyone who carries on a business that does not consist of the surname and all the given names (or the initials) of the owner(s) to register a *business name* before the business can trade. The reason for requiring registration of a business name is to enable the public to find out who is operating under a business name. It also serves to avoid confusion by ensuring that no two businesses have registered the same or similar names. After your business name is approved and registered, it must appear on every business letter, invoice, and receipt.

A *company name* must be registered with the ASIC. If a company does business under a name other than its registered company name, then the business name must also be registered.

A *domain name* is the address for a website on the internet. Domain names in Australia are administered by .au Domain Administration Limited (auDA). Registration gives you the exclusive use of that address for an agreed period of time. A list of authorised resellers can be found on the auDA internet site at ***auda.org.au***. Your business name might be used as a hashtag and it will be the URL for your website, so make sure you choose a name that can be used online.

Your name is a valuable asset, so it is worth the time and effort to get it right. Begin by thinking about your target market and what they value. Your name is the first thing most customers will know about your business. Make certain it tells them what your business does and avoid names that are vague about what you do. The key is to have a short name that is easy to recall and less likely to be confused. Choose a name that is easy to spell, especially when customers are trying to find your website. Limit your name to one or two syllables because it will be easier to remember. Do an internet search for commercial websites that are used to generate potential business names. When you have two or three candidates, try them out on your family and friends. It is informative to see how other people react to a proposed business name.

BUSINESS REGISTRATION SERVICE

The Business Registration Service at *register.business.gov.au* is an innovative and valuable service. It minimises the hassles that are part of getting into business because you can apply for most of your key business and tax registrations in one place.

Australian Business Number

An Australian Business Number (ABN) is a unique 11-digit identifying number that businesses use when dealing with government and other businesses. For example, you generally need to put your ABN on your invoices and other documents relating to sales. You also need an ABN in certain dealings with the Tax Office and other government agencies. Registering for an ABN is not strictly compulsory, but you will need one for things like registering a business name, registering for the GST, confirming your business identity to others when ordering and invoicing, avoiding pay-as-you-go withholding tax on payments you receive, and to register an Australian domain name. Also, some businesses will only deal with you if you have an ABN because it is regarded as evidence that you are a genuine business. If you choose a company structure, you will be issued with a nine-digit Australian Company Number (ACN). When you register your company for an ABN, you will be asked for your ACN. The ABN issued to your company will be the company's ACN plus two extra digits.

Registering a Business Name

You cannot register a business name that is identical to one that has already been registered. There is a tool on the Business Registration Service website to find out if a proposed name is available. When you apply to register a business name, you will be asked for your ABN, personal details, and your business address. You only need to register your business name once. When it is approved, you can use it

Australia-wide. If you ever decide to make any changes to your business name, you will need to re-register it as a new business name.

Registering a Company

A company and a company name can be registered through the Business Registration Service. However, there are a number of important legal considerations and you should consult with your solicitor before registering a company. You will be given an ACN by the ASIC that you need when you apply for the company's ABN. When you register a company, you will need to appoint the company directors and other office holders. Each of the company directors will need to have a *Director Identification Number* available from the ASIC.

Tax File Number

A Tax File Number (TFN) is issued by the Australian Taxation Office (ATO) to identify each taxpayer. If you operate your business as a sole proprietorship, then you will use your individual TFN for both your personal and business dealings with the ATO. If you operate your business as a partnership, company, or trust, then you will need a separate TFN and you can apply for it through the Business Registration Service.

GST registration

The GST is a broad-based tax that is currently 10 percent of the value of the supply of most goods and services consumed in Australia. If your annual turnover is $75,000 or more, then you are legally required to register for the GST and you will need an ABN to do this. Your ABN will also be your GST registration number. You should consider the benefits of registering for the GST even if your turnover is less than $75,000. Then you will be entitled to claim tax credits for the GST included in the things you buy to use in your business. If you are not registered, you cannot claim the tax credits.

LICENSES AND PERMITS

Licences and permits come under a complex variety of commonwealth, state, and local government jurisdictions. These requirements vary from one location to another and they involve a number of different government departments. This is one of the more frustrating experiences in store for new small business operators and one that requires a great deal of patience.

Your first stop should be the Australian Business Licence Information Service (ABLIS) website at *ablis.business.gov.au*. It provides a one-stop service for licences, permits, approvals, and registrations from all three tiers of government. It not only identifies what you require but also enables you to download most of the forms. This is an enormous help in complying with the red tape involved in obtaining licenses, permits, approvals, and registrations. You may nevertheless need professional advice before you complete and submit some of the forms.

Although many regulations are enforced through commonwealth and state government authorities, you need to pay particular attention to local government zoning and building regulations. Local councils prepare planning schemes that create 'zones' for specific purposes such as residential, industrial, or commercial use. In addition, councils also control the construction and use of buildings. When you have located potential premises, even if you plan to use your own home or garage, you need to ensure that you conform to the local council's planning scheme.

INSURANCE

Part of the start-up process is to consider what financial risks you might face and how you can protect yourself. *Liability risks* include the possibility of personal injury or property damage caused to someone by you, your employee, your product, service, or professional advice. *Property risks* include the possibility of damage to your premises, equipment, vehicles, and contents from fire, flood, earthquake, hail, storms, or theft. Other risks include the possibility of disruption to trading and the loss of revenue as a consequence of things like fire, flood, earthquake, power failure, equipment failure, or computer failure. It also includes the loss of a key person, including yourself, due to sickness, disability, or death. These are risks that can be covered by insurance.

General Liability Insurance

When you operate a business, you are subject to the laws governing negligence to customers, employees, and anyone else with whom you do business or who is on your premises. The types of risks that can be covered by general liability insurance include the following:

- Injuries to others while on your premises.
- Injuries to others from the use of motor vehicles or equipment from your premises.
- Damage to other people's property.
- Injury or damage as a result of the purchaser's use of your product or service.

Failure to recognise the dangers of not carrying liability insurance can be a serious mistake. One big claim could be enough to wipe you out. Most of the risks are covered under a general liability insurance policy, sometimes referred to as a 'comprehensive liability policy.' Some risks are excluded from general liability policies and need to be covered separately. These include third-party motor vehicle insurance, product liability insurance, and workers compensation insurance. If you are a contractor or you tender for government business, it will usually be a condition of the contract that you hold public liability insurance for a specified minimum value.

Commercial Vehicle Insurance

Every vehicle used on public roads must carry compulsory third-party motor vehicle insurance. It covers bodily injury to persons other than the driver of the vehicle. It needs to be supplemented by *comprehensive motor vehicle insurance* to cover other risks associated with the operation of a motor vehicle in your business. A comprehensive motor vehicle policy insures you against loss or damage to the vehicle itself due to accident or theft, and it covers damage to the property of others caused by your motor vehicle. If you are using your private vehicle for your business, you need to discuss this with your insurer. Undeclared business use may invalidate the insurance policy.

Product Liability Insurance

Product liability insurance protects you against damage or injury to a person or another business caused by your product or service. Product liability insurance is usually sought by manufacturers of products that may cause injury or damage to consumers. However, even if you only sell or deliver goods, you may still be liable. Services such as repair and maintenance services can also cause damage and are subject to product liability.

Workers Compensation

In each state, workers compensation legislation makes it compulsory for employers to obtain a policy of insurance covering all of their employees. The legislation is based on the principle that the employer, regardless of negligence by any party, must provide a monetary benefit to an injured employee subject only to proof of work-related injury.

An employee can receive payment for doctors' bills and medication as well as hospital expenses and lost wages. Injuries resulting in permanent damage make an employee eligible for payment to compensate for the loss. Compulsory workers compensation insurance protects you against these liabilities up to certain statutory limits. You should review your exposure to these risks to determine if you need to increase your coverage beyond the statutory minimum.

Property Insurance

Property insurance provides coverage for your business against loss or damage to buildings and contents such as machines, tools, furniture, fittings, and stock. Examples of the risks that can be covered by property insurance include damage caused by

Fire	Water
Explosions	Flood
Storm and tempest	Earthquake
Riots, strikes, and vandalism	Electric current (fusion)
Impact by vehicles, horses, or cattle	Aircraft

The most convenient way to buy property insurance is to combine all of your coverage under one policy. You are less likely to duplicate your coverage, settlement of claims is easier, and the total premium is usually lower. There may be some risks that are not covered by a property insurance package that you need to insure separately or by an extra endorsement to your policy such as theft or e-commerce insurance. If you are running a business from home, be aware that home and contents policies do not normally cover business losses. In fact, running a business from home could possibly invalidate your domestic policy.

Other Insurance

When your business is shut down as a result of a fire or flood, you may be protected for loss of property but not for the loss of operating revenue to pay the bills while you rebuild. Similarly, if a partner or a key employee dies, you may not be able to keep operating without their skills.

Business interruption insurance, sometimes called consequential loss insurance, will reimburse you for part of the lost profit and a proportion of the fixed costs of your business while you are out of action. It will never cover the full amount of the loss, but it is one way of making sure you have the funds to stay in business when you are temporarily unable to trade.

Partnership insurance provides immediate cash to keep a partnership business intact in the event of the death of one of the partners. Since the death of a partner legally ends a partnership, the proceeds of this insurance can be used by the surviving partner to buy the deceased partner's interest from their estate. *Key person insurance* is the same as partnership insurance except that the beneficiary is the business entity itself. This is sometimes considered when the loss of a key person may put the survival of the firm in jeopardy. It is designed to cover the extra expenses that a key person's death would cause such as finding and recruiting a replacement, training costs, and lost sales to important customers.

When you are self-employed or a subcontractor, you are not usually covered by workers compensation insurance. Therefore, you should have your own *personal accident, sickness,* and *disability insurance* through a private insurer. Income protection or disability insurance covers a portion of your normal income if you are prevented from working through sickness or accident.

Buying Insurance

There are three ways to buy insurance. You can deal directly with an insurance company, you can deal indirectly with an insurance company through its agent, or you can deal through an insurance broker. An insurance agent is acting on behalf of an insurance company. Brokers are independent of the insurance companies and it is their job to shop around for the most suitable policies, provide advice, arrange the paperwork, and assist you with claims. Insist on seeing the policy document and ask for a cover note or written confirmation of your instructions showing details of the insuring company, the period of the cover, and the amount insured. If an event occurs that triggers a claim, notify your insurer immediately and consult with them before taking any steps that may affect your claim.

SUMMARY

This chapter outlines the process of getting established in business. It consists of important questions that need to be considered, decisions that need to be made, and paperwork that needs to be completed. What is the right legal structure for your business? Will you operate as a sole proprietor, with others in a partnership, as a company, or as a trust? What will you call your business? The Business Registration Service is a central website where you can apply for most of your key business and tax registrations in one place. This is where you get an Australian Business Number, register a business name, register a company, get a Tax File Number, register for GST, and more. The Australian Business Licence Information Service is also a one-stop website for licences, permits, approvals, and registrations for your particular type of business. Part of the start-up process includes identifying the financial risks you could face and how to protect yourself with insurance.

Five
Business Plan

A successful small business is the product of a clear plan that minimises wasted effort and maximises results. Developing a business plan is a process of exploring opportunities, identifying and evaluating options, and arriving at how you are going to achieve tangible results. The purpose of this chapter is to describe how to construct a business plan. It begins by dispelling some of the myths about business plans and explains why planning is worth the effort. The main part of the chapter is devoted to suggestions for creating each section of your business plan including an introduction, marketing plan, operating plan, and financial plan. This is followed by an example. The chapter concludes by describing how a business changes over time and how to adapt your business plan as a result.

MYTHS AND REALITY OF PLANNING

Planning is important because it helps you work smarter rather than harder. It keeps you future-oriented and motivates you to achieve the results you want. Moreover, the process of doing a business plan enables you to determine what commitment you are prepared to make to the business. Planning significantly increases the likelihood of survival and prosperity by focusing your attention on the following areas in which small business operators sometimes get lost:

- Realism—It is human nature to be optimistic about a new idea. Planning helps to prevent you from viewing the future in ways that the facts do not support.
- The need for outside advice—Planning enables you to recognise problems that call for outside sources of information and assistance.

DOI: 10.4324/9781032676616-9

- Recognising change—The nature of markets and customer preferences are always changing. Planning cannot predict change, but it helps you to recognise it and to adjust your business strategy accordingly.
- Balancing growth—Small businesses either tend to grow too fast for their capital base or too slow to maintain cash flow. Planning helps you achieve smooth growth and avoid unexpected crises.
- Measuring results—A business plan enables you to compare your results against a set of goals.
- Obtaining finance—When someone puts money into your business, they want to know what to expect. A business plan not only helps you anticipate your capital needs, but it also provides the information that a banker or investor needs to evaluate your proposal for finance.

Most of the articles and books that have been written about business planning are designed for cash-hungry start-up situations in which a 100-page document is needed to pry money out of a tight-fisted venture capital organisation. That kind of business plan is simply not relevant for the vast majority of small businesses. It has resulted in a number of myths that leave some small business operators feeling a bit daunted. Let's examine them and consider the reality.

- ***My business plan has to be a formal exercise.*** The reality is, your plan can be as simple as a set of informal notes. The value of a business plan is in putting the ideas on paper and creating action steps that will get you where you want to go. Planning in a small business needs to be a practical road map that outlines where you want to be and how you want to get there. Stick to a short planning period of one or two years. Write it down, but don't make it long or complicated.
- ***Once I've done my business plan, I'm tied to it like a ball and chain.*** Some business owners feel like once it's on paper, their business plan can't be changed. Wrong! The reality is that it should be a rolling plan that gets reviewed and updated. You're

the owner, you wrote the plan, you know what's happening in your market, and you can make whatever changes you wish.

- *I don't have to do a business plan myself because I can pay a consultant or my accountant to do it for me.* The reality is that a business plan is a reflection of your vision and your aspirations. You can ask your accountant for advice and you can engage a consultant for specialised expertise, but you cannot expect them to make a strong personal commitment to planning your business. If you do not create the business plan yourself, then it is not really your plan. If it is not your plan, then how do you know you can depend on it? A genuine planning exercise might save you from yourself by persuading you to abandon a bad idea while your mistakes are still on paper.

- *Doing a business plan is a guarantee of success.* The evidence is clear that a growing number of small firms do plan and their chances for survival and prosperity significantly increase with the frequency and quality of planning. However, the reality is that no matter how carefully you do your business plan, there will always be a risk of failure.

- *I'm too small to worry about a business plan.* The reality is, even a one-person business can benefit from a simple rolling business plan. It helps you to think about your options and make decisions about how you want to operate your business.

PUTTING YOUR PLAN ON PAPER

Developing a business plan represents an opportunity to examine every aspect of organising and operating your business. It is a way to explore the consequences of different strategies and determine what resources are necessary to launch or expand your business. A business plan also contains the information needed by others if you are asking for finance. Here are some suggestions for how to organise your business plan.

Introduction

If your plan is going to be used as a financing proposal, then you need an introduction that identifies who is asking for finance, how much money is required, how the funds will be used, and how they will benefit the business.

Overview

Briefly describe your business. What is its name, how is it organised (proprietorship, partnership, company), and what are its main activities (retailing, service, manufacturing, wholesaling, or some combination)? Is this a start-up, an expansion, or the purchase of an existing operation? Describe the location and facilities. Relate anything of importance about new products, new markets and customers, and regional or economic trends that could have an impact on your business. Financial backers, including business angels and financial institutions, are interested in the people behind a business as much as the business itself. For this reason, you need to demonstrate your capacity to organise and operate the business. Outline the personal history of each owner and explain how their skills and experience relate to the business. Also be sure to list external advisers such as your solicitor and accountant.

Marketing Plan

The marketing plan is usually the most difficult part to prepare, but it is the key part of every business plan. Describe your product or service. Explain its primary use and any important secondary uses. Emphasise the things that make your product or service unique or superior to whatever is currently on the market. Discuss any opportunities for the expansion of your product line or the development of related products or services.

- Identify your market. Divide your market into segments and explain your rationale. Which market niche(s) are you targeting?
- Identify your customer profile. Who are your customers? What are their buying motives such as price, quality, service, convenience, or perhaps necessity?
- Determine the size of your market. How many potential customers can you reach within your trading area? How much should they spend on your product or service? Can this market be expanded?

- Assess the competition. Who are your nearest competitors? What is their share of the market? What have you learned about their operations? Explain why you think you can capture a share of their business or keep them from capturing a share of yours.
- Show how your overall marketing strategy follows from your assessment of the market. It should identify your market niche, explain how you are going to satisfy your customers, and indicate your plans for pricing, promotion, and distribution.

Estimating Sales

Estimating sales is important because it defines the level of activity in the business and it impacts every aspect of the business plan. It consists of calculating the expected annual sales for all potential customers in a target market area and estimating what share of this market you expect to capture. Sales can be measured in different ways such as the number of units sold per customer, the number of transactions per customer, or the dollar sales per customer. The number of customers can be measured in terms of individuals, household units, business units, or some other customer unit. Here is a step-by-step example:

Step 1: What is the customer unit for this idea? *Let's say, households.*

Step 2: How many households are in the target market? This information is available from the Australian Bureau of Statistics. *Let's say, 10,000 households.*

Step 3: What is the average annual household demand for this type of product? Consult the Australian Bureau of Statistics' Household Expenditure Survey. *Let's say, ten units per year.*

Step 4: What is the average price that customers would be willing to pay for this product? *Let's say, $30 per unit.*

Step 5: What is the annual market size for this product in this target market area? *10,000 households × 10 units per household per year × $30 per unit = $3,000,000 per year.*

Step 6: What share of this market do I expect to capture? *Let's say, 40 percent.*

Step 7: What will be my forecast annual sales? *$3,000,000 annual sales* × *40 percent market share* = ***$1,200,000.***

Another approach is to estimate market size using an equivalent or similar substitute. Try looking for information about a comparable product in the same market. Alternatively, look for information about the same product in a different market. Estimating market size by making comparisons like this works well for existing products and services. For example, a product that is sold in the United Kingdom can provide clues about market size for the same product in Australia. Similarly, sales turnover for a franchise in Newcastle can be adjusted for differences in demographics to estimate market size in Hobart.

Estimating market size for a completely new product or service is more difficult because there is no information about similar products or comparable locations. There is generally information about how many customers there are but very little information about their propensity to make a purchase. Think about what customers need, the way they will use your product or service to fill this need, the number of potential customers in the target market area, and how much they might be prepared to pay.

Operations Plan

The operations plan explains how a business will go about performing its tasks. The building blocks of an operations plan can be thought of as place, processes, programs, and people.

- Place includes location such as retail premises, workshops, or warehousing. It also includes equipment, from office furniture and computers to manufacturing machinery.
- Procedures vary greatly depending on the nature of a business. For retail and service businesses, they may range from

low-volume custom-made to high-volume on-demand. For manufacturing businesses, they may range from jobbing to mass production.

- Programs refer to the means by which place and procedures are brought together. They include planning, coordination, and integration.
- People include number of staff, locations, skills, recruitment, and training. The more specialised the skills needed, the more effort you should put into describing how you expect to go about finding them.

Financial Plan

A three-year financial forecast is probably as much as most small businesses can realistically project. The financial plan is concerned with liquidity, profitability, and financial position.

- Liquidity refers to the need for cash so you can pay your bills as they become due. Liquidity forecasts are based on the projected amounts and timing of cash receipts and disbursements arranged in the form of a cash flow budget. For many small businesses, a cash flow budget is the only financial forecast that really matters.
- Profitability forecasts are based on the sales estimates in your marketing plan and the expenses related to achieving those sales. They consist of forecasted income statements.
- Financial position consists of forecasted balance sheets, which show the assets you need to operate the business and the way you expect to finance them.

It is important to avoid overestimating sales or underestimating costs. It is also important not to confuse cash flow with profits. Since financial information is sometimes tedious, put the headline results into the body of your business plan and include the forecasted financial statements as supporting exhibits.

Supporting Exhibits

If your business plan is used to seek finance, you need to include copies of documentary evidence to substantiate your claims. Here are some examples of supporting exhibits:

Résumés of the owners	Legal documents
Credit information	Census or demographic data
Quotations or estimates	Financial forecasts
Leases or buy/sell agreements	

SAMPLE BUSINESS PLAN

What follows is an example of a business plan based on this format. It contains enough information to use as a proposal for finance.

TASMANIAN GOURMET VENISON

Tasmanian Gourmet Venison is planning to invest $300,000 to establish an organic venison butchery in Hobart, Tasmania. This investment will position the business to target a lucrative market for quality venison products. The funds will be used for

New equipment	$130,000
Leasehold improvements	$100,000
Website development	$10,000
Working capital	$60,000
	$300,000

The owners of Tasmanian Gourmet Venison are Mr Richard Amos and Mr Edward Davis. Richard has been on the land in Tasmania and he has managed the breeding and grazing operation at Tasmanian Gourmet Venison for 12 years. Edward was born in Sydney and worked for ten years in specialist butcher shops in the United Kingdom before joining

---

the meat products division of a large food company in Australia. He has direct experience with operations in meat packaging and marketing.

Richard is well known among Tasmanian organic food producers and throughout the rural community. He is particularly experienced in the agricultural and wholesale sides of the business. Edward is experienced in the retail trade and will manage a new outlet in Hobart. Profits will be distributed equally between the two owners. The following professional advisers have been engaged:

Accountant	Mr George Scribe, CPA
Solicitor	Tony Justice, LLB
Bank	Antipodean National Bank

Overview

Several developments suggest the market for organic venison in Tasmania is expanding:

- Higher prices for organic meat products make organic venison more price competitive than it has been previously.
- There is increasing demand for lean meat that is free from hormones and antibiotics.
- Tasmanian Gourmet Venison is in a position to produce sufficient volume to ensure a consistent supply of product to customers.

Tasmanian Gourmet Venison is the only organically certified grazing property in the Tasmanian highlands. Our deer enjoy clover-rich pastures, lightly wooded valleys, and bracken covered slopes – truly a deer's paradise. They live their entire stress-free life on the farm and are processed in our on-farm certified abattoir. Tasmanian Gourmet Venison has been expanding the size of the deer herd and now has sufficient breeding stock to enable us to offer a consistent supply of organic venison products to Tasmanian customers. The business is ready to take the next step by vertically integrating the operation into retail distribution.

Product Line

Venison, once the meat of kings, is gaining popularity in today's health-conscious consumer market. It is an extremely lean meat and it is the perfect addition to a well-balanced diet. Venison has far lower fat and cholesterol content than beef, lamb, pork, or chicken. It is high in polyunsaturates, which are important in building a healthy body and lowering harmful cholesterol. Venison is also high in protein and iron. Tasmanian Gourmet Venison carries a complete line of organic venison products including

Venison rump steak	Venison rib joint
Venison topside	Venison silverside
Venison haunch joint	Venison loin chops
Venison loin	Venison shin
Venison escalopes	Diced venison
Venison cutlets	Venison neck

For retail customers, we will offer venison box selections including

Monthly box selection	Introductory box selection
Winter box selection	Mini venison box selection
Thrifty box selection	Seasonal box selection
Steak selection	

Our venison box selections are packaged in a variety of boneless packs, so there is no waste. After ageing, the venison is prepared by a specialist game butcher. It is vacuum packed in individual cuts to ensure it remains in perfect condition. Recipes are included with every venison box selection plus tips on how to cook venison.

Target Market

Tasmanian Gourmet Venison is committed to providing premium quality organic venison at competitive prices to customers within the greater Hobart area. According to census figures from the Australian Bureau of Statistics, there are approximately 100,000 households within reach of the planned Hobart outlet. The number of customers increases significantly during December and January when holidaymakers come to Tasmania.

The Australian Bureau of Statistics report average weekly household expenditure on all organic meat products in Tasmania is $3.41, or about $177 per year. It is also estimated that organic venison products account for 12 percent of organic meat sales. Therefore, potential annual demand for organic venison products in the Hobart retail market is over $2 million. Existing wholesale sales to Hobart restaurants has been $500,000 annually. The sales forecast for the first year is included in the financial plan.

Marketing Plan

Tasmanian Gourmet Venison has developed an image and reputation for quality, fresh organic venison at competitive prices. We will continue to convey this image to our two market segments – retail and wholesale.

To the retail trade, we will promote our new convenient location, the health benefits in the diet, and the unique taste of organic venison. We will complement our quality image with clean, attractive facilities and excellent service. We will develop a website to make online purchasing easy, including gift packs, followed by next-day delivery anywhere in the greater Hobart area. Promotion will be based on online advertising, newspaper advertising, lifestyle magazine features, and retail display.

We will continue to make direct approaches to the 47 restaurants in the greater Hobart area. We will emphasise consistency of supply, convenient location, daily delivery service, impeccable quality, and volume discounts. We will have a username and password-protected wholesale section on our website to service the restaurant market.

Operating Plan

Tasmanian Gourmet Venison can lease a retail property in Hobart for five years with options to renew the lease for a further two five-year terms. It will require leasehold improvements including interior decoration and installation of a walk-in cold store. The building includes a 135 m^2 sales area, a 12 m^2 cutting room, and a further 80 m^2 of space that is currently unused and available for expansion. We will consider establishing a second location in Launceston when the Hobart outlet is fully operational and cash positive.

Tasmanian Gourmet Venison will initially employ two full-time specialist game butchers to prepare organic venison products for both the retail and wholesale trade. A full-time delivery driver will also be employed. Four part-time sales assistants will be engaged at award casual rates whose duties will be selling organic venison products over the counter to retail customers.

Financial Plan

The financial plan consists of a cash flow forecast for the first year. The new venture will exceed its cash break-even point in the first year of trading with a year-end cash position of over $60,000. The initial investment in stock, equipment, and improvements will be complete. This will see Tasmanian Gourmet Venison positioned to generate greater sales, profits, and cash flow in the following year.

Table 5.1 First-Year Cash Flow Forecast

	Month before start-up	July	Aug	Sept	Oct	Nov	Dec	Jan	Feb	Mar	Apr	May	June	Total
Receipts														
Sales		45,000	67,500	78,750	90,000	101,250	135,000	112,500	101,250	101,250	101,250	101,250	90,000	1,125,000
Capital	300,000													300,000
TOTAL	300,000	45,000	67,500	78,750	90,000	101,250	135,000	112,500	101,250	101,250	101,250	101,250	90,000	1,425,000
Disbursements														
Purchases	45,000	29,700	44,550	51,975	59,400	66,825	89,100	74,250	66,825	66,825	66,825	66,825	59,400	787,500
Wages		5,000	7,500	8,750	10,000	11,250	15,000	12,500	11,250	11,250	11,250	11,250	10,000	125,000
Marketing		4,500	6,750	7,875	9,000	10,125	13,500	11,250	10,125	10,125	10,125	10,125	9,000	112,500
Fixed costs		5,625	5,625	5,625	5,625	5,625	5,625	5,625	5,625	5,625	5,625	5,625	6,750	68,625
Equipment	130,000													130,000
Buildings	100,000													100,000
Website	10,000	250	250	250	250	250	250	250	250	250	250	250	250	13,000
BAS				5,000			7,500			7,500			6,000	26,000
TOTAL	285,000	45,075	64,675	79,475	84,275	94,075	130,975	103,875	94,075	101,575	94,075	94,075	91,400	1,362,625
Cash flow	15,000	−75	2,825	−725	5,725	7,175	4,025	8,625	7,175	−325	7,175	7,175	−1,400	62,375
Cash balance	15,000	14,925	17,750	17,025	22,750	29,925	33,950	42,575	49,750	49,425	56,600	63,775	62,375	62,375

ADAPTING TO CHANGE

The life of a small business consists of a number of phases, each with a different set of goals and requiring a different managerial mindset. It is not only important to learn how to construct a business plan, but it is equally important to recognise when to change it. You always want to have two strategies – one that capitalises on the forces that are naturally at work and a second that acts as a safety net if the first one does not succeed.

Start-Up Phase

The start-up phase is characterised by tremendous uncertainty. You will probably lack confidence and your decisions may be a little compulsive, erratic, and inconsistent. A new business will almost certainly face a cash crisis caused by the huge cash drain that normally occurs early in its life. A large proportion of closures occur during the start-up phase. The main goal is to survive and stay in business.

A small business operator needs to be an innovator, organiser, and troubleshooter during the start-up phase. An idea has to be transformed into reality. That means generating enough innovative inspiration and persuasiveness to appeal to your customers while you work towards creating a strong competitive advantage.

Entry strategies are designed to get into business. They may be aimed at a new business of a new kind or a new business of an existing kind. The avenues for entry include starting from scratch, buying an existing business, or perhaps buying a franchise. Effective entry strategies rely on a strong competitive advantage.

Exit strategies are designed to get out of business during the start-up phase if the competitive advantage turns out to be weak. They consist largely of minimising the losses associated with discontinuing operations. Inasmuch as the business does not usually have significant assets to liquidate, the focus is on how to handle the existing obligations and how to avoid any further liabilities that may arise from winding up.

Takeoff Phase

The takeoff phase is characterised by a sharp increase in sales volume. The dominant goal is to capitalise on your competitive advantage. You will need to invest in more resources to support increased sales volume, and it may aggravate any lingering cash flow problems left over from the start-up phase. After an agonising period of losses, the business finally turns the corner.

Now your business may be too big for one person to handle. If this turns out to be the case, overwork and stress may begin to take a toll. A delegation crisis will occur unless you make the transition from being an owner to an owner manager. It is time to develop and implement procedures that will guide staff in your absence. During the takeoff phase, a small business operator learns how to delegate responsibility while exercising sufficient control to ensure that the business stays on track.

Growth strategies are designed to achieve a big increase in sales. The rapid increase in sales means that the business needs to invest in more assets and more staff to support greater sales volume. Growth strategies also include sophisticated refinements to entrench your competitive advantage.

Concentration strategies are designed for recovery when a growth strategy loses its competitive advantage. The objective is to refocus the assets on a slightly different market niche in order to improve short-run cash flow and long-run profits. It usually means selling off some of the assets and concentrating new investment in those areas where the business will have its greatest competitive advantage.

Harvest Phase

When the growth in sales volume begins to stabilise, the business will be entering the harvest phase. This can be a very prolonged period in which the dominant goal is to make profits. Internal matters like cost control and efficiency will occupy more of your time. Your competitive advantage will be entrenched and your business will settle into a more predictable routine. You will be increasingly distant from the day-to-day operations and you will get things done through your staff. In this phase, a small business operator learns to become an effective administrator, manager, and leader.

The inevitable growth of administrative detail and paperwork may eventually sap your enthusiasm, and prolonged prosperity may cause you to lose sight of the fact that in order to continue harvesting, you also need to be sowing the seeds for future crops. Complacency may lead to a void in leadership and you could find your competitive advantage endangered.

Profit strategies are designed to make the best use of your competitive advantages and existing resources to produce large profits and positive cash flows. The focus shifts from acquiring new customers and new assets to exploiting existing customers and efficiently utilising existing assets. The ultimate profit strategy is the eventual sale of the business as a going concern for a price that reflects its long-term profitability.

Contraction strategies are designed to reduce the investment in a business while maintaining its profitability. Contraction strategies are called for when the asset base is too large for the sales and profits that it generates. Contraction strategies improve return on investment when profits are static by selectively selling surplus assets and taking the cash outside the business.

Renewal Phase

The renewal phase begins with the recognition that a firm's competitive advantage has been eroded. This often coincides with the owner wanting to withdraw from the business. Renewal requires overcoming resistance to changing the way things have been done in the past. The business is in danger of withering away unless the owner gets a new burst of enthusiasm or finds a successor. The goal is to renew the firm's competitive advantage and restore its ability to harvest.

In this phase, a small business operator will be a reorganiser and a revitaliser. The objective is to breathe new life into a business by reasserting its competitive advantage and recapturing its ability to harvest. A reversal in declining sales, profits, and cash flow will occur when the firm's assets begin to pay their way again.

Turnaround strategies are designed to reverse the declining fortunes of a business on the premise that it is worth saving. Turnaround strategies are usually based on revenue-increasing measures or cost-reducing measures depending on which have the greatest and most expedient effect on cash flow.

Liquidation strategies are the result of a decision to abandon a business. They are designed to generate as much cash flow as possible while methodically withdrawing from the business. Liquidation strategies work best when you can control the situation. They consist of liquidating the firm's assets and winding it up or attempting to sell the business as a potential turnaround opportunity for a new owner.

SUMMARY

This chapter describes how to construct a business plan. It begins by dispelling some of the myths about business plans and explains why planning is worth the effort. The main part of the chapter is devoted to suggestions for creating each section of a business plan. If a plan is going to be used as a financing proposal, then it needs an introduction that describes who is asking for finance, how much money is needed, and how the funds will be used. The next section is an overview of the business including whether it is a start-up or an expansion of an existing business. The marketing strategy is the key part of a business plan. The strategy identifies the product or service, the target market, pricing, promotion, distribution, and the estimates for sales. The operating plan lays out how the plant, processes, programs, and people will be organised. The financial plan is concerned with liquidity, profitability, and financial position in the form of a cash flow budget, a forecasted income statement, and a forecasted balance sheet. The chapter concludes by describing the ways in which a business changes over time and how a business plan can be revised as a result.

Reflective Exercise: Evaluating the Risks

Risk is an unavoidable part of being in business. It can be managed and its damaging outcomes can be minimised. Some risks are common to all businesses, and others may only be crucial for a few businesses. Risks also vary in terms of the *likelihood* that they will actually happen and the potential *consequences* if they do. Likelihood refers to how probable an event is to occur.

- If it is *unlikely* to ever happen, rate it as 1.
- If it is *possible* that it will happen, rate it as 2.
- If it is *likely* that it will happen, rate it as 3.

Consequence refers to the damage that will ensue if an event does happen. Think of it in terms of the financial loss.

- If it is a *minor* financial loss, rate it as 1.
- If it is a *moderate* financial loss, rate it as 2.
- If it is a *significant* financial loss, rate it as 3.

By multiplying the likelihood rating and the consequence rating together, you have a relative measure of how important each risk is to your business. This draws your attention to the most likely and the costliest events first.

DOI: 10.4324/9781032676616-10

Risk Importance

Consequence / Likelihood	Minor (1)	Moderate (2)	Significant (3)
Unlikely (1)	1	2	3
Possible (2)	2	4	6
Likely (3)	3	6	9

Major risks in the range from 6 to 9 are serious and require serious attention. Medium risks in the range from 3 to 4 are less urgent but nevertheless will need to be managed. Minor risks are in the range from 1 to 2 and you may decide to simply accept these risks or else take steps to eliminate them altogether.

At this stage, it is anticipated that you have an idea in mind that could become a business. The purpose of this reflective exercise is to identify and evaluate the risks associated with your business idea. We distinguish between those risks that are outside the business and those risks that are inside the business. External risks are generally beyond your control and may have the potential to restrict the commercial potential of the business. Internal risks are related to the way a business is organised and operated, and there is more you can do to manage them. In this exercise, you are asked to evaluate ten types of risk that could affect your business idea. When you are finished, reflect back on your responses and consider their collective impact on the overall risk of your business idea.

EXTERNAL RISKS

External risks restrict the commercial potential of an idea because they limit the ways in which it can be exploited. There is little that can be done to change the nature of external risks, but it is possible to position a business to minimise their effect.

Compliance Risk

Compliance risk covers nearly every aspect of business including competition, financial transactions, health, safety, the environment, and more. Compliance not only includes legal restrictions imposed at commonwealth, state, and local government levels but also regulation by non-government agencies and industry associations. Laws and regulations made by government and other regulatory bodies can significantly increase the cost of operating a business, reduce the attractiveness of making an investment, or change the market potential of an idea.

In terms of the relevant laws, standards, and other regulations, will my business idea meet them without any changes, require some changes, or possibly not meet them at all?

Technology Risk

Technology is the basis for many new business opportunities, but it also represents a significant source of risk. Many high-tech ideas fail because the developer falls in love with the technology and ignores the market that it is intended to serve. Technological change can also overtake the market for inferior technology, putting existing businesses at risk. Perhaps the biggest technological risk for every business is failing to embrace technology in the face of competitive pressure from businesses that do.

Will the technology on which my business idea is based be very stable for the foreseeable future, subject to some disruptive developments, or likely to be replaced by new technology relatively soon?

Economic Risk

The business cycle consists of periods of economic expansion and contraction. The three main economic risks for new business ideas are changes in consumer and business confidence, inflation, and interest rates. Changes in consumer and business confidence are driven by things that affect their purchasing power including taxes, employment, inflation, interest rates, government spending, and exchange rates. When inflation stays at an acceptable level, prices remain stable and consumers and businesses are more likely to be confident. When inflation rises, consumers and businesses lose purchasing power and curtail their spending. Changes in interest rates affect how much consumers and businesses are prepared to borrow and consequently how much they are prepared to spend.

Will the near-term outlook for the economy be positive, neutral, or negative for my business idea?

Political Risk

Proposed changes in government policy can alter the feasibility of a business idea. These include policy decisions about taxes, spending, regulation, exchange rates, trade tariffs, industrial relations, environmental regulations, and more. Political risk not only includes policies at the commonwealth government level but also at the state and local government levels. When governments decide to change a policy, it alters the risk-reward tradeoff for those businesses that are affected. Policy decisions in other countries can also create political risks.

Will the extent to which my business idea might be at risk from current or proposed government policy be very low, moderate, or very high?

Dependence Risk

Dependence occurs when a business idea must rely on some other product, process, service, system, person, or organisation to make sales. If dependence is low, then you will have greater control over your marketing strategy and more scope to exploit an opportunity. If dependence is high, then you will have less control over your business for what will be produced, what will be sold, or how it will be sold.

Will my product or service depend on another product, process, service, system, person, or organisation? Will the dependence be low, moderate, or high?

INTERNAL RISKS

Internal risks result from the way in which a business is organised, so it is important to know what they are and what you can do about them. You have a great deal more control over managing internal risks than for external risks.

Planning Risk

Planning risk is not knowing how you are going to make the transition from your initial business idea to a successful operation. Planning significantly increases the chances for success. It helps to prevent you from viewing the future in ways that the facts don't support, and it exposes problems early before they become a crisis. Planning cannot predict change, but it helps you to recognise it and construct a strategy accordingly.

Has a plan for my business idea been finalised, is work on one under way, will I do one sooner or later, or is it unnecessary because it is all in my head?

Marketing Risk

Marketing risk means not fully understanding the characteristics of your target market and how it can be captured. Without customers, there is no commercial potential, and without satisfying a genuine need or want, there will be no customers. The risk is that you may not have enough information that is accurate and complete. The goal is to know how you are going to deliver exactly the right benefits to the best customers.

Has the market research for my business idea been completed, has it been put off for now, or is it unnecessary because it is all in my head?

Deliverable's Risk

There are two parts to deliverable's risk. The first part relates to whether an idea will be fit for its intended purpose. For a product, we are interested in things like operating characteristics, features, flexibility, durability, conforming to standards, serviceability, aesthetics, and quality. For a service, we are interested in things like timeliness, courtesy, consistency, convenience, completeness, and accuracy. The second part relates to the process that creates the product or service. Some business ideas are simple and easily managed with standard operating procedures. Others are complex or vary considerably, resulting in greater deliverable's risk.

Will I be able to deliver my product or service consistently at a very high standard, at an acceptable standard most of the time, or I'm not sure without further investigation?

Liquidity Risk

Liquidity risk means running out of money. Initially, money may be needed for research and development, market research, setting up distribution channels, training, equipment, premises, production, packaging, promotion, and working capital. The more money it takes to get the doors open, the greater the chance there will not be enough money to keep going until the business becomes cash flow positive.

Will the money available for my business be enough to get started, will I require some borrowing, or I'm not sure without doing more investigation?

Personal Risk

It is one thing to recognise the commercial risks involved in a business idea, but there are also personal risks. Going into business can create an enormous strain on your finances, your family, your social life, your emotions, and sometimes your health. You need to consider the personal risks involved and ask yourself if this business idea is going to be within your comfort zone.

Will the personal risks involved in going into this business be totally within my comfort zone, at the limit of my comfort zone, or outside my comfort zone?

Part C
Marketing Plan

Marketing is a way of thinking that encompasses just about every aspect of how a business is organised and operated. The key to a marketing plan is to understand who your customers are and what motivates them to buy your product or service. The objective is to position your business as the preferred choice in your market niche by creating a marketing mix that matches your customers' needs and wants. Before technology and the internet, traditional marketing was the primary way business was conducted. Traditional marketing is still an important part of a marketing plan including direct marketing, newspapers, magazines, radio, television, outdoor advertising, publicity, sponsorship, and personal selling. The marketing landscape changed when digital marketing was introduced. It has created entirely new types of businesses, and it has introduced new opportunities for existing businesses. Digital marketing includes having your own website, listing in search engines and electronic directories, email marketing, online advertising and promotion, social media marketing, and marketing via mobile devices. The combination of traditional and digital marketing means that for every small business there is a marketing strategy that matches their market niche.

DOI: 10.4324/9781032676616-11

Six
Marketing Strategy

Marketing is a topic that has always been shrouded in mystery. Most small business operators know that marketing is probably the most important element in their business, but they are not sure about what strategies to use or where to begin. The first step in creating a marketing strategy is to do some research so you understand who your customers are and what motivates them to buy your product or service. You need this information to decide how you will position the business so it becomes the preferred choice in your market niche. Having established the foundations for a marketing strategy, your objective is to create a marketing mix that is aimed at your target market. The marketing mix consists of the products and services you decide to offer, the ways you distribute them, the methods you choose for advertising and promotion, and the pricing practices you adopt. The purpose of this chapter is to consider each component of your marketing strategy and how they can be combined to achieve the best results.

UNDERSTANDING YOUR CUSTOMERS

Understanding your customers means identifying their buying motives. When customers go shopping, they don't buy goods and services; they buy benefits. For example, when they decide to buy new tyres, some are buying safety, some are buying road-handling performance, while others are buying a sporty image. New and improved products and services regularly appear on the market, but customers' buying motives such as health, beauty, safety, comfort, convenience, economy, and enjoyment remain constant. Buying motives not only determine what customers buy but also how they buy. For example, what do you offer people who can only shop in

DOI: 10.4324/9781032676616-12

the evenings or on weekends? You open at times that are convenient, thereby offering a benefit that appeals to one of their buying motives.

Understanding customers also means gaining an insight into their buying role. The buyer for a one-person household decides what is needed, what will be bought, and where it will be purchased. In larger households, these roles are often played by different individuals. It helps to anticipate who has the need, who influences the purchase decision, and who actually decides what and where to buy. For example, a family decides they want to buy a takeaway meal on the drive home. Dad wants to go somewhere that has easy parking, Mum wants something that isn't deep fried, and the kids want a fast food venue that offers loyalty points they can redeem for music downloads. Each plays a role in the buying process. A business strategy works best when it is squarely aimed at satisfying customers' buying motives, and the only things you should be selling are the benefits your customers want to buy.

CUSTOMER INFORMATION

To understand your customers, you need information. Customer information enables you to choose the right products and services, determine the size and characteristics of your market niche, and establish the best ways to promote sales. After your business is established, you will need more customer information to decide where to grow, where to cut back, and where to change emphasis. Customer information does not have to be expensive to be good. In fact, if you are already in business, some of the best information will be from your existing customers. However, customer information is only useful if it is focused on answering important questions such as:

Who . . . uses your product or service?
decides to make the purchase?
actually makes the purchase?
buys from you?
buys from a competitor?

Where . . . is your product or service used?

do customers find information?

do customers decide to buy?

do customers actually buy?

are the customers located?

What . . . benefits do customers want?

is the basis of comparison with other products or services?

is the rate of usage?

price will customers pay?

is the potential market for your product or service?

The Australian Bureau of Statistics at **abs.gov.au** is a great source for obtaining census and demographic information. You can use census data and household expenditure survey information to compile a profile of your market. For example, you can establish the age distribution of the local population, average income, size of families, if they own or rent their home, if they have a car, and the number of school-age children. You can also establish how much the average household spends on a variety of goods and services. Studying this type of information will help you construct a picture of your target market. The limitation of statistical information is that it is based on historical data, which may change in the future.

Find Your Niche

To develop a marketing strategy, you need to aim at a specific market niche. *Market segmentation* is the process of dividing the overall market into groups with similar characteristics. The objective is to select segments that match your strengths and are large enough to support your business. This does not mean that you ignore the other market segments. It simply means that a high proportion of your sales will come from the market segments you target. One of the strengths of being small is the ability to play 'nichemanship' in ways that large competitors cannot match.

Suppose you are interested in the packaged food business and you want to create a new approach for this market. One way to begin is by segmenting households according to the dominant way in which their meals are chosen, prepared, and consumed.

- Country cooks prepare three meals from scratch every day and occasionally make dessert. This market segment is relatively small and it is not interested in packaged food.
- Functional feeders look first for convenience in food preparation and then for variety and taste. This segment is growing at about the same rate as the population.
- International eaters are seeking new and exotic ways to authentically recreate ethnic foods. They are influenced by travel and cooking programs on television, specialised cookbooks, and the ethnic diversity of Australia's restaurants. This market segment was slow to develop, but it is now growing and evolving as new trends in food styles emerge.
- Healthy households place their emphasis on natural food, a balanced diet, and fitness. This is the second fastest-growing market segment.
- Grab-its are characterised by people who have an obsession with free time and leisure activities. This is the typical fast food, frozen dinner, takeaway eater. It represents the fastest-growing market segment.

Each market segment represents a different group of customers with different buying motives. The objective is to identify the market segment that best matches your competitive advantage. An effective marketing strategy is based on a clearly defined market niche, a thorough understanding of your customers' buying motives, and knowing exactly how your product or service is going to provide the benefits they want.

POSITIONING YOUR BUSINESS

Market position is the image that customers have of your business. When they decide to make a purchase, they mentally rate the businesses that are most likely to carry what they want and offer the kind of services they prefer. They have an image of each business that sums up their feelings about it and they will go first to the business they rate best. The perfect market position is the one that clearly establishes you as the preferred choice in your market niche.

Every business has a market position whether it is intentional or not. The decor of the business, the style of the sign outside, and the way in which staff dress, answer the phone, and greet customers all express the personality of a business. These impressions tell customers a great deal about a business in the first few seconds. When you choose a market position for your business, make sure that it accurately reflects the buying motives of your market niche. Emphasise the things customers value most so that your market position exactly matches the benefits they want.

PRODUCTS AND SERVICES

The easiest and most profitable products and services to sell are the ones that your customers want to buy. The path to establishing a marketing strategy starts by identifying your customers' needs and then shaping an offering of products and services accordingly. A *product line* is a group of products or services that have similar characteristics and uses. For example, you would expect a computer store to offer product lines in desktops, laptops, printers, and software. The product lines that the computer store carries is called its *product mix*. The key to deciding on the best product mix is how well it meets the needs of customers.

The number of product lines on offer is called *product breadth*. If a computer store carries only hardware, then its product mix is narrow. If it carries every possible computer-related product line, then its product mix is wide. The assortment within a product line is called *product depth*. For example, the more models of laptops that a computer shop has for sale, the more depth it has in that product line. *Image anchors* are products that you promote heavily because they define the image of the whole product line. They are usually from the higher end of the product line range.

Decisions about product lines, product mix, product breadth, and product depth constitute your product choices. These decisions should be consistent with the way you have segmented your market and positioned your business.

DISTRIBUTION

If products or services are not available where and when customers want them, then the sale is lost. Your goal is to identify the best way to get your products and services to your customers. Depending on the nature of your business, your distribution may be simple and direct or it may be complex and involve multiple steps.

Your choice of distribution channels is determined by how your customers want to buy from you. Would they prefer to buy directly from the manufacturer, or would they prefer to buy from a retailer? Perhaps they would rather buy over the internet? What do they need in terms of technical advice, installation, or service? Which distribution channel provides customers with the kind of information they need to make a purchase decision? Your choice of distribution channel will also be influenced by cost. Distributors charge a markup or commission for carrying your goods. This may be fair compensation for their services, or it may be unacceptably high in terms of the final price to the customer or the loss of your own profitability.

Distribution choices are not restricted to products. It can be equally important when selling services. Hotels, for example, not only sell their rooms (a service) directly, but they also sell through distributors such as travel agents, tour operators, airlines, tourism offices, and centralised online booking systems. You may also need more than one distribution channel to serve different market segments. For example, customers for food supplements can buy them through a variety of distribution channels including health food stores, chemists, grocery stores, direct mail, and on the internet.

Direct marketing means dealing with customers yourself. The main advantages are you don't have to share your profits and you have complete control over the marketing process. There are other reasons why you might want to sell direct. You may be the only person who can demonstrate your products, offer detailed information, and provide the right kind of after-sales service. If retailers or other distributors are not willing to handle your products or services, then you may have no choice but to sell direct. The flip side is that direct marketing can also be more of a hassle than using a distributor. A distributor may have more resources and better expertise to sell your products and they may be able to do it at a lower cost.

Beyond direct marketing, distribution is more complex and can take place on several levels. A one-level strategy uses just one intermediary. For consumer goods, it is usually a retailer, and for industrial goods, it is usually a distributor or agent. In larger markets, a two-level strategy might be more appropriate in which a product is sold to a wholesaler who in turn distributes to retailers.

The choice of distribution is a tradeoff between the cost of using intermediaries to achieve wider distribution versus the greater control and higher margins of selling direct. It has significant implications for your profit margins, marketing budget, final retail pricing, and selling practices. If you are starting out, try to avoid costly or complex channels of distribution in favour of more direct strategies in which volume requirements are lower and promotion is less expensive.

PROMOTION

Promotion is built on a thorough understanding of your customers' buying motives and the way you position your business. The objectives are to decide what to promote, where to promote, and how much to spend on promotion.

What to Promote

If you have spent considerable effort in trying to create an image, then it is important to keep this in mind when selecting products and services for promotion. Deciding what to promote means focusing on customers' buying motives and developing a promotional theme around them. Here are some examples of buying motives:

- Safety—People want to protect themselves and their property from harm.
- Savings—People are not only interested in the lowest price but also in savings through less frequent replacement, lower maintenance, or lower operating costs.

- Health—People buy products and services like exercise bikes, organic food, sunglasses, and aerobics classes to protect and maintain their health.
- Status—People buy things in order to be recognised. A fashion-conscious individual, for example, may be more concerned with the designer's name on the label than with the garment itself.
- Pleasure—People download movies, go to football games, eat out at restaurants, and buy books for pleasure.
- Convenience—Many products and services make the routine chores of life easier. Examples are takeaway food, house cleaning services, and car washes.

Where to Promote

Different products and services lend themselves to different media. If an item has news value, use newspaper advertising. If an item has strong and desirable visual qualities, show it off in your window and store displays. If it can be easily described in words, promote it on radio. If an item meets the requirements for both displays and radio, consider using television. If digital marketing fits into your strategy, there are a variety of ways to promote products and services such as online advertising, email, and social media.

Your market area and your advertising budget will help you determine what medium, or combination of media, to use. There are media outside your business and inside your business. Outside media include newspapers, magazines, direct mail, outdoor signs, cinemas, radio, television, and the internet. Examples of inside media are window displays, interior displays, blowups of advertisements, brochures, manufacturers' literature, gift novelties, signs, posters, and merchandise attachments such as tags and labels.

How Much to Spend

Deciding how much to spend for advertising and promotion is not only an important part of your marketing strategy, but it is also a key element in the cost side of your business. If you are already in business, look at previous advertising and promotion to see what sales volume it produced. What factors may have changed? What is your sales target for the same period this year? What sort of promotional effort is needed to achieve your sales target and what will it cost? Here are some features you may want to consider:

- Age—A new business needs more promotion to announce its opening than an established business.
- Products—A shoe store needs more promotion to attract customers than a pastry shop that relies on passing foot traffic.
- Size in a community—A small business in a large community needs proportionally more advertising than a larger business in a small community.
- Location—A neighbourhood bookstore needs more promotion to attract customers than an airport bookstore that relies on a captive market.
- Trading area—A farm equipment dealer serves a wider area and therefore needs wider promotion than a city sandwich shop that only serves a few nearby office buildings.
- Competition—More promotion may be needed in one situation than in another to cope with competitive pressure.

Promoting Services

Promoting services follows the same principles that are used for products. However, you also need to be sensitive to the differences between tangible goods and intangible services. Here are some suggestions:

- Focus on recognisable tangible benefits in your advertising and other promotion to compensate for the intangible nature of a service.
- Services need greater explanation to make them fully understood.
- Promise only what you can deliver.
- Maintain a continuous promotional presence to remind customers of your service.
- Ensure that you maintain continuity of theme and style because these are important in developing an image and positioning a service business.

One of the distinctive characteristics of a service business is the importance of personal referrals and word-of-mouth recommendations. Customers are usually involved with the provision of a service and they experience its nature and quality. They form an opinion that will be sought by others who are interested in buying the same service. Word-of-mouth recommendations are one of the most potent sources of new customers and they outweigh all other forms of advertising and promotion. Dissatisfied customers, on the other hand, tell many people about their poor experience and they can severely damage a service business. That is why you must only promise what you can deliver and then deliver on time every time.

PRICING

Pricing is initially influenced by your product and service decisions. Depending on whether you are positioning your products and services as the low-cost leader or the high-quality leader, you will set your prices accordingly. Too many small business operators undervalue their products and services. Profit is the reason you are in business and profit is what enables you to stay in business. The objective is to set your prices to maximise profits, not to maximise sales turnover.

The relationship between price and sales volume is referred to as *price elasticity*. It describes the effect that a change in price has on the amount of a product or service customers will buy. When a product or service has high price elasticity, it means a small change in the price will have a strong impact on the amount purchased. Therefore, with a price cut, sales volume will increase significantly, and with a price hike, sales volume will fall off sharply. Low price elasticity means that changes in price have little effect on sales volume. In very competitive businesses with little product differentiation, price elasticity tends to be high. In specialised businesses with highly differentiated products, price elasticity tends to be low.

Approaches to Pricing

An understanding of your target market combined with a knowledge of the main approaches to pricing will help you set your prices.

Pricing practices vary between industry sectors and, to a lesser extent, within sectors.

Full-cost pricing sets the price to cover labour, materials, a proportion of the overhead costs such as rent and electricity, and a percentage for profit. Few businesses adhere rigidly to full-cost pricing because consumer demand and market factors exert a stronger influence on pricing. *Flexible markup pricing* is a more common practice in which full costs establish a 'floor' to which flexible markups are added. Not only can you adjust markups to reflect changes in demand or competition, but this approach also provides for variations in the markup that you put on different product lines. *Going-rate pricing* is not based on the underlying costs. Although costs are not ignored, the focus is on what the competition is charging and what prices people are willing to pay.

Gross margin pricing is the customary practice in retail firms by calculating a markup on the wholesale cost. The amount of the markup is called the gross margin. The same markup is not applied to all items, nor do you use the same markups at all times. The aim is to match the markups to consumer demand in an effort to maximise profits. *Suggested pricing* is used by some businesses that prefer not to make their own pricing decisions. Particularly in retailing, there is a tendency to accept the prices suggested by manufacturers or wholesalers for their products.

Promotional pricing is designed to bring customers into a business. *Discounting* a popular item to generate traffic is one form of promotional pricing. *Bundling* is two or more different products or services offered at a price that is lower than if they were purchased separately. Similarly, *multiple pricing* offers two or more of the same product or service for a lower price than if they were purchased separately.

Retailers rely mostly on suggested pricing or going-rate pricing, with flexible markup pricing or gross margin pricing on more competitive product lines. Service firms calculate prices on the time to perform a service multiplied by an hourly labour rate plus the materials used marked up to a retail price. The hourly labour rate is calculated to cover full costs and return a profit. Wholesalers' pricing practices are heavily influenced by the extent to which their distribution rights are exclusive. Therefore, their basic pricing practice will be suggested pricing with going-rate pricing in those lines in which they have competition. Manufacturers tend towards full-cost pricing on exclusive lines and flexible markup pricing on competitive lines. Don't forget to add GST to your prices.

Pricing Services

When customers buy a product, the price is usually clearly stated and they can evaluate the tangible benefits that the product offers. When they purchase a service, however, they tend to underestimate its value. Customers generally equate the price for services with what they think is a fair wage for the labour involved. They do not think of overheads, equipment, materials, and profit margins.

It is important to have a standard pricing policy for services in order to avoid unnecessary customer squabbles over price. Nothing destroys a service business faster than customers discovering they paid different prices for the same service. Wherever possible, published prices should be used to calculate your charges. Even if customers believe the prices are high, they find comfort in the fact that they are being charged the same price as others for the same service. One approach to setting your prices is to look at your competitors' published price lists in conjunction with your cost base.

Some service businesses do not lend themselves to standardised pricing because there is considerable variation from one job to another. In these cases, you need to evaluate each job individually and prepare a quote or bid price. The trick to bidding competitively is to prepare your bid based solely on the nature of the job and not according to what you think your competitors might bid. Each job needs an examination of all the factors that might affect the cost of doing the job. Winning a bid that results in a loss is no win at all.

MARKETING MIX

The objective of managing each component of the marketing mix is to create a coordinated marketing strategy that generates large profitable sales. It is like adjusting the components in a racing car so they work perfectly together to maximise performance. The way in which you combine the components of the marketing mix depends on the nature of your target market and the way in which you choose to position your business. Here is a retail example of how the marketing components can be combined depending on the market position that is chosen:

Marketing Mix

Position	Products	Distribution	Promotion	Pricing
Exclusive	Monopoly	Personal	Services	Highest
Speciality	Narrow/deep	Distinctive	Quality	Higher
Standard	Conventional	Central	Availability	Going rate
Discount	Broad	Expansive	Price	Lowest

An *exclusive* retail market position is usually the sole outlet for a particular product or service. The location need not be highly visible, but inside, the atmosphere is plush and personal. Advertising is low key, refined, and never refers to prices. Customers expect many extra services and they are willing to pay high prices for them.

A *specialty* retail market position depends on a narrow and very deep product line. The location and premises are distinctively related to the nature of the product. Advertising is primarily based on quality. Customers expect the firm to be expert in its line of business and to offer quality products and services for which they are prepared to pay higher-than-average prices.

A *standard* retail market position carries conventional product lines but not the depth of a specialty outlet. Location is in a central shopping area where complementary businesses are also found. Regular advertising is based on product availability and sometimes on price. Fewer services are offered and customers expect them to be priced separately. Pricing policy follows suppliers' recommended retail prices with some adjustments for competition.

In a *discount* retail market position, customers expect little or no services in return for the lowest possible prices. Large amounts of advertising emphasise low prices, broad product lines, and convenient hours. Location can be virtually anywhere so long as the premises are extensive and accessible.

SUMMARY

This chapter explains the components of a marketing strategy and how they can be combined to achieve the best results. The first step in creating a marketing strategy is to do some research so you know exactly who your customers are and what will motivate them to buy your product or service. You need this information to determine how you will position the business to1 become the preferred choice in your market niche. Having established a solid foundation for your marketing strategy, the goal is to consider how each component of the marketing mix can be managed for the best results. The products and services you offer need to match what your customers want to buy. Distribution is determined by how your customers want to buy. Promotion is focused on what to promote, where to promote, and how much to spend on promotion. Pricing is largely determined by the industry you are in and your product and service decisions. The objective of managing each component of the marketing mix is to create a coordinated marketing strategy that generates large profitable sales.

Seven
Traditional Marketing

Generating sales is the most important function in business. Without sales and the revenue stream it produces, none of the other business functions really matter. The purpose of this chapter is to examine the traditional marketing tools that are used to generate sales. Direct marketing methods including brochures and flyers, direct mail, and newsletters. Advertising media include newspapers, magazines, radio, television, and outdoor advertising. There is no simple way to create the perfect advertisement, but there are some simple rules for writing advertising copy. Publicity and sponsorship can also be used to lift the profile of a business. Personal selling is an essential part of being in business and it can be done in a way that is positive and rewarding. Each of these tools is a part of traditional marketing and they are used to generate sales by informing, persuading, and reminding customers about your business and what it offers. In the next chapter, we will turn our attention to digital marketing.

DIRECT MARKETING

Direct marketing relies on targeted communication with individual customers rather than the scatter-gun approach through mass media advertising. It is usually characterised by a call to action in which the customer is urged to respond by contacting or visiting the business. Direct marketing consists of brochures and flyers, direct mail, and newsletters.

Business Card

Before you think about advertising and promotion, make sure you have a business card that describes you and your business. Your business card needs to say as much as possible about your business in

DOI: 10.4324/9781032676616-13

a very small space. It not only needs to contain important details about who you are, what you do, and how you can be contacted, but it also needs to project your image. A business card is a selling tool, and you design it just like an advertisement.

Brochures and Flyers

Brochures and flyers are an important tool for retail and service businesses and the most economical means of small-volume advertising. They are more readily controlled than other forms of promotion because they are distributed directly by the business doing the advertising and they are inexpensive to produce. Brochures and flyers can be distributed over a specific area that is expected to give the greatest return and they can be passed out in the store and inserted in packages.

Direct Mail

Direct mail has many of the advantages of brochures and flyers and it is also more dignified and personal because it can be directed to an individual customer. Direct mail is more selective than brochures and flyers. To ensure adequate but controlled coverage, use a mailing list compiled from your own business records or from commercially available mailing lists. Direct mail is more expensive than brochures and flyers, but you can say more, you can try novel ideas on selected clients, and you can have a more personal touch.

Newsletter

A newsletter can be a potent promotional tool. Properly executed, it is an effective way to keep customers informed about your products and services. A newsletter can range from a single-page one-colour format to a 12-page four-colour design. You can have your newsletter written and produced by a professional, or you can do it yourself using a desktop publishing package on your personal computer.

Newsletter information should reinforce your image. Items commonly found in newsletters include a message from the owner, news about the business, calendar of events, articles on new services or products, special promotions, and stories about employees. It should be information that is important to the reader. If you are positioning your business as friendly and down to earth, then your newsletter should be consistent with that image. If you are positioning your business as a high-tech operation, then you want a state-of-the-art publication. A newsletter should be published on a regular basis such as monthly, bimonthly, or quarterly. Keep in mind that it takes time and effort to prepare a newsletter, so the more frequently you decide to publish, the more time you will need to devote to it.

Most newsletters are now distributed by email. This almost eliminates distribution and production costs. If all of your newsletters are distributed this way, use a full-colour design because there are no printing costs. For hard-copy distribution, a newsletter can be a self-mailer, or envelopes can be printed. If you have a large volume of hard-copy newsletters, you may want to use a distribution service or the services offered by Australia Post. Be sure to keep your mailing list up to date.

MEDIA ADVERTISING

Media advertising operates through a third party to communicate your message to a wider target market. It includes newspapers, magazines, radio, television, cinemas, and outdoor advertising. When you choose advertising media for your business, the main focus is on your target audience, the nature of your message, and the size of your budget.

Select media that will cover your market area and allow you to tell your story effectively. If you are located in a small town where most people come to shop, then advertising in the local media should give you good coverage without wasting money. On the other hand, if you are located in a large capital city where it would be inconvenient for people from other parts of the city to shop, then it would not make sense to pay for readers or listeners who cannot conveniently come to your business.

Newspapers

Using local newspaper advertising depends on how much of your market area is covered by the newspaper's circulation. If the bulk of your business is drawn from only a small portion of the area that the paper covers, then you will be paying a premium for advertising that is wasted. Very small neighbourhood businesses might consider the possibility of using neighbourhood or shopping papers. Some neighbourhood papers are read with great interest, but others are thrown away or regarded as a nuisance.

You may think you cannot afford to advertise in the newspaper because the volume of your sales will not support the advertising expense. By using only one newspaper and by following a prearranged advertising schedule, you may be able to buy regular advertising at a lower rate. You can also get help by working with your newspaper's advertising department.

Getting a good position for your newspaper advertisement is desirable but not always possible. Only rarely can you get a guarantee for a specific location, but you can usually arrange to have it appear on a certain page or in a given section. Occasionally, you may find your advertisement at the bottom of the page or next to one of your major competitors. That is why it is more important to depend on layout, design, and copy than to rely on a specific location.

Magazines

General consumer magazines are not only an expensive advertising medium, but their coverage is too wide for a local market. Special interest magazines are less costly and you can reach people when they are actively thinking about what they need to pursue their particular interest. Examples include magazines for gardening, photography, skiing, golf, boating, cooking, weddings, parenting, and computers. Special interest magazines are especially useful for small manufacturers who need to back up their retailers with national advertising and mail-order firms that target a national market with a narrow product line. Locally based magazine-type media include visitors magazines, theatre programs, and the newsletters of local organisations.

Radio

Radio advertising is almost entirely local advertising. Some products can be advertised better by voice than in print. Other products benefit from radio advertising as a complement to print advertising.

The human voice can establish a rapport with listeners. A woman announcer can impart a feminine character to your message, or you can record your own radio commercials to give them a personal touch. The human voice can also convey a sense of urgency. If you want an immediate response, you can ask your listeners to phone you immediately. Radio listeners remember messages that are spoken in a conversational manner and repeated frequently.

Your customers must be listening to the radio for your message to get through. That is why choice of station, choice of broadcast times, and repetition are important. Use a station that has strong listener appeal for your type of customer. Each station defines its listening audience by age, musical taste, news and information interest, and geographical market. For example, if your target market is teenagers, then you would select a station that plays their music. Try to get time slots when your customers listen to the radio. For example, commercials for a plant nursery would reach better prospects if they run during a gardening program. The non-visual message is short-lived, and many radio listeners are 'tuned out' or concentrating on something else while they listen. That is why the key is to repeat your message frequently.

Television

Television stations have brought the cost of television advertising within the budgets of small firms. Sight, sound, colour, and motion make this medium the closest thing to personal selling, and it takes place right in the customer's own home. Like radio, you need to be very careful to select the station and the broadcast times that match your target audience. Television is a medium that can carry action, so you should capitalise on it. For example, a boat dealer should feature a boat slicing through the water as opposed to a still picture.

Repetition in television advertising is different from radio. It is boring to see the same television commercial repeated too often. Think in terms of short, interchangeable segments that can be mixed and matched to make your television commercials appear different. The beginning and the end of every commercial should consistently identify your business and its image, but the message in the middle can change for variety and interest.

Cinema Advertising

Cinema advertising consists of slideshow ads or video ads. Slideshow ads are either silent or voice-over advertisements that play on the screen while the audience is coming into the theatre and finding their seats. Video ads usually play before the movie trailers and they are the same as a commercial on television.

Outdoor Advertising

Outdoor advertising was previously associated with billboards, but now it also includes a range of other formats designed to reach customers where they live, work, play, drive, shop, and commute. Outdoor advertising formats include digital billboards, traditional billboards, and posters. Transit advertising appears on buses, railways, trams, and taxis. There is also outdoor advertising on street furniture such as bus and train shelters, kiosks, phone booths, and seating. Visit the Outdoor Media Association website at *oma.org.au* for ideas about how outdoor advertising might be useful in your business. Vehicle signage is popular among retail and service businesses. Couriers, removalists, and home service operators with distinctive vehicle signage are advertising their services while they are working.

WRITING ADVERTISING COPY

Pursued with taste, vigour, and imagination, advertising can attract new customers, help you retain existing customers, and establish your image firmly in the minds of the public. There is no single way of creating the perfect advertisement, but there are some simple rules that will help you produce effective advertisements.

Make Your Ads Easy to Recognise

The secret to immediate recognition is consistency. This can be done with a distinctive logo, a consistent art technique, a certain typeface, or a distinctive border. Sometimes the shape of the advertisement, such as one column wide by the full depth of the page, gives you instant recognition.

It is not only important to make your advertisements easy to recognise but to do it in a way that reinforces your image. For example, a bold, cluttered border around an advertisement tends to convey an image of low prices while a clean, conservative border tends to suggest quality and service. Using the same border every time you advertise helps to create recognition. People reading your advertisements will associate the border with your business before they even read the advertising message.

Use a Strong Headline to Create Interest

A good headline says, 'This message is for you, so read on.' It is most effective when it promises a benefit that matches your customer's buying motive. Here are some of the ways that headlines are used to create interest: *How to* headlines offer the reader a promise of specific practical information.

- HOW TO EAT AND STAY SLIM
- HOW TO INVEST YOUR MONEY
- HOW TO WIN AT CHESS

Question headlines offer the reader an answer if they read on.

- TIRED OF PAYING TOO MUCH TAX?
- WOULD YOU LIKE A FREE HOLIDAY?
- ARE YOU SICK AND TIRED OF BEING SICK AND TIRED?

Reason why headlines offer the reader a solution to a problem.

- THREE REASONS WHY YOU NEED A NEW PAIR OF SUNGLASSES
- WHY YOU WILL NEVER NEED TO PAY FOR HOT WATER AGAIN
- WHY I BUY . . .

Command headlines tell the reader to take clear action.

- BUY YOUR SCHOOL SHOES NOW
- COME TO OUR GRAND OPENING TOMORROW
- ENTER OUR COMPETITION TODAY

Don't fall into the temptation of using the name of your business as the headline. Customers are attracted most by the benefits you offer them. The most persuasive words used in headlines are *easy*, *free*, *guarantee*, *health*, *love*, *money*, *new*, *proven*, *safety*, *save*, *you*, and *win*.

Use a Simple Copy Layout

Having gained the reader's attention with a strong benefit headline, the copy layout takes over to guide the reader through the advertisement. We are accustomed to reading a page from the top left-hand corner to the bottom right-hand corner. The same rules apply to the way the eye moves through an advertisement. Pull the reader's eye across the headline, draw it down through the explanation copy, and finish by reminding the reader who you are, where you are located, and when you are open. Use a picture or illustration only if it relates directly to the benefits offered by your product or service, otherwise the artwork may get the reader's attention, but it will not direct their buying behaviour.

If a good layout guides readers through your advertisement, it is the body copy that holds them. The body copy builds on the benefit in the headline. Since people are generally accustomed to reading short sentences, this is usually the best format to use in your body copy. Keep it simple and direct and try not to use unusual or difficult words.

Make sure the body copy is complete. Nothing ruins an advertisement more than the omission of an important fact that the reader needs to take action. Be sure to include all of the necessary information about what you are selling, where you are, what hours you are open, where customers can conveniently park, and which credit cards you accept. A 'just arrived,' 'one day only,' or 'while stocks last' creates a sense of urgency and gives your reader a reason not to put off a visit.

Make Use of White Space

Some small business operators try to cram every bit of advertising space full of print in an attempt to get the most for their advertising dollars. The practice usually leads to advertisements that are not read because they are too 'heavy.' The more white space you leave in your advertisements, the 'lighter' they appear. Light advertisements are easier to read, easier to digest, and more pleasing to the eye. The white space in your advertisement acts like an oasis where the eyes can pause for a rest. Cluttered advertisements convey an image of low prices and sometimes low quality. Examples can be found in supermarket and discount store advertising. Advertisements with plenty of white space, on the other hand, produce a stronger image of quality.

Practise on Other Advertisements

The key to writing good advertisements is to develop a sense for what works. The next time you pick up a newspaper or magazine, study a few advertisements and evaluate their effectiveness by asking the following questions:

- Does it offer products or services having wide appeal, special features, price appeal, and timeliness?
- Is the newspaper or magazine the best medium for the advertisement or would a different medium be more appropriate?
- Is the advertisement located in the best section and position?
- Is it large enough to do the job expected of it? Does it omit important details, or is it overcrowded with non-essential information?
- Does the headline express the single major idea about the product or service? The headline should be an informative benefit statement and not simply a label.
- Does the illustration (if one is used) reinforce the idea that the headline conveys?
- Does the copy contain enough information, or does it leave out things that would be important to the reader such as location, opening hours, website, or phone number?
- Does the layout of the advertisement and the use of white space make it easy to read? Does it stimulate the reader to look at all of the copy?
- Does it appeal to customers' buying motives?
- Is it written and presented from the customer's perspective?
- Does it seem honest, or is it exaggerated or phoney?
- Does it use a distinctive typeface that is easy to read or a logo that is easy to recognise?
- Does it stimulate prompt action?

PUBLICITY

Publicity is an important supplement to advertising that can be used to lift the profile of a business. There are a number of important events that are used to generate publicity:

Staff promotions	Staff appointments
Opening new premises	Expansion
Remodelling of premises	Launching new products
Honours or awards	Community projects
Change in opening hours	Change in ownership
Safety record	Anniversaries

You can tell these stories with paid advertising, but with publicity, you get your story before the public for free. The newspaper will publish your story if it is news. What you do makes better news than what you say. It is up to you to write a press release. Lots of badly written press releases end up in the editor's rubbish bin. The best way to learn about writing press releases is to study the publicity that appears in your newspaper every day. Here are some tips:

- Use the word processing software on your personal computer to produce eye-catching letters and press releases.
- Use simple words and short sentences. Try to avoid jargon and technical terminology. Give your press release a headline.
- Keep the press release to about 300 words, or about one page, and talk about your most important items first. Include a picture if it helps to tell the story.
- Email your press release rather than post it so the newspaper can simply cut and paste.
- Remember to cover who, what, when, where, and why. Look for the unique, rare, or individual ingredient that makes your story newsworthy. A quote always gives personality to a story.
- Issue a press release before and after an event, but keep in mind that Mondays are not good days for press releases.

- Be sure that your contact details, especially your name, phone number, and email address, are clearly printed at the top or bottom of the press release.

SPONSORSHIP

Sponsorship consists of underwriting an event like a fundraiser or an arts festival. Sponsorship support can be in the form of money, in-kind services, or products. Event sponsorship can yield a number of marketing opportunities, especially if you work closely with the event organiser to make sure you receive appropriate credit in publicity releases, brochures, advertising, program books, street banners, and posters. The key to sponsorship is to match the event you sponsor with the nature of your business. Here are some things to consider:

- Demographics—What do you know about the event's audience and do they represent your target market?
- Exclusivity—Will there be many sponsors, or will your business stand out clearly as the sponsor of the event?
- Credits—What kind of exposure will you receive in terms of signs, event advertising, promotions, and public relations? For example, as a naming rights sponsor, your business name should appear on all event material.
- Credibility—Does the event manager have a good track record for creating and managing successful events that stimulate a positive response from participants?
- Organisation—Are there enough staff, volunteers, and resources to run the event?
- Timing—Is it the right time to sponsor this event? Will it be popular?

PERSONAL SELLING

What is it about selling that worries so many small business operators? Some avoid selling because they have a fear of rejection. Others dislike selling because they think it consists of tricking or coercing a customer to buy something they don't really need. Selling is an essential part of being in business and it can be done in a way that is positive, rewarding, and enjoyable. If your product or service truly meets the customer's needs, then everyone benefits as a result of a sale. It means taking the time to build a relationship with your customer rather than just focusing on making an immediate sale.

Customers want to be served by someone they can trust. Have you ever walked away because you didn't trust a salesperson? On the other hand, do you find yourself going back again and again to someone who is helpful and honest? How do you build trust? One way is let your customers get to know you. Tell them why you started your business and why you believe in what you are selling. Another way to build trust is to keep your word. From follow-up calls to delivering on time, simply keeping your word is a powerful sales tool. If something unavoidable happens, you can still keep the level of trust intact by telling your customer what has happened and asking what you can do to minimise the inconvenience. When customers know you sincerely care about them, they will feel secure that they are making the right decision to buy from you.

Something extraordinary happens when you give a customer your undivided attention. This means listening and not interrupting them or impatiently waiting to talk next. If you do all the talking, how will you ever learn anything about your customer? When you listen more than you talk, customers realise that you are genuinely interested in them and you are trying to understand their individual situation. They will become increasingly comfortable with you because they realise you are on their side. Part of listening includes recognising body language. Knowing how to interpret a customer's folded arms or eye contact will give you extra insight into how comfortable they are and whether they are ready to make a purchase decision.

Personal selling is a way of doing business that is flexible, cooperative, and professional. It also enables you to operate as an ethical, considerate, and genuinely helpful person. The following steps are a basic guide to personal selling:

- **Know your product or service.** Before you begin a conversation with a customer, it is essential that you clearly understand your products and services and why people should want to buy them.
- **Make the initial contact.** A courteous greeting establishes rapport between you and your customer. The traditional 'May I help you?' often results in an answer like 'Just looking,' which fails to get the ball rolling. Simply, 'Good morning, what may I do for you?' is a more positive greeting. A better approach is to comment on whatever it is the customer is examining such as, 'These new synthetic brushes are very popular with professional artists.' Another alternative is to ask about the customer's reason for shopping such as, 'Are you looking for something for yourself, or is it a gift for someone special?'
- **Exchange information.** This step consists of asking questions, uncovering buying motives, giving information, and determining how your product or service will fulfil the customer's needs. Find out why the customer has an interest in buying a particular product or service. For example, the answer to a question like 'How long have you been playing tennis?' may help you direct a customer to the right brand of tennis racket. The most effective questions are those that are not answered with a simple 'yes' or 'no.' Instead, try using open-ended questions that get the customer talking. These are questions that begin with words like 'why,' 'what,' or 'how.'
- **Propose a solution.** Once you are comfortable with the relationship you have created, propose how your product or service will solve the customer's problem or fulfil their need. When you describe a product or service, focus on the link between its features and benefits. A feature is a distinctive characteristic of a product or service. A benefit is the way the customer's buying motive is fulfilled by the feature. Customers' buying motives vary widely and they can buy the same product or service to gain different benefits.
- **Confirm the sale.** Rather than focusing on 'closing the sale,' a term that indicates the end of the process, confirming the sale

means you are reviewing the customer's willingness and ability to make a commitment. It is a natural extension of a sales relationship built on a foundation of trust, respect, and rapport.

- **Deliver the goods.** Actually delivering the product or service is a very important step. First, if you don't deliver, then you haven't completed the sale. Second, during this step, you have an excellent opportunity to continue to build trust and to cement your relationship with the customer.

- **Follow up promptly.** Find out how the customer likes your product or service. This provides you with an opportunity to create repeat business and to ask for referrals to new customers. If there is a problem, then you are there to correct it.

One of the main reasons that small business operators shy away from selling is because they don't like to be rejected. This is a basic and understandable human reaction. A customer will generally say 'no' for one of two reasons. Either they don't trust you yet, or they genuinely do not want to buy what you are offering. If you focus on building a genuine relationship, then you can avoid rejections for the first reason. If you get a 'no' for the second reason, then remember that this customer may return to make a purchase later or they may refer others who are interested.

SUMMARY

This chapter describes the traditional marketing tools that are used to generate sales. Your business card is your initial selling tool and it needs to be designed with the same intent as an advertisement. Direct advertising consists of brochures and flyers, direct mail, and newsletters. They rely on targeted communication with individual customers. Media advertising operates through a third party to communicate your message to a wider target market. It includes newspapers, magazines, radio, television, and outdoor advertising. Although there is no single way of creating the perfect advertisement, there are some simple rules that produce good ads. Publicity and sponsorship can also be used to lift the profile of a business. Personal selling is an essential part of being in business, and the chapter concludes by showing that it can be done in a way that is positive and rewarding. Each of these traditional marketing tools can be used to generate sales by informing, persuading, and reminding customers about your business and what it offers.

Eight
Digital Marketing

Traditional marketing lost its monopoly on the Australia public when we began using the internet. As we rely less on the conventional media, digital marketing has emerged offering potent new marketing channels. Even word-of-mouth recommendations are becoming turbocharged by the social networks that have been spawned by online media. Digital marketing has not only created new business opportunities, but it also represents new ways of marketing for existing businesses. The purpose of this chapter is to examine how digital marketing fits into the overall marketing strategy for a small business.

WHAT IS DIGITAL MARKETING?

There are many ways to engage in digital marketing. *Brick-and-click* digital marketing can be used by an existing business that wants to go online as part of their overall marketing mix. *Pure-click* digital marketing is conducted wholly in cyberspace without any need for a physical shopfront. Email, online promotion, and social media are forms of digital marketing that can be targeted at specific customers. Smartphones and other emerging mobile technology are the most recent addition to the digital marketing arsenal. Digital marketing is not only an important tool for conventional small businesses, but it has also created enormous opportunities for totally new types of online businesses.

A retail business that is marketing online is called an *e-tailer*. A pure-click e-tailer only operates online. A catalogue e-tailer operates a traditional mail-order business with a web-based catalogue. A brick-and-click e-tailer operates a traditional retail establishment augmented by a website. A manufacturing business that sells its products online can

DOI: 10.4324/9781032676616-14

reach more buyers directly, thus shortening the distribution channel and capturing greater retail margins.

Digital marketing has been effective in bringing buyers and sellers together. Some websites act as a virtual broker with a full range of services including listing, negotiation, transaction, payment, and delivery. Some websites conduct auctions for sellers, and others search out hard-to-find goods and services for buyers. There are also websites that facilitate transactions between buyers and sellers by providing comparison shopping information and services without actually engaging in the exchange of money or goods. High-volume websites such as Amazon and eBay offer hosting services for small online retailers known as *virtual shopping malls* or *online marketplaces*.

Digital marketing has spawned completely new types of businesses. For example, some deal in virtual products such as music downloads or smartphone apps. Others create content that attracts targeted users who *click through* to other businesses that pay for the click-throughs. Some charge a subscription fee for access to text, audio, or video content. A powerful new force in digital marketing is social networking in which users have the means to connect with other like-minded individuals. The resulting high-volume traffic provides enormous opportunities for targeted advertising, subscription services, and premium content.

DO I NEED A WEBSITE?

According to the Australian Bureau of Statistics, about 40 percent of small businesses have a website and 27 percent use one to generate orders. A website is the cornerstone of digital marketing. If digital marketing genuinely fits into your marketing strategy, then you not only need to have a website, but you also need to make sure it is accessible by a variety of digital devices including desktop computers, laptops, tablets, and smartphones. If, on the other hand, your customers get most of their information from traditional advertising and promotion, then you may be better off concentrating your efforts on those media.

Having a website does not mean that people will automatically come flocking to it. You need to encourage traffic through active promotion online as well as in your traditional media. Put your website address on all of your marketing and sales materials including your business cards, stationery, advertisements, brochures, newsletters, and product literature. Anything that normally contains your phone number should also contain your website address and your email address.

Digital marketing is an extension of traditional marketing principles. The main differences are the new channels that can be used to reach a target market and the ability to engage in two-way communication. A digital marketing strategy consists of three parts. The first part is *attraction* in which you attract prospects to your website using a variety of channels such as search engines, email, online promotion, and social media. The second part is *engagement* in which visitors become engaged with the content of your website, including the opportunity for two-way communication, that leads them toward a purchase decision. The third part is *conversion* in which you convert visitors into customers by making shopping with you an easy and positive experience.

SEARCH ENGINES AND DIRECTORIES

It is essential to list your website in the leading internet search engines. If customers can't find you, then they won't know you exist. Search engines are the equivalent of the *Yellow Pages* on the internet. In Australia, the majority of search traffic comes from three search engines:

- Google at ***google.com.au*** is by far the dominant search engine with over 90 percent of the search engine traffic in Australia.
- Bing at ***bing.com*** is Microsoft's search engine with less than 5 percent of the search engine traffic in Australia.
- DuckDuckGo at ***duckduckgo.com*** has less than 1 percent of the search engine traffic, but it is popular with some users because it doesn't track user activity.

You can list your website yourself. Each search engine has its own guidelines for submission. Generally, you only need to list your home page. The search engine then sends out its automated 'spider' to retrieve the other pages of your website and put them in its database. Search engines vary in the depth to which they catalogue pages, so you might want to register all of your important pages separately. *Search engine optimisation* (SEO) is an important tool to maximise traffic to your website. The goal is to push your website toward the top of search results pages. SEO gets a bit technical for some small business operators and you may want to get some help.

There are commercial services that will submit your website to major search engines and directories. You fill out an online form that includes your site's title, its URL, keywords, and other information and the service handles the submission process. You can also buy internet promotion software that performs a similar task. Although these methods can save you time by automating the registration process, they don't give you much flexibility in terms of how you describe your website or which pages you register.

In addition to the top search engines, list your website in online directories that fit your business profile. These include industry search websites that focus on businesses in a single market, regional directories that list businesses in a specific geographic area, or trade association websites that have searchable member listings. These listings won't generate the same volume of traffic as the large search engines, but they give you access to a targeted audience for the products and services you sell. Examples include Yelp Australia, TrueLocal, Yellow Pages, StartLocal, Hotfrog, and AussieWeb.

EMAIL MARKETING

Email marketing is a bargain compared with direct mail. Response rates on email campaigns are also much higher. Nearly everyone has an email address and they use email every day. Email marketing is a way to:

- Stay in contact with your existing customers.
- Create personalised contact for individual customers.
- Promote an awareness of your business and what it offers.
- Encourage traffic onto your website.
- Create timely promotional campaigns.
- Make direct sales.

Decide who should receive your emails, what will appeal to them, and what action you want them to take. This enables you to craft emails that are aimed directly at your target market, containing a message that interests them, with a clear call to action. The emphasis may be to create an awareness of your business, develop a relationship with customers, promote your products and services, or achieve direct sales.

Having a customer's email address means they have already showed an interest in your business. There are email strategies designed to make immediate sales. Examples are the 'limited time' offers that create a sense of urgency. Other email campaigns are not after immediate sales. They engage with customers and prospects with a view to creating a longer term relationship. These emails are used to direct readers to content that may be on your website, in a newsletter, on a social media platform, or your blog posts.

The main challenge in email marketing is building a list of contacts. Sometimes called a 'subscriber' list, it is the keystone of email marketing. Getting permission to communicate by email is part of marketing best practice. An opt-in form is a reliable way to build a quality email list. Keep in mind that a prospect needs a clear incentive before they will sign up, and the process needs to be quick and simple. Here are some examples:

- Put an opt-in button on the landing page in your website. When visitors land on your website, it increases the likelihood that they will sign up for your emails.
- Include an opt-in button in your social media posts. Prospective customers regularly find the businesses they are interested in through social media. Ask your followers to share your opt-in link with others.
- If you are buying online advertising, tell prospective customers about the content they will receive if they sign up for your email list.
- Offer exclusive information about an important topic that the user cannot access until they sign up for your email list.
- If you are using hard copy brochures or direct mail, include a QR code that will send prospects directly to your opt-in page.

Focusing on value is what encourages prospects to sign up for emails because they want to see what they contain. If your content gains their interest, you have an opportunity to convert them into a customer who is engaged with your business and the products and services you offer.

A *promotional email* informs customers and prospects about what you are offering or showcasing and how they can get it. It could be a new product, a seasonal promotion, or a 'flash sale.' The goal is a 'call to action' that results in sales.

A *newsletter email* is different. Its goal is to become a source of trusted information that results in an ongoing relationship with the customer. They are read more carefully when they offer information that is genuinely useful rather than merely selling products or services. The goal is still to make sales, but the approach is different.

An email that begins with a subject line that grabs attention is much more likely to be opened. Make the subject line short, to the point, and focused on what a customer would like to see. The body of the email contains the promotional message and a call to the reader to do something such as 'See the deals on our website,' 'Come into the shop this weekend,' or 'Order today.' Images add visual appeal in the body of the email. It could be your logo, a quality photo, or something from an imaging service such as Shutterstock or Getty Images.

Limit each email to just one message. If it is not simple and to the point, the reader will move on. If you want to cover more, then send multiple emails at appropriate intervals targeting different topics. A newsletter is another way to cover multiple topics. Make sure that every email includes important information such as where you are located, a link to your website, or when you are open. Too many emails end up in the spam folder. Limit them to things like important announcements or significant events.

If you decide to use email marketing on a regular basis, consider using the email marketing tools that are available. These include email templates, customised emails, automated mailouts, and tracking information. Examples of email marketing services are Mailchimp at ***mailchimp.com*** aimed at beginners, Benchmark Email at ***benchmarkemail.com*** aimed at small businesses, and

Constant Contact at ***constantcontact.com***, which has the highest delivery rate.

ONLINE PROMOTION

Conventional advertising attempts to *push* a message out to the largest possible audience in hopes of catching the attention of a few potential customers. Although push advertising will not disappear, the advertising and promotion landscape is changing. Online customers can choose which websites to visit, they can choose what to click on, and they can choose what information they *pull* onto their screen. The internet provides them with broad and deep access to detailed information about the products and services that really interest them.

Some websites provide targeted content mixed with advertising messages such as banner advertisements. Other websites are designed to be an online version of classified advertising. There are also websites that use video and audio segments like a television infomercial, and there are a few with interactive advertising that requires users to respond to the advertisement before reaching the content they are after.

There are websites that sell advertising banners that link to your website. Banner advertising gives you creative flexibility in colours, fonts, images, sound, and video. Look for banner ad space on established websites that cater to your target market. Contact the webmaster at these sites to find out about their ad requirements as well as their costs. In general, banner rates are based on the number of times the ad is served called *impressions*. The amount you pay per thousand impressions is based on the site's ability to deliver a target audience.

The big search engines and other platforms like LinkedIn, Twitter (now X), Pinterest, and Facebook offer paid link advertising. You pay an advertising fee to have your online ad appear in a sponsored link area when a user searches on particular keywords. You are charged a click-through fee if the user clicks on the ad and jumps to your website. This is a good way to drive traffic to your site. However, the click-through fees can easily mount up, so make sure you are getting quality traffic that results in sales.

When you see a related business with a website that complements yours, send an email to the webmaster and ask them if they would like to include your website in their links page. Offer to reciprocate by placing a link to their website on your links page. Make sure their image corresponds to yours and that you share similar customers. You can also seek links with vendors, suppliers, and providers of complementary products and services. Your goal is not to generate high-volume traffic but high-quality prospects who will be interested in visiting your website.

SOCIAL MEDIA

Social media is one of the best word-of-month tools online. There is a range of social media that are used for customer ratings and reviews, user recommendations and referrals, and sharing the experience of shopping online. One of the great benefits of digital marketing is that customers can read reviews, which could be from experts or simply fellow shoppers, about a particular product or service. Peer recommendations on social media play a key role when online shoppers are getting ready to make a purchase. You can include customer reviews on your own website or provide links to established social media platforms. The key to using social media is identifying your target market, what they need, and formulating posts that address their needs.

Social networks are all-purpose social media platforms in which people can interact and share information and experiences. The objective is to make prospects aware of your business and create an incentive for them to visit your website. Social network platforms that can be used by a small business to share their story include:

YouTube	Pinterest	Tumblr
Facebook	Twitter (X)	TikTok
Instagram	LinkedIn	Snapchat

Not all social networks will be right for your business. For example, professionals and businesses that sell to other businesses tend to congregate on LinkedIn, while TikTok and Snapchat are more likely to appeal to a younger market. To pick a social network for your business, find out where your target market spends most of their time. Using a platform that you enjoy can also make it easier to engage with your audience. You can use more than one social network, but consider how much time you are prepared to devote to this.

Social networking platforms enable customers to share their online purchasing experience and to make and receive personal recommendations. In some platforms, customers can bring products or services to the attention of their online friends and followers using a *share* or *like* button. Some businesses only use social networks to make posts, but it is increasingly common to see paid social media promotion including:

Facebook ads or promoted posts   Shoppable pins on Pinterest
Promoted tweets on Twitter (X)   LinkedIn ads or promoted posts

These are generally accompanied with phrases like *paid post, presented by, sponsored by, promoted,* or *advertisement.* Sponsored content differs from traditional promotion because it is designed to be compatible with the type of content that appears on that particular social media platform.

Blogs are another form of social media. These are websites in which users can have an informal conversation about a particular topic. The blog owner usually writes an opinion piece and invites readers to respond with their comments. A conversation is known as a *thread.* You can create a blog on your own website, or you can participate in blogs that are related to your line of business. *Forums* are more formal online discussion sites in which messages can be posted. These differ from blogs because the messages are usually moderated before they are posted. Only target blogs and forums that cover topics associated with your products and services. Provide some useful advice, not just an advertisement, and announce that your website has more information on the same topic. The main caveat with social media is only post when you have something of value to say and don't have too many posts.

Content marketing consists of valuable information that you offer to customers. The objective is to attract their attention and create an ongoing relationship in which they regularly return. The information can be published on your own website or on content hosting platforms, and it can be promoted using social media, email marketing, and search engines. It is used to present information, photos, audio, or video content that provides an engaging presentation leading to your products and services. For example, a garden centre can post change-of-season gardening information leading to the appropriate products. *Podcasts* are downloadable audio files that are used to provide sound such as talks and speeches. *Photo-sharing* applications, such as Flickr, can be used to present still pictures. *Video-sharing* sites, such as YouTube, enable you to present video content.

The risk with social media is you cannot control what other people may have to say about your business, your products, or your services. If their comments are complimentary and they recommend you to others, then it will trigger a viral response that is better than any advertising you can buy. If you attract criticism, however, then the damage can be enormous. It is usually better to learn from negative feedback than to ignore it. By monitoring compliments and criticisms, you can learn much about how to improve your business and your image.

MOBILE MARKETING

The reinvention of the mobile phone as a touch-sensitive handheld computer has made mobile marketing a practical reality. If digital marketing is part of your marketing strategy, then the chances are you will need to consider mobile marketing as well. Here are some reasons why:

- Nearly everyone has a smartphone. Mobile marketing means you can reach a vast pool of prospects directly.
- You can take your message to where your prospects are. For part of every day, they are on their phone.
- People use their smartphones for all sorts of tasks including searching for product information and making purchases. You can put your message in front of them when they are ready to buy.

- Mobile marketing gives prospects an opportunity to engage with you. Interesting and useful content encourages them to dig deeper into your products and services.
- Mobile marketing is cost effective. It is less expensive to run than most forms of digital advertising, and it costs less to create because there is less content.
- A smartphone is a personal device, and the messages received on it feel like they are directed to each user individually.

If your target market is under the age of 30, then mobile marketing is essential because there is a whole generation that perceive the internet as something that only happens on their phone. They might not even own a desktop computer, and their expectations point to a future in which mobile technology may become the dominant form of digital marketing. They use their smartphone to search for products and services, read reviews and recommendations, shop around, compare prices, and eventually make a purchase. An example is mobile ticketing in which theatre tickets are booked and cancelled on a mobile device using an app or by accessing the portals of various agents. A customer presents their smartphone with a QR code in place of a ticket.

To make the most of mobile marketing, it needs to be tailored for this medium and presented in the way users expect to see it. If you want your website to be mobile friendly, then it needs to incorporate a *responsive* design. This means it will be optimised for whatever device your customer uses including desktop computers, laptops, tablets, and smartphones. The alternative is to develop an app for mobile users instead of a website.

Mobile search ads are the equivalent of desktop search ads. They are the ads that automatically jump to the front of the queue resulting in higher click-through rates. Increasing numbers of mobile users are using voice search. For example, an Apple user might say, 'Siri, where is the nearest chemist?' It is important to make ad content mobile friendly using shorter sentences, engaging headers, and quality images or videos.

Brick-and-click retailers can take advantage of mobile marketing by using applications such as location-based services, barcode scanning, and push notifications to improve the customer's shopping experience. These enable customers to access the benefits of shopping online such as product reviews and information while shopping in-store. It bridges the gap between online shopping and in-store shopping, and it is a way for retailers to compete with the lower prices typically available online.

There are a variety of ways to introduce mobile marketing into your business. The main ones are text message marketing, app-based mobile marketing, in-game mobile marketing, location-based mobile marketing, and QR codes.

Text Message Marketing

Text messaging, or SMS, is the main technology carrying mobile advertising and marketing announcements to mobile users. It is often used in combination with other applications such as location-based marketing. There are SMS best practices in the same way as there are email best practices.

Text messages arrive with a notification that the user has a message waiting. The text is usually opened and read within a few minutes, making text message marketing faster and more reliable than most other marketing channels. They can be used for a variety of purposes such as promoting a sale, inviting people to subscribe to your email list, or jumping to your website. Text messages are limited to 160 characters. By keeping them short and to the point, you improve the chances that your target market will actually read them and understand the message.

App-Based Mobile Marketing

Because users spend more than half of their mobile time on apps, these are a crucial part of mobile marketing. This is mobile advertising that is embedded within an app. Having your own custom mobile app fosters ongoing engagement with customers and keeps them coming back. To create an app for your business, consider working with someone that has skills in app development, content, promotion, and customer engagement. The alternative to having your own dedicated app is to use the Google AdMob service, which helps businesses place ads in third-party apps, or Facebook's

Promoted Post ads, which appear in Facebook mobile app users' news feeds.

In-Game Mobile Marketing

Gaming apps provide entertainment, and in-game marketing gets your ads in front of users who are not only engaged but regularly return. Mobile ads for gamers consist of banner ads, full-page ads, and video ads. Gamers will usually see your banner ad at the top of the screen during a game. The response rate for banner ads is low, but the repetition increases recognition. Full-page and video ads appear between loading screens during a game. They have proven to be more successful because they are more engaging.

Location-Based Mobile Marketing

Location-based marketing uses a mobile's current or past location to display content that is relevant to a location. Some systems use the internet protocol address to find the location, and other systems use the device's global positioning system. Platforms like Facebook and Snapchat use *geofencing* to push ads to users when they are within range of a business like a restaurant or a shop. Other applications of location-based services include announcing entertainment or social events in a particular area, finding a business or service, or getting navigation instructions to an address. Location-based marketing is not only a good way to target high-value prospects, but it is also good timing for making a sale. A Google Business Profile is another way to take advantage of location-based marketing. It ensures that people who are searching Google for your products or services in your local area will find you during a search. Any business with a physical location can boost traffic using location-based mobile marketing.

QR Codes

QR codes are the square images that can be scanned by a smartphone. They appear almost anywhere including brochures, signs, magazines, newspapers, buses, business cards, or on products themselves. They can take the user to a web page, dial up a phone number, download an app, send email content, give directions to an address, and more. They are a fast and easy way to deliver a large amount of information. You can create your own QR codes using one of the online generators.

GETTING HELP

There are several government and private sector organisations that can help you go digital. Here are some examples:

- A comprehensive website designed to help kick-start businesses that want to get online is *business.gov.au/online/digital-tools-for-business*.
- The Australian Communications Authority at *acma.gov.au* has important information about the SPAM Act 2003 and SPAM regulations.
- Information about cybersecurity for small business can be found at *cyber.gov.au*.
- The Australian Web Industry Association at *webindustry.org.au* has a directory of private sector organisations that can help with your website.
- Search Engine Watch at *searchenginewatch.com* has detailed information about how to use search engines.
- Google has a free interactive course at *learndigital.withgoogle.com*. There are 26 modules, all created by Google trainers, that are packed full of practical exercises and real-world examples.

SUMMARY

This chapter explores how digital marketing offers important new marketing channels for both new and existing businesses. A website is the cornerstone of digital marketing and it needs to be accessible by a variety of digital devices including desktop computers, laptops, tablets, and smartphones. The channels that bring customers to your website include search engines and directories, email, online promotion, and social media. Some websites provide targeted content mixed with advertising messages such as banner advertisements. Other websites are designed to be an online version of classified advertising. There are websites that use video and audio segments like a television infomercial, and there are a few with interactive advertising that requires users to respond before reaching the content they are after. Nearly everyone has a smartphone. If mobile marketing is going to be a part of your digital marketing strategy, then consider the features of text message marketing, app-based mobile marketing, in-game mobile marketing, location-based mobile marketing, and QR codes.

Reflective Exercise: Capturing the Target Market

The purpose of this reflective exercise is to evaluate the viability of the target market you want to capture. You are looking for evidence of demand, how potential customers might react to the product or service you plan to offer, and what your competitive strengths and weaknesses are likely to be. Your responses will help you form a judgement about whether the market for your business idea can be captured.

ANTICIPATED DEMAND

Questions about demand are easier to ask than to answer because we need to know how the marketplace operates. There is always a certain amount of judgement involved about the factors that are important in influencing demand. Nevertheless, demand can be examined in the early stages by looking into the general behaviour of the marketplace and how related products and services are selling.

Market Size

Evaluating the relative size of the market is an essential part of anticipating demand. What we are looking for is information about the overall size of the market even though not every customer is going to buy from us. The target market might be a neighbourhood or a suburb, a town or city, a region, a state, Australia-wide, or global. The number of customers can be in terms of individuals, households, businesses, or some other customer unit. The larger the market, the more likely there will be significant demand.

Will the size of the target market for my business idea be relatively large, medium size, or small?

DOI: 10.4324/9781032676616-15

Market Growth

An expanding market clearly implies more opportunities and the possibility of greater financial returns. A declining market usually means the opposite. Trying to estimate market growth faces the same obstacles as trying to estimate market size. For existing products and services, there is usually information about past sales and the rate of growth. For new products and services, estimating market growth is more complicated. Sometimes estimates can be inferred from the growth rates of comparable products or comparable markets.

Will the target market for my business idea be likely to increase, remain constant, or decline?

Market Stability

Market stability refers to the pattern of demand. Almost all products and services face fluctuations in demand. For some, variations in seasonal demand can be foreseen with reasonable accuracy, permitting forward planning for inventory and staff to cover surges and lulls. Unstable demand that does not behave according to any well-defined seasonal or cyclical pattern is a more hazardous proposition. The important point is that some business ideas are more susceptible to demand instability than others.

Will fluctuations in demand for my product or service be stable, predictable, or unpredictable?

Commercial Life Span

Some business ideas will have a short commercial life whereas others might enjoy a long one. One might last only a few months, like a fashion accessory, compared with more than a century for the motor car. Commercial life span can apply to a product, a process, a service, a business, a brand, a style, a fashion, or a fad. It characterises how a business idea moves from inspiration to exhaustion over its commercial life. It does not make sense to make a long-term financial commitment to a business idea with a limited commercial life span.

Will the commercial life span for my business idea be likely to last for a long time, a moderate period of time, or a brief period of time?

Spinoffs

Spinoffs are additional products or services that can be derived from the original business idea. If it can be extended into other products or services, then it has greater commercial potential. More than half of the new products and services introduced each year are spinoffs of other products or services. The benefits that come from spinoffs include more customers, more sales to existing customers, greater marketing efficiency, greater production efficiency, lower costs, and greater profits.

Will the potential for additional related products or services be high, moderate, or limited?

MARKET ACCEPTANCE

Market acceptance explores how potential customers might react to the product or service you plan to offer. Does it fulfil a genuine need? Will the benefits be easy to recognise? Is it compatible with existing attitudes and patterns of use? Is it complicated to consume or use? Will it be difficult and/or costly to distribute? If customers like your product or service, then you will make sales. But if they don't like your product or service, then the size of the target market doesn't really matter.

Need

A successful business idea fulfils a genuine need. A need can take different forms such as a functional need, psychological need, economic need, social need, or informational need. The most basic needs include things like safety, savings, health, status, pleasure, or convenience. Needs have different degrees of importance ranging from essential to

Reflective Exercise

non-essential. Successful businesses have an intimate understanding of what these needs are and how they can meet them. Some products and services fulfil an essential need that is highly valued. Other ideas may fulfil a need but not necessarily one that is highly valued. And some are simply novelties that are easily forgotten.

What need is fulfilled by my product or service? Will customers consider it essential or non-essential? Will it be highly valued or not highly valued?

Recognition

Customers must be able to recognise the features and benefits of a product or service before it can gain their acceptance. The cost and effort required to explain the features and benefits vary substantially. Will customers find your product or service easy to understand? Can they try it out before committing themselves? Can they observe its performance before they buy it? Can it be favourably compared with something in which they have had some experience?

Will the features and benefits of my product or service be completely obvious, require some explanation, or require a great deal of explanation?

Compatibility

Compatibility is the way in which a product or service is consistent with customers' existing values, past experiences, and perceived needs. Even though an innovation may represent an improvement, it can put a business idea outside the normal expectations of potential buyers. If the expectations of potential customers are entrenched, then it is important to protect compatibility in order to achieve market acceptance.

Will the compatibility of my product or service with customer expectations be high, moderate, or low?

Complexity

Complexity refers to how difficult a product or service is to use or consume. The amount of learning needed to overcome complexity directly affects market acceptance because it introduces an element of risk in the customer's mind. The more complicated the product or service, the more customers have to learn. The more customers have to learn, the more difficult it is to gain their acceptance. Complexity can also be a barrier to market acceptance if the process of making a purchase decision is confusing.

Will the degree of complexity in learning how to use, consume, or purchase my product or service be low, moderate, or high?

Distribution

Distribution is an important part of achieving market acceptance. You can distribute directly to customers, or you can distribute through intermediaries. The right choice depends on the nature of your product or service, the size and proximity of the market, the bargaining power of intermediaries, and the costs involved. Exactly where will customers expect to find your product or service? Who in the existing distribution channels is already dealing with these customers? How many stages must your product or service go through before it gets to the end user? What sort of markups will need to be given away at each stage, and will there be enough profit left over? How much technical support, promotion, or training has to be provided?

Will the distribution method for my product or service be simple and inexpensive, about average in effort and cost, or complicated and costly?

MARKET STRENGTH

A business idea not only needs to gain market acceptance, but it also needs strength in a crowded market environment. Differentiation and value are the two most important drivers underpinning market strength. Negotiating power with customers and suppliers also determines how securely it is entrenched in the marketplace. And the capacity to stand up to direct and indirect competition makes a crucial difference to long-term success.

Differentiation

Differentiation is the way in which a product or service offers features, benefits, or performance that satisfies a need or solves a problem better than the alternatives. A sales method that gives customers easier, more convenient, less disruptive, or less time-consuming access to your product or service will also differentiate it from competitors. Clear-cut differentiation means an idea is not only different but also superior in some way (better, faster, cheaper, etc.) to whatever is currently offered.

> **Compared with the alternatives, will customers consider the features and benefits of my product or service to be better, the same, or inferior?**

Value

Value means getting the same benefits at a lower cost or greater benefits at the same cost. Cost is not just the price but also non-financial costs such as wasted time, confusion, inconvenience, or the uncertainty of making a mistake. Benefits are solutions to problems such as saving money, ease of use, superior quality, improved health, more fun or greater convenience. The goal is to plan a business idea around the features and benefits that customers value most so the product or service becomes the go-to solution for their problem.

> **Compared with the alternatives, will customers consider the value of my product or service to be better, about the same, or worse?**

Customers

Not all customers are good customers. Customers who are in a strong position to negotiate for a lower price or for more features at the same price diminish the market strength of your product or service. Price concessions decrease revenue, more features increase costs, and both have the effect of reducing profits. If the customer's negotiating power is not strong, then you have greater control over pricing and terms of sale.

Will the negotiating power of my customers be low, moderate, or high?

Suppliers

Not all suppliers are good suppliers. Suppliers who are in a strong position to dictate the price, quality, or availability of the inputs you need for your product or service diminish its market strength. If their negotiating power is not strong, then you have greater control over the cost and availability of your inputs.

Will the negotiating power of my key suppliers be low, moderate, or high?

Competitors

There is rarely a business idea in which there are no competitors. Direct competitors sell the same or similar products or services, and indirect competitors sell something that acts as a substitute. The objective is to identify who the potential competitors may be, determine what threats they pose, and find out as much as possible about their relative strengths and weaknesses.

Will competition for my product or service be low, moderate, or high?

Part D
Operations Plan

There is enormous diversity in the way small businesses are organised and operated. However, they are all intended to achieve the same result – to supply a product or service to a customer and earn a profit. The practices that underpin day-to-day operations differ between service businesses, retail businesses, online businesses, and manufacturing businesses. Although each category has many things in common, they also have individual circumstances that drive decisions about how to operate. The location and layout of premises makes a significant contribution to a smooth and efficient operation. Decisions about location and premises not only depend on the nature of the operation, but they are also subject to compliance with local government regulations such as planning approval, permits and licences, and health and safety requirements. Fewer than half of small businesses in Australia employ staff in their operation. For those that do, there is much to learn about the role of being an employer.

DOI: 10.4324/9781032676616-16

Nine
Operating Practices

Small businesses vary in what they do and how they do it. Nevertheless, there are operating systems that have stood the test of time. Service operations can be automated, standardised, customised, or bundled. Retail operations are concerned with managing the purchasing cycle, controlling stock, and use of selling space. Online operations are focused on creating visibility, converting visitors into customers, and fulfilment. Manufacturing ranges from flexible small-batch operations to specialised high-volume operations. The purpose of this chapter is to examine some of the important practices that underpin service operations, retail operations, online operations, and manufacturing operations.

SERVICE OPERATIONS

A service business performs a task for the customer. The task generally requires specialised training, experience, or equipment. The key drivers in service operations are productivity and reliability. Service business operations tend to follow one of four practices:

- *Automation* is an operating practice that is provided by a machine rather than a person. An automatic car wash is an example.
- *Standardisation* is an operating practice that minimises costs, maximises productivity, and produces a uniform service. A fast food franchise is an example.
- *Customisation* is an operating practice aimed at providing a tailored service for each customer. An interior decorator is an example.
- *Bundling* is an operating practice designed to offer multiple services. A lawn care business that offers mowing, fertilising, weeding, and pest control is an example.

DOI: 10.4324/9781032676616-17

Other than automated services, a service business generally relies on the expert knowledge, skills, and experience of an individual. Unlike tangible goods, a service is not easily separated from the individual who provides it. Service customers' buying motives are price, value, and quality. The objective is to offer services that are highly valued and affordable, superior in quality, and capable of being effectively advertised and promoted.

Challenges

Service businesses face challenges that differ from those faced by retailers and manufacturers. Services tend to be intangible in the sense that they are not easily seen, touched, or tasted. Instead, they consist of tasks, acts, or experiences. Advertising and promotion is more challenging because there is nothing to show the customer. Customers may have different perceptions about what constitutes the service. Price setting may be more subjective, and justifying prices is more difficult. Consequently, neither the cost nor the value of a service is readily apparent to customers.

Services pose a number of other challenges because they are typically produced and consumed simultaneously in the presence of a customer, such as a makeover by a professional makeup artist. The customer may not have an opportunity to evaluate the service prior to purchase, leading to potential dissatisfaction if they receive something that is different from what they expected. It may also be difficult to detect and remedy errors before the customer sees them. If the customer actively participates in delivering the service, such as aerobic exercise instruction, the quality of the service depends on the customer's contribution as well.

Unlike physical goods, services cannot be put into inventory for future use. For example, when a bus drives off with empty seats, the revenue is lost forever. Revenue is also lost if the demand for services at a point in time exceeds the capacity to serve customers. Because service businesses have no inventories with which to smooth out these imbalances, they need to pay careful attention to matching the timing of supply and demand.

Services are also variable in the sense that the same service is not always delivered in exactly the same way, such as a re-upholstering service that varies with each piece of furniture. The more it is labour intensive, the more variable a service becomes. The variability of a service can play havoc with customers' expectations if they don't know what to expect in the first place. Variable services also lead to inefficiencies such as having to do some things over, wasted materials, and spending too much time on some jobs. Since the quality of most services depends largely on the performance of the individual providing them, labour costs are a big part of service business costs.

Competition

Some service businesses compete directly against other service businesses in the same line of work such as an accountant, dry cleaner, or hairdresser. Some service businesses compete indirectly with related businesses such as a cinema competing with a playhouse theatre for entertainment revenue. Some retail and manufacturing businesses offer services as an addition to their products such as installation and repairs. Some service businesses have to compete against government agencies that offer similar services such as the parcel delivery services that compete with Australia Post.

New customers rely on your image, reputation, and word-of-mouth recommendations to decide whether to buy from you. Repeat customers rely on past experience to decide if they will buy from you again. Unlike tangible goods, competing services are not likely to be found sitting together on a retailer's shelf. This means it takes more effort for a customer to compare services and service providers. A key element in service operations is a continuous marketing effort to encourage new customers to try your services and reminding existing customers about why they should buy from you again.

Consumers are more inclined to provide their own services than to manufacture their own goods. Lawn care, home maintenance, tax preparation, childcare, and food preparation are examples. Similarly, business customers might prefer to do their own cleaning, market research, and deliveries. Customers who want to provide their own services represent formidable competition for a service business. Successfully competing with do-it-yourself customers means understanding why they choose to perform these services themselves and then positioning your service so that the package of costs and benefits is more appealing. The obvious opportunities are providing services that do-it-yourself customers do not want to do or do not have the time, skills, space, equipment, or know-how. Similarly, you can provide a service that is safer, quicker, or more convenient than they can provide for themselves.

One reason why service businesses appeal to many aspiring small business operators is because the start-up costs are usually low compared with retailing and manufacturing. However, this low entry cost also attracts poorly qualified operators and others who lack a genuine commitment to providing quality service. They typically reduce their prices by cutting service quality to get business. Ironically, it is poor quality and low profit margins that eventually drive them out of business. This churn of competitors who continuously come and go makes for a chaotic and testing competitive environment for genuine service businesses.

RETAIL OPERATIONS

A retailer buys goods from manufacturers or wholesalers and resells them to consumers. The biggest challenge for small retailers is keeping up with the big retailers and franchise outlets. The Australian Retailers Association at *retail.org.au* is Australia's peak industry association for retailing. They have current information and advice about retail operations. Retail operations are primarily concerned with purchasing, stock control, the design and use of selling space, and point-of-sale technology.

Purchasing

In most retail operations, the biggest cost is the stock purchased for resale to customers. Not only do you need to control this cost, but clever purchasing is also important for maximising sales. The *purchasing cycle* is a systematic approach for buying the right stock, of the right quality, in the right quantity, at the right price, and at the right time. It consists of determining your stock needs, selecting your suppliers, negotiating purchases, and follow-up.

Different categories of stock call for their own approach to determining what and how much to buy. Some lines are staples that are always in demand with little change in models or styles. Determining what you need involves looking at your current stock and your current rate of sales. Other lines may be seasonal, perishable, or affected by style changes. For these categories, you have to make risky decisions about which styles to select and how much of each to buy. You don't want to get stuck with a lot of old stock if a particular style is no longer popular or a food item is past its use-by date. The goal is to maintain stock at the lowest level possible and still have a sufficient variety of colours, sizes, flavours, or models available. Look for ways to improve the selection of stock that your customers want to buy, and look for clues to help you time changes in your stock lines.

Find out what lines and quantity discounts are available from all of the vendors and what kind of deals your supplier has been doing with your competitors. Make the supplier's representative work for you even if you are fully prepared to buy from them anyway. Negotiation not only involves the purchase price but also includes quantities, delivery dates, single or multiple shipments, freight and packing expenses, guarantees on quality, promotion and advertising allowances, return policy, and special deals.

Stock Control

You need a practical system for maintaining stock to help you to order the right quantities and assortments, simplify buying, assist in selecting items for special promotion, and expedite the liquidation of slow-moving items. One method divides stock into three categories according to how closely they need to be controlled.

Maintained reorder items are usually of a staple nature that are consistently available from your supplier. They don't change styles or models often, and your stock position can be adjusted gradually. For example, an assortment of men's socks in standard colours will be a staple item for a men's wear store.

Maintained selection items normally come in a variety of styles, colours, or sizes. Whenever an order is placed, the entire customer selection needs to be reviewed. These style items require a careful review to select new styles whenever purchases are made. Variations in the stock position need to be corrected before maintained selection items are no longer popular. Jeans are an example of a diverse product line that also changes over time according to cut and style.

Fast-turning selection items are usually the least predictable but the most profitable. Stock planning for these items needs to be very flexible and set up to change rapidly. Overbuying is costly because mistakes cannot be reduced gradually and severe price reductions may be necessary to move stock that is no longer popular. Young women's clothing, for example, is not only seasonal, but it is subject to short-term trends resulting in a fashion cycle as short as a few weeks.

Display

Have you noticed how some retailers make it easy for you to shop while others make it frustrating? How you display your merchandise makes a big difference to sales. Customers must be able to see and identify every item you have for sale at a glance.

Your display space is your most valuable asset. It should be apportioned among your product lines according to their contribution to sales and profits. Your best-selling products deserve the best space compared with the merchandise you keep on display simply to complete the product line. For example, eye-level shelf space is a prime position compared with knee-level shelf space. That is why it is common practice to arrange each product line vertically because most customers scan the shelves horizontally. The vertical arrangement causes customers to scan more product lines quickly. They stop when they see the product line they want, looking up and down to find the brand or model they are looking for.

Signs inside a shop can also be used to promote products as well as guide customers through your selling space. Inside signs can be as big as a banner or as small as a price tag. Big signs convey a high-volume, low-cost image, whereas small discreet signs tend to convey a more exclusive image. With new techniques in instant printing and computer graphics, inside signs are no longer a drab hand-lettered card but colourful and exciting graphic art.

How you use colour forms a symbolic background in which you can express the image and mood of your business. The colour scheme should make it easy for customers to identify your business and it should complement your other marketing material. Colour can help you create a buying mood by enhancing the feel of your selling space and highlighting the merchandise. Generally, a colour scheme should be subtle and blend well with the store fixtures. Depending on the interior of the store, colour can help to give the illusion of greater size, or it can be used to offset undesirable factors. For example, light colours add depth to a small space and dark colours help to make a large space look smaller.

Lighting catches the customer's eye and calls attention to the merchandise. The objective is to encourage customers to examine the merchandise and buy it. Good lighting does not call attention to itself; it accents selling space, makes the merchandise stand out, and brings out the natural colours. Lighting is a blend of art, engineering, and experience. Architects, interior designers, and lighting equipment suppliers are all capable of giving you advice. Remember that customers are attracted most by sight, and the role played by proper lighting can make a difference to your sales.

Point-of-Sale Technology

A retail point-of-sale (POS) system, or the checkout, amounts to an electronic cash register. A POS system typically includes a computer, screen, barcode scanner, credit card reader, cash drawer, receipt printer, and a customer display. It can also incorporate other devices like a weight scale. Retail POS systems include touch-screen technology, and the computer is built into the screen chassis for an all-in-one unit designed to save counter space. POS systems can handle a variety of customer functions including:

Sales	Gift cards	Promotional sales
Returns	Gift registries	Manufacturer coupons
Exchanges	Loyalty programs	Foreign exchange
Lay-bys	Quantity discounts	

The back-office functions of a retail POS system are a powerful management tool that include purchasing, receiving, inventory control, customer accounts, GST, and profit reporting. Most POS systems have an interface that is used to transfer information to your accounting system. Given the expense involved and the variety of retail POS systems on the market, make sure you understand your current needs as well as your future needs before you buy or lease one.

ONLINE OPERATIONS

The five uncertainties that affect online shoppers are how to find product information, how to place an order, how to make payment, how delivery will take place, and if they can trust you to have a secure website that protects their privacy. An online shopping trip is a lot like a conventional shopping trip. Customers want to browse through your products, put the items they want into a shopping cart, and proceed to the checkout. At the checkout, delivery arrangements and payment are completed. If these steps are smooth and uncomplicated, then customers will find it easy to shop with you. If any part of the process is not easy, such as a confusing payment system or inconvenient shipping options, then you give customers a reason to drop out in the middle of the transaction and you lose the sale. The essential drivers for creating an online operation are:

Visibility. If you don't show up on a Google search, then customers will not find you. The best way to boost your visibility is to invest in *search engine optimisation* and cultivate valuable links with other websites. The objective is to attract quality traffic to your website.

Converting visitors into customers. You need to have a modern, user-friendly, trustworthy, and secure website that conveys a genuine value proposition. The objective is to get visitors' attention, encourage them to engage with you, and become customers.

Customer experience. Customers expect a great deal and they want to know all about your products and prices. Is information easy to find? Is the website easy to navigate? Is the checkout straightforward? Is there a fair, fast, and easy way for returns and refunds. The objective is to create an experience that is smooth and hassle free.

Fulfilment. Filling orders involves managing the inventory, picking and packaging the goods, and shipping them to the customer. It can be a costly and time-consuming process. An alternative to doing it yourself is to outsource fulfilment or use drop shipping to ease your workload and streamline the customer experience.

Security. Customers need to be confident that your website is safe and their personal information is secure.

Going online is not limited to a pure-play operation. Service and retail businesses can gain significant benefits from adding an online component to their existing operation. They can be open 24/7, they can have a new and convenient way for customers to make purchases, and new prospects can be reached who otherwise may not know you exist. An online operation creates new ways for promotion, such as announcing in-store events, or extra services like online ordering and pickup or delivery. Information and assistance about getting started online is available on the Australian Small Business Advisory Service Digital Solutions website at *business.gov.au/asbas*.

Building a Website

If you want to have your own website, a lot depends on what you want it to do, your own level of technical expertise, and the investment you are willing to make. You can create one yourself or have a website developer build one for you.

If you want to do it yourself, then using a *website builder* enables you to create your website without having to hire a professional website developer. With only a little technical expertise, you can create a professional-looking website in less than a day using a pre-designed set of web pages in which you plug in your own content. Website-building programs, such as *Wix, Weebly, Squarespace, web.com, GoDaddy, Shopify*, and others, enable you to set up your website directly online through a web browser. Some offer hosting services and connection to a payment gateway as well.

Building a custom website from scratch means you will have one that runs exactly to your specifications. The disadvantage is the time it takes and the cost involved. Unless you have the technical skills, you will need to hire a website developer. Start by making an outline of your vision for the website. Writing the page copy and gathering your images before you contact a developer will speed up the process. The more precisely you explain your needs to the developer, the more time and money you will save. If you are a bit tech-savvy, you may want your developer to build your website using a content management system such as *WordPress*. It gives you greater flexibility and less dependence on the developer when you want to make changes.

The term *hosting service* refers to a business that stores your website on their computers and connects it to the internet. There are several types of web hosting services and each differs in terms of storage capacity, the technical knowledge required, speed, reliability, and cost. If it is your first website, consider starting out small with a shared hosting account. It is the least costly, is easy to maintain, and is sufficient for most new sites. You can always upgrade later if your website needs more capacity. You can learn more about hosting services by visiting Web Hosting Reviews at ***webhostingreviews.com.au***.

Virtual Marketplaces

If you simply want to sell your goods online and you don't want to have your own website, then the alternative is a virtual marketplace. Websites such as *eBay, Amazon*, and *Etsy* are virtual marketplaces in which large numbers of individuals and businesses contribute to the mix of products on offer. There is more than one operational model for a virtual marketplace, but the most common method consists of a website that displays your wares, collects your orders and payments, forwards the orders to you, tracks delivery, and releases payment to you after deducting a fee. You are generally responsible for maintaining inventories, making delivery, supplying product descriptions, and pricing.

Amazon is the biggest virtual marketplace giving you worldwide exposure. It has warehousing and distribution facilities in Australia that firmly establish it as the top online shopping website and the first choice for many new online operations. Its high standards have made Amazon one of the most trusted virtual marketplaces in the world. However, Amazon's fees are also among the highest, meaning you need to decide if the costs are worth the exposure. Amazon stocks and sells a wide range of its own product lines, which means your products could potentially face some stiff competition from Amazon itself. To learn more about becoming an online seller on Amazon, visit their international website at ***services.amazon.com***.

eBay is the biggest auction site and it is one of the easiest platforms to use. Many sellers have seen an item go for twice, even three times, its listed price because of a bidding war between two enthused buyers. Although you will not directly compete with eBay in the same way you could with Amazon, you will almost always be competing with hundreds of other sellers. Standing out from the crowd can be difficult if you are offering a common product. On top of eBay's regular fees, there is also a removal fee to take an item off the site. To learn more about selling on eBay, visit their Australian website at ***ebay.com.au***.

Etsy is the leading virtual marketplace for anything handmade. It has a reputation for being an easy virtual marketplace to use, and unlike eBay and Amazon, Etsy uses a fixed-fee model that makes it far easier to keep track of your costs. If what you are selling is not handmade, however, then it will probably not be suitable for Etsy. To learn more about selling your handmade goods and craft supplies on Etsy, visit their Australian website at ***etsy.com/au***.

The main reason virtual marketplaces are attractive is because they have a huge volume of traffic compared with what you are likely to attract on your own website. Moreover, using a virtual marketplace avoids having to design your own website, engage a hosting service, connect a payment gateway, and set up accounting software. You can switch marketplace providers whenever you wish, and there is nothing to stop you from using more than one provider.

MANUFACTURING OPERATIONS

Manufacturers make consumer products that are sold to the public and industrial products that are sold to other businesses. Small manufacturers generally find it difficult to compete directly with large manufacturers and usually depend on a specialised niche market to prosper. The drivers of successful manufacturing operations are:

- Low unit cost—minimising the costs of labour, materials, and overheads.
- High quality—products that meet or exceed design and customer specifications.
- Prompt delivery—minimising the time between receiving an order and making shipment.
- Low investment—minimising the amount of capital invested in plant, facilities, and inventories.

The layout and equipment in a manufacturing operation depend on whether it is going to produce a variety of low-volume products with the same equipment or if whether it is going to be a more specialised high-volume operation. Once the plant is established, manufacturing operations consist principally of production scheduling and stock control.

Production Scheduling

Production scheduling is important to ensure customers receive their orders on time. In some manufacturing operations, production scheduling amounts to 'when we get the orders, we make the products.' In other firms, it means, 'we produce for the season, so we have enough stock available when the season starts.' Either way, customers drive the production targets. Production scheduling starts with a forecast of sales. How much do you expect to sell? When do you need to make delivery? Forecasting sales is straightforward if you only manufacture against orders or if the demand for your product is stable. In other circumstances, sales forecasts are less predictable and a cause for uncertainty. Production scheduling consists of determining the work that needs to be done, scheduling the people to do the work, scheduling the equipment to be used, scheduling the materials to be used, and integrating the work, people, equipment, and materials to create a smooth flow of production. There are computer packages that give a small manufacturer the same tools as the big manufacturers for scheduling production.

Stock Control

Stock control applies to raw materials, components, work in progress, and finished goods. It includes knowing when to order and how much to order. If you keep too few raw materials and components, you run the risk of shutdowns in production caused by shortages. If you keep too few finished goods, then you run the risk of lost sales to customers who are unwilling to wait for delivery. On the other hand, if you purchase or produce too much stock, then you will have dead stock and extra costs. The purpose of controlling stock is to provide the maximum service to your customers at the lowest cost to your business. Your aim should be to achieve a rapid turnover of stock without running out. The less money and space you tie up in raw materials, components, work in progress, and finished goods, the better. Production scheduling software will also have a module for controlling stock.

Pricing

Too many small manufacturers try to compete on price alone. A better strategy is to avoid competing on price and focus on benefits such as quality, service, performance, delivery, design, and packaging. These are the benefits that give small manufacturers a competitive advantage. You may be surprised to find that sales are not price sensitive if you emphasise non-price benefits in promoting your products. Therefore, the first rule in pricing a manufactured product is not to compete on the basis of price unless you happen to be the lowest-cost producer. It is

Operating Practices

the market that sets a *price ceiling* above which customers will not buy, and it is your costs that determine a *price floor* below which you cannot sell without incurring losses. The range between the price ceiling and the price floor determines the choices available for your pricing.

Information and Assistance

Running a manufacturing business does not mean you must be an expert on every step in the process. There are state and common-wealth sources of information and assistance, trade associations that cater to different types of manufacturing industries, as well as commercial services that can be used to outsource some of the work. Visit ***business.gov.au*** and run a search for 'manufacturing' to see all the information, grant programs, expertise, advice, events, and news for manufacturing businesses. Manufacturing software and internet services makes it possible for a small manufacturer to use the same tools that are used by larger firms. Capterra at ***capterra.com.au*** contains a free directory of manufacturing software vendors and their products in Australia.

SUMMARY

This chapter describes some of the important practices that underpin service operations, retail operations, online operations, and manufacturing operations. Service operations can be automated, standardised, customised, or bundled. The key drivers in service operations are productivity and reliability, and they generally rely on the knowledge, skills, and experience of the individual who provides them. Retail operations consist of managing the purchasing cycle, maintaining a system for controlling stock, and maximising the use of selling space. Retail operations generally depend on point-of-sale technology for a retail information system. Online operations are focused on visibility, converting visitors into customers, the customer experience, and fulfilment. They may have their own website, or they may prefer to operate through a virtual marketplace. Manufacturing ranges from flexible small-batch operations to specialised high-volume operations. Operating decisions in manufacturing are aimed at achieving low unit cost, high quality, prompt delivery, and low investment.

Ten
Location and Layout

The location and layout of your premises makes a big difference between an average business and one that is genuinely successful. A poor location prevents a business from reaching its potential by adversely affecting sales and unnecessarily adding to costs. Similarly, the layout of premises is fundamental to a smooth and efficient operation. Establishing premises is subject to local government regulations including land use zoning, building codes, health regulations, fire restrictions, and environmental requirements. The majority of small businesses lease their premises, and there are a number of provisions that you and your solicitor should carefully examine. The purpose of this chapter is to survey important elements to consider in selecting your premises.

TEMPORARY PREMISES

You may need to look for temporary premises until you are ready for something more permanent. Examples are serviced offices and business incubators.

Serviced Office

An alternative to setting up your own office is to rent space in a serviced office. Serviced office complexes provide furnishings, answering service, word processing services, photocopying, fax, postal, and courier services. They often provide a reception area and a boardroom or meeting rooms. Trained staff are employed by the serviced office centre who are available on a casual basis. The major advantage is that you only pay for what you need and you do not pay for unused space or idle staff when business is quiet. When things get busy, however, you have extra capacity at your fingertips.

DOI: 10.4324/9781032676616-18

Business Incubator

Business incubators are usually targeted towards the needs of firms engaged in light manufacturing, services, or research and development. They are seldom suitable for retail businesses. Incubators offer office and factory space with onsite expert advice. The idea is to provide an environment in which a new business can achieve self-sufficiency before they become independent and move on to other premises. Like a serviced office, you can rent the space you need for a short period and you only pay for services that you use. You are not locked into a long-term lease and you have access to guidance and advice.

Most business incubators are sponsored by government or non-profit organisations. Some are affiliated with universities to commercialise technical innovations. A few are joint ventures with private investment groups. Inasmuch as business incubators vary in the services they offer and the fees they charge, the following criteria may help you determine if an incubator is the right place for your business:

- What are the charges for space and services and how do they compare to commercial rates? Do the location, space, shipping and receiving, parking, telephone, security, and other basic services meet your needs? Is there room for your business to grow?
- What is the scope and quality of the services available? Does the incubator management understand the needs of your business and can they offer onsite assistance?
- How long has the incubator been open? What is the experience of other firms who were part of the incubator and have subsequently moved on? Who are the current tenants? Ask for references.
- What are the policies and procedures of the incubator? What services are provided for free? How long can you remain in the incubator? Does your rent increase and, if so, on what basis? Can you leave easily?

HOME-BASED BUSINESS

As a result of the pandemic, there has been an enormous increase in home-based businesses. A home-based business may be a temporary arrangement until you move into commercial premises, or it may be your permanent place of business. About 70 percent of home-based businesses operate *at* home and the remaining 30 percent operate *from* home.

Many people are attracted to a home-based business by family and lifestyle considerations. The hours lost commuting, the long working hours, and the stress of abandoning young children to day care centres have prompted many individuals to review their career aspirations and what they want out of life. They can have an office at home with no overheads, they can be close at hand for the family, and their working hours can be as flexible as they like. Technology is perhaps the most powerful force behind the growth in home-based businesses. Relatively inexpensive and powerful computers, email, mobile phones, and the internet have helped to make the home-based business not only functionally feasible but also financially realistic.

There are also a few pitfalls to consider if you want to work from home. Be sure that your local council approves of the use of residential premises for business purposes. You could find yourself in violation of zoning regulations. Ensure that your business activities do not attract complaints from your neighbours because of traffic, parking, noise, pollution, or other reasons. Make sure you have enough space to operate satisfactorily without intruding on other members of the household. You can obtain tax benefits from your home-based business, but this can also lead to a loss of part of your tax-free capital gain when you sell your home. It is easy to succumb to the inevitable distractions and interruptions when you work at home, so you will need self-motivation and self-discipline to establish an effective work routine. Working at home can also be a lonely lifestyle if you are accustomed to the social interaction of a workplace.

RETAIL PREMISES

A major factor in selecting retail premises is the nature of the business and the amount and type of traffic needed to sustain it. Some retail businesses depend on foot traffic and must be located within walking distance of the people they serve. Other retail businesses cater to a mobile clientele and can be located some distance from the customer.

Retail Location

There are four types of retail trading areas, and each has advantages and disadvantages for particular types of retail businesses.

- A *wayside area* usually appeals to transitory customers. Operating costs are low and so are the rentals. The merchandise is usually of a mixed nature, and there is extensive parking, long hours, and personal service.
- A *neighbourhood or suburban shopping area* draws local customers. Operating costs are low and so are the rentals. Consisting mostly of smaller businesses, they feature personalised service and plenty of parking.
- A *central shopping area* draws customers from a wide area. Operating costs are much higher and so are the rentals. It is an area of keen competition, mostly larger stores, and crowded parking with limitations on freight access.
- A *shopping centre* is a little different from finding a place on Main Street or in a neighbourhood shopping area. To customers, shopping centres have a distinctive appeal. Parking is easy, and they can walk conveniently to a variety of stores. However, operating costs and rentals are very high.

Locating the right retail premises involves more than simply finding a vacant shop. Have you ever noticed that the big retailers and franchise operations always seem to select the best locations? That is because they make a painstaking survey before they select a site. What you sell also affects the choice of a retail location. Customers tend to behave differently depending on whether they are buying convenience goods, shopping goods, or specialty goods.

Convenience goods are usually inexpensive, bought by habit, purchased frequently, and available in many outlets. Examples are milk, newspapers, and confectionery. If you handle convenience goods, the *quantity* of pedestrian traffic is most important. Convenience stores have a limited ability to generate their own traffic, so it is more effective to locate a store within a traffic pattern than to try to generate it yourself.

Shopping goods are usually higher priced, bought infrequently, purchased on the basis of price and feature comparisons, and only available in selected outlets. Examples are clothing, kitchen appliances, and cosmetics. If you handle shopping goods, the *quality* of pedestrian traffic is most important. Convenience goods are purchased by everyone, but shopping goods are purchased by only certain segments of shoppers and you want to be positioned to intercept them.

Specialty goods are usually expensive, bought very infrequently, require a special effort on the part of the customer to make the purchase, and are sold in exclusive outlets. Examples are camper vans and quality furniture. Specialty goods are sought by customers who are already pre-sold on the product. If you handle specialty goods, you can use isolated locations because you will generate your own customer traffic. Specialty stores that are complementary to shopping goods outlets may want to locate near them.

Minimum time and effort largely determines the retail trading area that customers will go to first. If your business requires a high volume of traffic, then it needs to be highly visible and accessible. Is it easy to enter and exit from the footpath or the street? Is there plenty of handy parking? Is the area a short drive from the customer's home or business? The size, character, and location of surrounding businesses are also important. A good retail trading area has a balance of other types of businesses that create extra draw. Businesses that are complementary tend to cluster together and draw mutually beneficial trade into an area.

Shopping Centre

If you locate in a shopping centre, you will be expected to contribute a pro rata share of the centre's operating budget, maintain store hours, light the store windows, and use signs in accordance with shopping centre policies. You will need to observe the centre's requirements regarding the use of shared facilities such as loading docks. You pay for whatever is needed to prepare your space such as floor coverings, light fixtures, counters, shelves, and whatever decorating needs to be done. Sometimes you install your own air conditioning and heating units. The centre manager will assist you in planning for the storefront, display signs, and even the interior colour scheme. However, this is done to ensure some continuity of decorating styles throughout the centre.

To decide if the advantages of locating in a shopping centre outweigh the costs, you need to do your homework. Check to see if the shopping centre attracts enough people to achieve the turnover that is necessary to justify the cost of setting up and operating there. Make sure your product or service is not too far up-market or too far down-market for the type of customers who come into the shopping centre. Seek independent professional advice from people who specialise in shopping centres. This includes advice on the terms of the retail tenancy agreement to ensure that they are reasonable and comply with the retail tenancy legislation in your state or territory. Ask for a copy of the most recent customer survey and market research for the shopping centre. Talk with existing tenants about the shopping centre and the centre management.

Retail Layout

Destination traffic are customers who know what they want. *Shopping* traffic has nothing particular in mind and is usually 'just looking.' Destination traffic moves directly toward what they want to buy, while shopping traffic is more unpredictable. Your job is to control the store traffic so that it not only separates destination and shopping traffic but also encourages the smooth circulation of both groups throughout the store.

Shopping traffic has a tendency to shop the perimeter of a store, moving from place to place as their attention is caught by the merchandise on display. Destination traffic goes directly to the merchandise they planned to buy before they entered the store. Research has shown that shopping traffic usually drifts towards the right when they enter the door. Destination traffic, however, tries to avoid the slow movement of the shoppers and drifts to the left. You can take advantage of this traffic pattern to maximise sales and minimise congestion.

- *Impulse* goods are bought on the spur of the moment and should be conveniently located to the right of the entrance, on the ends of aisles, and near the checkout.
- *Convenience* goods are bought frequently in small quantities and should be located with easy access to the left near the front.
- *Utility* items are bought for basic use in the home and they can be located toward the back of the store because easy access is not required.
- *Necessities or staples* are bought to satisfy a need. They can be located centrally or on the sides.
- *Speciality* goods are purchased after a great deal of planning and require more emphasis on personal selling. They should be located where they have easy access to a salesperson.

Creating a store traffic pattern is an exercise in finding the path of least resistance between the customers and the merchandise. Make sure that your fixtures and signs are placed so that customers instinctively know how to find what they want. Save your worst-selling space for the office and storage. Trade associations, retail design services, and suppliers of store fittings can help you with retail layout designs.

SERVICE BUSINESSES

The diversity of service businesses leads to a variety of principles for establishing premises. Some depend on a specific location and tailored premises, some are more flexible and can establish in a variety of locations and commercial premises, some have a base from which they travel to their customers, and some are completely portable. Here are some examples:

- A childcare centre requires the right location and custom-built premises. It either needs to be near where the families live, near where the parent works, or conveniently along the commute in between. Premises are subject to a myriad of regulations including zoning, layout, health, and safety.
- An insurance broker and a hairdresser can locate in a variety of commercial premises. The insurance broker requires office space

that is located where clients can conveniently reach them. The hairdresser needs to find a more accessible location and premises that are more adaptable for their purpose.

- A catering business needs a base from which it travels to serve customers. It should be located in reasonable proximity to the majority of customers, and the premises will need to conform to the zoning and other requirements for a commercial kitchen. Access for a vehicle is also needed for deliveries.
- A mobile dog wash is completely portable. The main requirement is a vehicle, a custom-built unit that can be towed to the customer's location, and connections for water and power.

Some service businesses need to operate in a high-traffic location because their customers' basic buying motive is the convenience of location. Many others can locate more flexibly because they do not rely on customer traffic.

MANUFACTURING PREMISES

A manufacturing site generally means making a large capital commitment for a long period of time. Important location considerations include access to customers, access to a workforce, access to transport, access to raw materials and components, community support, and the relative costs. The layout of a manufacturing operation is concerned with the efficient flow of production.

Manufacturing Location

If your manufacturing operation needs to be convenient to your customers, then you are looking for the geographic centre of your market. If you do not need to be near your customers, then the choice of location can focus on other factors. For example, are workers available with the skills that you need? If the need is for skilled workers, then this may become a critical factor in choosing a location. If the need is for unskilled workers, then location is less critical.

What type of transport do you need to get raw materials or components in and finished goods out, and what access to transport facilities (airport, seaport, highway, rail service) does the site offer? If you have a low-value-for-weight product, such as concrete, then your location decision will be heavily influenced by transport costs. If you have a high-value-for-weight product, such as electronic parts, then transport costs will not be very important. Do you need access to a port facility or a rail siding, or can you tranship to these facilities by road? Road access is important for both incoming materials and outgoing goods. Is the road frontage adequate to accommodate larger delivery vehicles? Is there enough room for loading and unloading? Could traffic congestion be a problem, especially at peak times? The growth of air freight makes sites near airports attractive for some manufacturers.

Most manufacturing businesses require an industrial power supply. Check with the local electricity distributor about the availability, quality, and reliability of a suitable power supply. Some areas in Australia have problems with the supply of adequate water. If water is important to your business, check with the local water authority about availability, quality, and seasonal or other restrictions. The cost of waste removal and sewage treatment also affects some manufacturing businesses.

Some communities want new development and their eagerness to welcome new industry helps to minimise many of the problems that can arise. Does the community want your type of manufacturing business, and will local government cooperate in terms of zoning and operating restrictions? Avoid areas that clearly do not want industry, and concentrate on those areas that show enthusiasm for you and your business.

Is the cost of the site justified in terms of its potential productivity now and into the future? Cheap premises are not a bargain if the ongoing operating costs destroy the initial cost advantage, so it is important to consider the tradeoff between the initial expense and the costs of marketing, staff, and transport. Would it be better to lease, buy, or build the facility you need? Will your requirements change in the future? Do you want to commit a large proportion of your capital to plant and equipment? Can you secure a favourable lease with options that maintain your flexibility?

Manufacturing Layout

Designing the layout of manufacturing premises begins by identifying each of the functions that takes place and considering the most efficient relationship that each function should have with the others. These functions are generally located in the office, production and assembly area, maintenance area, testing and inspection area, and the receiving, shipping, and storage areas.

In many manufacturing operations, the front office is the showplace of the business because this is where a customer's first impression is established. The reception area, product display area, and offices create an image for the entire operation. A bookkeeping or accounting office needs to be adjacent to the front office, but it doesn't need to be on public display. A production office should be located so that it is in contact with the rest of the manufacturing operation without the need to pass through the front office.

The primary objective of a manufacturing plant is to produce a product. The main elements in production and assembly layout are the space required for each machine, the relationship of the machines to each other, and the efficiency of the overall production and assembly operation. The layout of a production and assembly area can be described as a process-type layout or a product-type layout. A process-type layout is suited to low-volume job-lot manufacturing because of its flexibility to produce different products with the same equipment. A product-type layout is best suited to high-volume manufacturing for products in which the same sequence of operations is required. The product-type layout is suited to a high and constant level of production, but it is expensive and not very flexible. For many small manufacturers, this option is simply not feasible or economical.

Even the smallest plant has a workshop or area adjacent to the main production area where maintenance operations are performed. As the size of a manufacturing operation increases, it becomes increasingly cost effective to have equipment repairs performed by your own staff. It also enhances your ability to make quick changes in jigs and other tooling.

The importance of testing and inspection depends on the nature of the product. Inspection and checking is usually performed before a product is packaged, crated, or otherwise prepared for shipment. If all items need to be tested, then adequate space that is clean and protected from shop fumes, noises, dust, or vibration should be provided.

Ideally, raw materials or components are received at one end of the plant, processed through the production area, and the finished goods stored and shipped out from the other end. In very small manufacturing operations, this may be difficult to accomplish, or the location of shipping and receiving areas may be dictated by road access or the location of the loading dock. One way to compensate for a single entry/exit point is to create a U-shaped manufacturing layout that brings the product back to the shipping area without having to backtrack.

LOCAL GOVERNMENT REGULATIONS

There are hundreds of local governments around Australia, and they have different approaches to regulating things like land use zoning, building codes, health regulations, fire restrictions, and environmental requirements.

Planning

Planning regulations represent a significant compliance burden for any small business that needs to make a development application or a building application and navigate the various processes leading to approval. Planning approval also includes local government regulations for things like noise, parking, and signage. Be prepared for lots of forms, reports, fees, and inspections.

Permits and Licences

Permits and licences involve more red tape and fees. These might include professional certification, equipment permits, certification of adherence to standards, forklift/heavy machinery, plumbing, electrical, and site permits. Others include permits to operate in a public place, special vehicle registration, loading zone and parking restrictions, street signage, street seating, and training required to maintain certain types of licences.

Health and Safety

Local government is responsible for administering a number of health and safety matters. These include some occupational health and safety standards, building reports, fire safety, food safety, various quality control and quality assurance matters, and transport and storage regulations. Some environmental issues are also part of local government responsibilities including dangerous goods and chemical management, waste management, and noise restrictions.

Get Advice

There are many reasons why local government requirements can be confusing and complex. Few small business operators understand local government regulations and how to navigate local government processes. For example, even a small home-based business may require permits or approvals, especially if parking, access, or signage issues are involved. Trying to find out what local government requires can also be difficult because there is usually no clear access point where you can ask someone to explain what you must do and how to do it. Even when you have determined what you need, local government decisions and approvals often involve lengthy delays.

Given these precarious circumstances, rather than spending your own time trying to satisfy local government requirements, consider getting professional advice. An architect or builder knows the planning system, you solicitor can help with permits and licenses, and your trade association knows about specific requirements for businesses like yours. You can save yourself a lot of time and frustration by engaging professionals who already understand local government requirements and procedures.

NEGOTIATING A LEASE

The majority of small businesses lease their premises rather than tying up capital in land and buildings. The first step in negotiating a lease is to evaluate the landlord. Talk to other tenants and ask them if the landlord responds to their needs. Does the landlord return calls promptly? Does the landlord send service people when they are

needed? Is it necessary to pester the landlord for routine maintenance? Does the landlord just collect the rent and disappear?

A lease is a legal contract. Once you and your landlord enter into a
lease, you are both bound by its conditions. Therefore, the lease
agreement should contain all of the promises that the landlord has
made about repairs, construction and reconstruction, decorating,
alteration, and maintenance. Be sure to have your solicitor review the
lease before you sign it. There are a number of key lease provisions
that you should examine carefully.

Rental Payments

Rent can be calculated in a number of ways. It can be a regular fixed
rental payment, a base rent with an annual increase determined by
movements in the Consumer Price Index, a base rent subject to an
annual market review that brings it into line with other rental values,
or a base rent plus a percentage of gross sales. For retail businesses, a
common method is a base rent plus a percentage of gross sales over a
base sales target. Suppose the agreed base sales target is $800,000 per
year and the lease terms are $50,000 per year plus 5 percent of gross
sales over the base sales target. If sales are below $800,000, then the
rental is $50,000 per year. If, however, actual sales turn out to be
$1,000,000, then the annual rental becomes $60,000.

Most lease agreements increase the base rental annually according
to a formula or in line with the Consumer Price Index. When the
base rental clause provides for annual increases, be sure that there is
also a compensatory increase in the base sales target. Try to avoid a
lease that is subject to an annual market review. If you are able to
negotiate a favourable rental, then you do not want to lose your
advantage in the first review. Some lease provisions include additional costs besides the rental. Be sure to identify all of these costs and
add them to the rental to find your true cost of occupancy.

Term of Lease

The term of a lease is the length of time you may occupy the premises. Traditionally, retail leases are offered for terms of three or five
years. During the term of the lease, you are liable for the agreed base

rental whether your business is operating or not. When the lease term expires, you may not be able to renew or extend it. If you have to move, you will lose the goodwill you have built up in that location.

When you spend money on new premises, you want to know that you can occupy them long enough for your investment to pay for itself. On the other hand, you do not want to lock yourself into a long lease in case you need to close down, move, or expand into bigger premises. The solution to this dilemma is to negotiate an option to renew the lease at the end of its term. For example, you may negotiate a three-year term with an option to renew the lease for a further three years. If you exercise the option, you may continue to occupy the premises for another three years. If you do not want to continue in that location, then you can simply let the option lapse. It is also important to have the right to sell or assign the lease. If you decide to sell the business, you need to be able to transfer the lease to the new owner. If you assign a lease, try to avoid any residual liability to the landlord if the new tenant defaults.

Permitted Uses

Permitted uses define the kinds of business activities that you are permitted to carry on. Make sure the permitted uses are stated broadly enough to accommodate any changes you may wish to make in the way you run the business. Permitted uses clauses are usually interpreted strictly, especially in shopping centres that try to maintain a balanced tenant mix. They include a number of restrictions that are designed to prevent a tenant from creating any nuisances, disturbances, or damage. Look for provisions that restrict the hours during which you have access to the building or that require you to be open for trading during specific times.

Other Provisions

If you are leasing space in a large established shopping centre, the landlord is unlikely to be very flexible about the terms and conditions of the lease. In most other circumstances, there is significant scope for negotiation. Ask for a rent-free period while you get established, stepped rental rates which start out low and increase later, and a contribution towards the initial fit-out. Here are some other provisions to look for in a lease:

- Compulsory membership in a tenants' association
- Parking provisions for staff and customers
- Access to common areas in a shopping centre
- Sharing of expenses with the landlord or other tenants
- General conduct of the business
- Storage of goods
- Disposal of waste
- Receiving and delivery of goods
- Repair and redecorating of premises
- Landlord's right to enter the premises
- Compliance with various laws and regulations
- Insurance
- Default conditions and remedies available

State and territory governments have implemented minimum standards for retail tenancy into their legislation and regulations. Ask your state or territory small business agency for a guide that covers leasing in your jurisdiction.

SUMMARY

This chapter considers important factors in selecting your premises. At first, you may need temporary arrangements until you are ready to move into something permanent such as a serviced office or a business incubator. Some small business operators choose to operate either temporarily or permanently from their home. Major factors in selecting retail premises are the type of retail business and the kind of traffic needed to sustain it. The interior of the selling space is a highly specialised area, and your trade association, retail design services, and suppliers of store fittings can help you with the design. Some service businesses depend on a specific location and tailored premises, some are more flexible and can establish in a variety of locations and premises, some have a base from which they travel to their customers, and some are completely portable. Manufacturing premises generally mean making a large capital commitment for a long time. Location factors include proximity to customers, availability of skilled or non-skilled labour, availability of transport, water, and a power supply. A production or assembly area is generally designed as either a process-type layout or a product-type layout. Complying with local government regulations is an important part of getting established in new premises. The majority of small businesses lease their premises, and there are a number of provisions that you and your solicitor should carefully examine.

Eleven
Employing Staff

It is one thing to be self-employed, but it is quite another thing to be an employer. The Australian industrial relations system and the changing nature of the employment environment can make employing staff a challenging proposition. Perhaps this explains why there are 1.6 million small businesses in Australia that employ no staff. Before you commit yourself to becoming an employer, think carefully about the consequences. Be prepared to devote a great deal of time, effort, and money to deal with the responsibilities of being an employer. The overall cost of employing someone is much greater than their pay packet, so you need to be clear about the cost compared with their contribution to your business.

Sooner or later you may find that you cannot be everywhere at once and you are no longer able to do everything yourself. If you want your business to grow, then you may eventually need to employ staff. From this point on, the greatest asset in your business will be the people who work for you. Unless you can find, attract, and develop people who will work in a productive and cooperative manner, your business is unlikely to reach its potential. The purpose of this chapter is to examine key elements of employing staff including the legal framework, designing a job, hiring new staff, motivation and performance, and staff turnover.

LEGAL FRAMEWORK

If you decide to employ staff, then you will need to acquaint yourself with the commonwealth and state legislation that covers you and your employees such as:

The Fair Work Act	Occupational health and safety
Anti-discrimination legislation	legislation

DOI: 10.4324/9781032676616-19

Superannuation legislation   Workers compensation legislation
Long service leave legislation   Taxation legislation

Fair Work System

The Fair Work System is the name used for the national workplace relations system. Key features of the Fair Work System are the National Employment Standards, awards that apply nationally for specific industries and occupations, the national minimum wage, and protection from unfair dismissal. The Fair Work System covers most Australian workplaces, but there are some exceptions that are covered by state legislation. The Fair Work website at *fairwork.gov.au* is a comprehensive source of information about current employment legislation and regulation. There is a special section called the *Small Business Showcase* that covers several key topics:

Hiring employees   Paying employees
Keeping the right records   Ending employment
Managing employees   Help and advice
Leave and other requests   Latest news

A feature of the Fair Work System is the National Employment Standards. They provide a set of minimum conditions for all employees covered by the national workplace relations system. The standards set out such things as maximum hours of work, various forms of leave, redundancy, and dismissal. Neither an award nor an enterprise bargaining agreement can be used to get around the standards. Information about the standards is available from the Fair Work website.

Awards

For some types of jobs or for employees of certain types of businesses, there is an award that sets out the minimum conditions for that kind of work. For example, there are awards for employees in retail or hairdressing. Awards may include conditions such as penalty rates and allowances, hours of work, and leave entitlements. Rates of pay are included in some awards while others refer to a separate pay scale. Visit the Fair Work website to find out if an award applies in your business.

Enterprise Agreements

Enterprise agreements are arrangements for pay and conditions that are negotiated between an employer and employees and they override an award that would otherwise apply. In some cases, multiple employer and employee groups may be involved. There is also scope for union participation in negotiating agreements. Enterprise agreements are different to awards because they can cover a broader range of matters and they can be tailored to a particular business's needs. However, enterprise agreements cannot remove the safety net conditions contained in the standards. To make an agreement, the parties must bargain with each other in good faith, genuinely agree to the conditions, and lodge the agreement with Fair Work Australia for approval. For information on the types of agreements and how to make them, see the Fair Work website.

Occupational Health and Safety

An employer is required to provide a safe place to work and establish safe work practices. Employees are obliged to conduct themselves in a safe manner including observing safety instructions and training, using safety equipment that has been provided, and not recklessly placing themselves or others at risk.

Workplace safety involves identifying and managing the risks in your business. For particular industries and types of jobs, there are codes of practice for how certain risks are to be managed such as the safety precautions required for asbestos removal. If there are no guidelines for a particular job or task, you are nevertheless required to take reasonable precautions and exercise due care. Some activities are considered highly risky and require specific training, licences, and permits for all employees involved in or overseeing those jobs.

For current information about occupational health and safety requirements in your state or territory, see the Safe Work Australia website at **safeworkaustralia.gov.au**. Some state and territory workplace safety authorities offer assistance to help you comply with occupational health and safety requirements. This may include workplace consultations to help assess risks or workshops on managing safety. Your industry association is also a potential source of advice and information on workplace safety because they may have training and resource materials designed for your line of business.

Workers Compensation Insurance

Employers are required to have workers compensation insurance for their employees. In the event of work-related injury or disease, there is an entitlement to claim for a range of medical costs and income support. The level of risk associated with an industry, an employer's record of providing a safe workplace, and the amount of wages paid to workers determine the premiums paid. Each state and territory has its own regulator that administers and gives advice on workers compensation. For information on insurance requirements, policy providers, and claims procedures, you can find your state or territory authority on the Fair Work website.

DESIGNING A JOB

Designing a job consists of analysing the tasks that need to be done and specifying the attributes you require in the person who will do them. This enables you to write a brief job description that you can use in recruiting and selection.

Task Analysis

Task analysis consists of setting out the work that needs to be done. Related tasks can be grouped together to make up a job. Here are some questions to consider in making your analysis:

- What physical and mental tasks need to be done? Examples are tasks such as grinding and cleaning or planning and directing.
- How is the task done? What are the methods, equipment, or applications to be used? Examples include using a metal lathe to shape parts or entering financial data into an accounting program.

- Why is the task done? This is the purpose of the task and how it relates it to other tasks. An example is recording sales data using an accounting package so the accountant can prepare the quarterly business activity statement.
- What level of responsibility is associated with the task? For example, is the task to be performed under supervision, or will it be done independently?

The amount of work to be done tells you how many jobs you need to fill. The attributes you require of the person who will fill the job consist of the skills, qualifications, and experience necessary to perform the tasks.

Attributes

From the task analysis, identify the skills that are needed. Should the person know how to operate special equipment? Will they need to have skills in retail selling? Carefully spell out the skills that the tasks require, and decide beforehand whether the person must have these skills before being employed or if you can teach them on the job. Remember that the tasks you give an employee need to be within a reasonable range of their abilities.

In addition to educational and training qualifications, some jobs require licences or certificates issued by government or other authorities such as a heavy rigid drivers licence or certification as a dive master. For other jobs, there may be no requirement for specific training or qualifications. However, an untrained person in a position requiring particular skills or knowledge is a potential liability to your business and a source of expense when you have to replace them. Filling a job with an overqualified person is no solution either because it is likely to result in frustration for the employee and unnecessary staff turnover.

Skills and qualifications are important, but you may also need staff with practical experience. For example, whereas a trade certificate may indicate competence at laying bricks, what you may need is a person who is capable of doing the job without supervision. On the other hand, you may be prepared to employ an individual to work under supervision while gaining experience.

Job Description

A job description is a concise outline of the job based on the information obtained from the task analysis and the attributes required to perform the tasks. Writing it down helps to clarify your thinking about the work that needs to be done and the kind of person you need to do it. A job description usually includes the following elements:

- Job title—keep in mind how important titles can be to some people.
- Work to be performed—a brief summary of its general nature.
- Major job duties—including responsibilities for quality and quantity of work, the supervision and safety of others, equipment to be used, and schedules to be met.
- Minor job duties—duties performed only occasionally.
- Relationship of the job to other jobs—whom the person would supervise and to whom they would be responsible.
- Skills, qualifications, and experience—the minimum skill level, formal qualification, and previous experience required for the job.

A job description serves more than one purpose. The obvious one is to outline the important functions of a job. When you evaluate applicants, you have a measure against which to match their skills, qualifications, and experience. Having a written job description will also help you to prepare an advertisement, develop interview questions, and provide a basis for determining wages. When you have hired a new employee, having a job description helps them to understand what is expected and how their job fits into your business.

HIRING NEW STAFF

Hiring new staff can be the beginning of a productive and mutually rewarding relationship. Getting the right person depends on how you recruit, interview, and select the best applicant.

Recruiting

Recruiting is easy when many people with the skills you need are looking for work. If qualified workers are in short supply, then you need to find ways to attract good applicants. If the position represents a promotion, ask your existing staff if they would like to apply. Otherwise, ask them if they know someone who is qualified that might be interested. It might also be worthwhile to contact former employees to ask if they are available for work again. A common recruiting tool is to advertise in the newspaper. If you place a 'blind' advertisement, one in which the name of your firm is not given, be sure to tell your current employees to avoid possible embarrassment. You can also place spot ads on the local radio station, put job advertisements on bulletin boards in places such as TAFE, or place an advertisement in the journal of your trade association. Ask your trade union representative if they can recommend someone. Ask suppliers and sales reps if they are aware of someone in the industry who is looking for a job, or perhaps you can lure someone away from one of your competitors. If you cannot find the right person on your own, list your job with an employment agency.

Conducting the Interview

The most common method for choosing a new employee is a personal interview. In addition to facts, an interview can also tell you something about the applicant's personality and character. To evaluate these less tangible qualities, you need to be skilful, observant, and objective. Plan for the interview by having a checklist of questions to ask each applicant.

Put the applicant at ease. Job applicants are usually tense and they will relax more quickly in an informal discussion and you will learn more about them. Provide the applicant with a copy of the job description and discuss it with them. Give the applicant plenty of opportunity to ask questions. Let them do most of the talking while you guide the conversation with open questions such as 'Tell me a bit about yourself' or 'Tell me about your last job.' Review the written application and probe the accuracy of the information contained in it. Pay particular attention to the reasons for leaving previous positions. Test the applicant's knowledge and skills required by the position.

Determine if the applicant has the personal characteristics required for the job. What are their aspirations and goals? Are they willing to accept the responsibilities of the job? Are they emotionally stable? Would they make a loyal employee? Do they demonstrate an ability to learn and to develop in your business? Ask the applicant how they feel about the position and note carefully any comments. Be sure that the financial rewards of the job are understood. Immediately schedule a second interview to hold a qualified candidate while you continue to interview the others. Write down your impressions of the applicant immediately after the interview.

People who feel that they have always worked for poor supervisors and unfair managers will probably find you to be the same. Those who tell you that they have enjoyed working with interesting people in their previous jobs are more likely to find them in your business as well. The interview is a good way to discover their attitudes towards supervision, workmates, and cooperation. Having another person with you at the interview, such as the person who will be their supervisor, is helpful because they may observe things that you have missed and they can help you to make a selection.

Selecting the Best Applicant

References should always be checked for those applicants who appear to be best qualified for the job. Using the phone has several advantages. It is quicker than using a letter, it sometimes turns up facts or opinions that a previous employer would not be prepared to set down on paper, and it may lead you to other referees who can offer more information. When written references are provided, it is a good idea to confirm them with the provider and ask questions about any matters that are not addressed on paper. When speaking to referees, ask specific questions rather than general ones. The information you get should be considered with judgement. Always evaluate the person from whom it comes and do not blindly accept either severe criticism or bountiful praise.

Review your interview notes in conjunction with the information you obtain from the applicant's references. If a clear preference does not emerge, try to narrow the field to two or three and ask them to come in for a second interview. Accept the fact that the selection process is a judgement about human nature. There are times when you may make a mistake and you will be faced with repairing the damage. Nevertheless, with a bit of experience, you will learn to recognise those applicants who represent the best fit with the needs of your business.

When you have made a selection, consider offering the job subject to an initial probation period to give you an opportunity to evaluate their performance. Probation periods of three to twelve months are common in some industries. Make it clear that there is a probation period and how long it will be. Clearly set out your expectations at the start of the probation period and provide training in your work methods and regular discussions to iron out any questions. If the new employee isn't working out, you are in a position to terminate the employment. Ask your solicitor to ensure that you are acting within the law.

Your staff will expect their pay to reflect the skills and energy they put into your business. If you want to attract and keep good staff, then you need to match the rates paid for comparable work by other firms like yours and the fringe benefits they offer. Wages should reflect an employee's contribution to your firm and they should be consistent within your firm. Job classifications enable you to establish a normal wage for each job and a regular scale for merit increases or length of service. Don't forget about the various government regulations and industrial awards when you set your wage rates.

Give some thought to how you will bring new staff on board. On their first day, complete the paperwork for their tax file declaration, workers compensation, and superannuation. Show them around the business, introduce them to the rest of the staff, give them an overall view of the operation, and explain how their job fits into the picture. This requires little effort and it can save you time and money in the long run. Even when you do a good job selecting new staff, you need to back it up with training. Every new employee, even those with previous experience, needs training in your particular ways of doing things. A common method of training is job rotation in which staff are trained in various jobs that require different skills or responsibility. You will have a more flexible workforce, you can easily fill vacancies or cover periods of leave, and you are able to demonstrate that your staff are being prepared to move ahead to better positions.

MOTIVATION AND PERFORMANCE

A small business has some built-in advantages for developing employee motivation. The most important advantage is the close relationship between you and your staff. Here are some motivating factors that engender a deep commitment to job performance:

- The work itself—the extent to which the work is meaningful and worthwhile.
- Achievement—the opportunity to undertake tasks that are a reasonable challenge.
- Responsibility—the authority to carry out a significant function.
- Recognition—knowing how highly one's contribution to the business is valued.
- Advancement—a genuine opportunity for promotion.

Despite your best efforts to motivate staff, your expectations may not always be met. If this happens, try to identify the problem to see if there is something you can do about it. For some problems, the solution will lie in changes to the working environment or the work procedures. For other problems, the solution will lie in your approach to human behaviour. Here are some examples:

- Fatigue and illness—People lose motivation when they exceed their physical capacity. It could be a result of working overtime, inadequate rest, tasks beyond their ability, or attempting to work when they are sick or not fully recovered from an illness or injury.
- Inadequate skill or training—When a person is doing a job for which they have inadequate skills or training, they are likely to lose confidence and become dispirited.
- Boredom—Routine tasks create boredom, especially when there is infrequent action required. Boredom can also occur in simple repetitive tasks, particularly if the job is paced by a machine.
- Unsatisfactory working conditions—Poor working conditions slow productivity and impede quality performance.

- Improper tools—It has often been said that a good worker never blames their tools. Nevertheless, if the necessary tools are inadequate or unavailable, then productivity and quality are going to suffer.
- Wrong information—People can only act on information to the best of their understanding. Errors occur if they are given the wrong information or if they misunderstand the information because it was unclear.
- Carelessness—When staff are rewarded for the quantity rather than the quality of their work, carelessness can creep into their performance. Careless errors can also result from 'don't care' or 'she'll be right' attitudes on the part of staff who are not interested in their work.

STAFF TURNOVER

All businesses lose staff and have to replace them. Some quit, some are dismissed, and others may become ill, start a family, or retire. For whatever reason, they leave your employment and you need to replace them. Meanwhile, you have a job that you must cover by working overtime and generally limping along. The vacancy may last for only a few days, or it can stretch out into weeks and even months. Finally, when you do get a new employee, they are likely to be untrained for your particular job, or at least your way of doing it. Losing one employee may not seem too serious, but losing three or four at once can be disastrous. Sometimes the causes of staff turnover are not immediately apparent and it takes some digging to put your finger on the problem.

- Placement—Different jobs call for different aptitudes and skills. Misplaced people can cause problems for themselves and for you. In a job for which they are unsuited, staff may eventually quit or have to be let go.
- Orientation—The purpose of an orientation program is to make new staff feel at home and to tell them what they need to know about your business. If the orientation is mishandled, either by neglect or by doing it poorly, it may result in things getting off on the wrong foot.

- Wages—How do your wages and benefits compare with other firms in your community? Can your staff look forward to moving up to a better job? If not, they will think of their job as a dead end.
- Working conditions—Employee dissatisfaction with their surroundings can result in turnover.
- Supervision—Poor supervision is a major cause of poor work quality and staff leaving. Look for unfairness, favouritism, or erratic discipline.
- Training—Everyone needs some training for a new job. Even if they have done the work before, your ways are probably a little different. If they have not done the work before, then training is imperative. If they move on, it could be because the training they received was unsatisfactory.

Although the emphasis is generally on minimising employee turnover, there may be an occasion when you are compelled to dismiss an individual. No one likes it, but sometimes you have no alternative for the good of others and for the good of your business. If you think you may be forced to dismiss an employee, make sure you comply with the procedures and conditions for dismissal set down in legislation and industrial awards. Review the 'Ending Employment' page on the Fair Work website, and ask your solicitor for advice.

First, try to salvage the situation. Discuss the cause of the problem as you see it and let the employee tell you the cause of the problem as they see it. Ask if there is a way you can help them to do a better job. Be helpful but firm. Give yourselves a reasonable length of time to work for improvement. Be sure the employee knows this is a formal warning and that failure to resolve the problem will result in dismissal. Provide a written warning that has been checked out by your solicitor.

If your warnings and attempts at counselling have no effect, then you will need to dismiss the employee. Choose the right time and place. Privacy and freedom from interruption are important. Plan to spend enough time so that the individual has plenty of opportunity to express their feelings and opinions. Discuss the problem only. Never comment on an individual's personality or character unless it is directly related to the problem. Make the meeting final. Be firm, calm, and reasonable.

Permit the individual to let off steam. Their reaction may not be logical, but don't argue with them. Have a face-saving approach in mind like offering to let them resign. Do not humiliate them in front of their workmates. When it is all over, ask yourself how you might improve your methods for recruiting, selection, training, and motivation to avoid a similar problem in the future.

SUMMARY

This chapter explains some of the important issues you face if you decide to employ staff. The Australian industrial relations system and the changing nature of the employment environment can make employing staff a challenging proposition. The Fair Work System is the basis for many of the employment rules and regulations. In addition to the National Employment Standards, there is legislation that covers awards, enterprise agreements, occupational health and safety, and workers compensation insurance. Before you begin looking for a new employee, you need to design the job. This involves analysing the tasks to be performed, identifying the attributes that the employee should have, and writing a job description. A job description underpins the processes of attracting applicants, conducting the interviews, and selecting the best candidate. Once you have a new employee on board, you can focus on how you will motivate their performance in the job. The chapter concludes with a brief discussion about staff turnover.

Reflective Exercise: Creating a Smooth Operation

The purpose of this exercise is to identify and evaluate the expertise and resources you need to create a smooth and efficient operation. Expertise includes marketing expertise, technical expertise, financial expertise, functional expertise, and managerial expertise. Resources include financial resources, physical resources, staff, information, and sources of help and assistance. Each question is designed to identify the gap between what you need and what you already have to get your business idea into operation.

EXPERTISE

The kinds of skills and experience you need depends on the sophistication of your business idea and the nature of the market it faces. Having a balance of skills and experience is just as important as depth of expertise in particular areas. The overriding premise is the circumstances of a business dictate the marketing, technical, financial, functional, and managerial expertise needed for a smooth operation.

Marketing Expertise

Marketing is not just about selling. It is a broader way of thinking and acting in which every decision is driven by an intense focus on how to deliver the right benefits to the right customers. This is particularly true of consumer products that need to be skilfully designed, packaged, promoted, priced, and distributed to gain the consumer's attention. Perhaps you will be able to develop a marketing strategy and carry it out yourself. Products and services that require a high level of marketing expertise are probably best tackled by those who have the skills, experience, and resources.

DOI: 10.4324/9781032676616-20

Will the gap between what I have and what I need call for no additional marketing expertise, some extra marketing expertise, or a high level of marketing expertise?

Technical Expertise

A business needs sufficient technical skills and knowledge to produce and deliver the product or service. Some are straightforward and require very little technical input. A product or service that requires a very high level of technical expertise needs to be in the hands of someone who knows what they are doing. It is easy to underestimate the technical sophistication involved in a product or service if you lack technical expertise or have not been in business before.

Will the gap between what I have and what I need call for no additional technical expertise, some extra technical expertise, or a high level of technical expertise?

Financial Expertise

Examples of the financial knowledge and skills that may be needed include things like bookkeeping, budgeting, cash flow, financing, cost control, and more. A modest level of financial expertise is generally enough for small-scale operations with little or no financing requirements and a simple accounting system. If you need help, engaging an accountant is one way to gain financial expertise quickly. Businesses that require a very high level of financial expertise need to have greater in-house expertise or outside professional assistance.

Will the gap between what I have and what I need call for no additional financial expertise, some extra financial expertise, or a high level of financial expertise?

Functional Expertise

Examples of functions requiring knowledge, skills, or experience include purchasing, production, service delivery, cost control, transport, supervision, negotiating, and information systems. Some functions consist of repeating a series of relatively straightforward tasks while others can be highly complicated. Functional expertise also varies between service businesses, online businesses, retail businesses, and manufacturing businesses.

Will the gap between what I have and what need call for no additional functional expertise, some extra functional expertise, or a high level of functional expertise?

Managerial Expertise

Managerial expertise is different from other skills and experience because the emphasis is working *on* the business rather than working *in* the business. Managerial expertise includes knowledge and skills in planning, sales and marketing, customer service, finance and accounting, legal and governance, and human resources. It is a rare individual who can lay claim to have mastered all of them. Nevertheless, developing a business idea into a successful enterprise means you will necessarily need to master some of them. Perhaps the best attribute of a good manager is the ability to recognise when to bring others into the business who can contribute the knowledge and skills that are needed.

Will the gap between what I have and what I need call for no additional managerial expertise, some extra managerial expertise, or a high level of managerial expertise?

RESOURCES

Start-ups typically suffer from insufficient resources. The result is it takes too long to get to market, they perform poorly when they do get to market, and they often fail to capitalise on the full potential of the original business idea. Avoid wasting resources by concentrating what you have on the issues that give your business the best chance for success. The purpose of these questions is to identify the resources you need to make your business idea operational.

Financial Resources

Having enough money when you start out means more than just being able to open the doors. You also need enough money to cover operations while you wait out the inertia of customers. Customers are creatures of habit and they are unlikely to change their behaviour just because a new product or service enters the marketplace. Financial resources consist of your savings, your borrowing capacity, and your ability to raise equity. The less money it takes to get into business, the less demanding will be the process of getting started.

Will the gap between what I have and what I need call for no additional financial resources, some extra financial resources, or a significant amount of financial resources?

Physical Resources

Physical resources are the tangible assets that are needed to operate a business such as location, premises, and equipment. Many of these are the everyday physical resources that are required to operate most businesses. Critical physical resources, however, are the ones that provide a commercial advantage, like the best location, state-of-the-art technology, or access to a limited source of supply. The need for physical resources can be modest for some business ideas and substantial for others.

Will the gap between what I have and what I need call for no further physical resources, some extra physical resources, or significant additional physical resources?

Staff

It is one thing to start out in business on your own, but it is quite another thing to become an employer. You can start out by engaging the services of temporary staff or outsourcing some of your work to another person or business. Eventually, you may find that you cannot do everything yourself and you need to employ staff. Before you do, however, make sure you understand the responsibilities and cost of becoming an employer.

Will the gap between what I have and what I need call for no extra staff, some additional staff, or a highly skilled workforce?

Information System

Information systems have become an essential tool for all businesses. Modern information technology offers streamlined systems for accounting, remote communications, a website, sales and marketing, desktop publishing, payroll, payments, and much more. Some information systems are tailored to meet the needs of particular types of businesses.

Will the gap between what I have and what I need call for no changes to my existing information system, a different information system, or I'm not sure what kind of information system I will need?

Help and Assistance

Going into business does not mean you are forced to rely entirely on your own skills and experience. There are significant benefits from building a network of organisations and people who have information, knowledge, and expertise that can help you. Initially, the formal part of your network will probably consist of professional advisers, your trade association, and government agencies. Later, you may want to engage specialist help.

Will the gap between what I have and what I need call for no further help and assistance, some extra help and assistance, or a significant amount of help and assistance?

Part E
Financial Plan

Success in a small business depends on the financial information your accounting system provides and how you use it. Without current, reliable financial information at your fingertips, it is difficult to make good commercial decisions. Modern small business accounting systems are designed to simplify and automate bookkeeping and reporting processes. An accounting system periodically produces a balance sheet and an income statement, and the information they contain is used to analyse and monitor financial performance. Managing liquidity is a critical concern because small businesses often operate with too little working capital and miss the implications of a cash flow crisis until it is too late. Managing profitability consists of identifying the key variables that drive profits and applying this information to your products and services, your customers, and your market channels. Financing and taxation issues occur less frequently than day-to-day money management. If you need more capital, you may want to consider borrowing money, leasing, outside equity, or apply for a government grant. The taxation system impacts just about every phase of business including the GST, income tax, capital gains tax, fringe benefits tax, and the superannuation guarantee.

DOI: 10.4324/9781032676616-21

Twelve
Financial Information

Your recordkeeping and accounting system should reflect the type of business you operate. It is important to seek advice from your accountant about which accounting methods will suit your operation and what records you need to keep for tax and statutory reporting purposes. The accounting system periodically produces a balance sheet and an income statement. The balance sheet tells you what the business owns, what it owes, and what it is worth to you as the owner. The income statement reports sales revenue, expenses, and the resulting profit. Information from these reports is used to analyse and manage financial performance. The purpose of this chapter is to explain how to set up your accounting system and how to use the information it provides.

PAPER TRAIL

Every small business operator resents having to keep the mountain of paperwork required by our overzealous bureaucrats. Nevertheless, you need to be able to substantiate the accounting entries that underpin your taxation returns, financial statements, and statutory reports. You do this by establishing a paper trail that leads back to the original documents.

Inasmuch as most businesses generate lots of paperwork, how you keep track of these documents is important. If you only have a few transactions, then you can get by with a simple filing and storage system. If you have many transactions, then you need to have a method for storing your documents that makes it easy to locate them again. You can scan the original documents and store them electronically using an index system. This avoids the requirement to keep the original documents and makes it easy to retrieve them. Ask your accountant for advice.

DOI: 10.4324/9781032676616-22

ACCOUNTING SYSTEM

Even if your accountant is providing you with a full bookkeeping and accounting service, it is important to understand how it works and what information it provides. The following illustration demonstrates how accounting systems are organised.

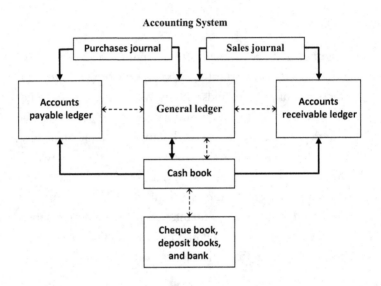

Figure 12.1 Accounting System

The *purchases journal* records the purchases that you make in conducting your business. It includes the purchase of goods for resale, equipment, supplies, and services. The summarised information from the purchases journal is transferred to the general ledger. Purchases that you have made on credit are also transferred to the accounts payable ledger.

The *sales journal* records the sales that you make to your customers. It may contain an individual entry for each sale or a batch of daily sales. The summarised information from the sales journal is transferred to the general ledger. Sales that you have made on credit are also transferred to the accounts receivable ledger.

The *accounts payable ledger* (sometimes called the *creditors* ledger) records the goods and services that you purchased on credit from your suppliers and the amounts that you owe them. From the *cash book*, the accounts payable ledger receives information on the amounts you have paid. The accounts payable ledger provides you with information to maintain good relationships with your suppliers.

The *accounts receivable ledger* (sometimes called the *debtors* ledger) records the goods and services that you sold to your customers on credit and the amounts they owe you. From the cash book, the accounts receivable ledger receives information on the amounts you have received. The accounts receivable ledger provides you with information to control credit and collections.

The *general ledger* is the place where all transactions are ultimately recorded. Most transactions come from the journals and the cash book. At the end of each accounting period, your accountant may make some further adjustments for non-cash items and accruals. The general ledger is where the information is gathered together to make up your financial reports.

The cash book records cash receipts and payments or the transfer of cash into and out of your business. The cash received information is transferred to the general ledger and to the accounts receivable ledger. The cash paid information is also transferred to the general ledger and to the accounts payable ledger. The cash book is regularly reconciled with your bank statements to ensure they agree.

The accounting system produces two key financial reports called the *balance sheet* and the *income statement* (sometimes called the *profit and loss account*). Essentially, the balance sheet shows what your business has, what it owes, and your investment in the business. It can be likened to a photograph, showing the financial position of your business at a point in time. The income statement is a summary of business operations. It can be compared to a moving picture. It reports the financial activity of your business over a period of time. In very general terms, the balance sheet tells you where you are, and the income statement tells you how you got there since the last balance sheet was prepared. We shall look more closely at these financial reports later in the chapter.

Chart of Accounts

The key to getting your accounting system set up correctly is the chart of accounts. It is a list of the accounts in the general ledger.

For a very small business with few transactions, a simple chart of accounts will do the job. For complex operations, the chart of accounts will be more elaborate. Some industry associations publish a recommended chart of accounts for their members and accounting software packages usually come with a selection of charts of accounts for different types of businesses. Ask your accountant for advice.

Each account is assigned an account number, but they are not in consecutive order making it easy to add more accounts later. The accounts are arranged in the same order as the balance sheet and the income statement. The following example is a chart of accounts for the financial reports discussed later in the chapter.

My Small Business
Chart of Accounts

Current assets

110	Cash
120	Accounts receivable
130	Inventory
190	Other current assets

Non-current assets

210	Plant and equipment
215	Accumulated depreciation plant and equipment
220	Vehicles
225	Accumulated depreciation vehicles
290	Other non-current assets

Other assets

310	Other assets

Current liabilities

410	Accounts payable
425	GST clearing account
430	Taxes payable
490	Other current liabilities

Non-current liabilities

510	Bank loan
590	Other non-current liabilities

Owner's equity

610	Contributed capital
690	Retained earnings

Revenue

710	Sales revenue
790	Other revenue

Expenses

810	Cost of sales
820	Salaries
830	Casual wages
840	Marketing expense
850	Occupancy expense
860	Administration expense
870	Interest expense
880	Depreciation expense
890	Other expense

Small Business Accounting Packages

Modern small business accounting systems simplify and automate the bookkeeping and reporting processes. They are designed for businesses that do the bookkeeping themselves and give the information to their accountant to complete the financial statements, business activity statements, taxation returns, and other compliance reports. They are also designed to be used by people with limited knowledge of accounting and only basic computer skills. There are scores of general-purpose and industry-specific accounting systems on offer, and your accountant can steer you in the right direction.

You can download accounting software over the internet together with the instructions on how to install and operate it on your computer. There are also short courses available that will train you to use these accounting packages. Make sure you have the right computer setup to run the accounting package you have selected. This includes the correct operating system, the right type of processor, enough RAM and hard drive capacity, and whatever peripherals are required.

You can also access accounting systems and store data online. Called 'cloud' computing, you use a hosted accounting package over the internet for a monthly fee without having to buy the software or install it on your own computer. Examples are QuickBooks, MYOB, Xero, Reckon, FreshBooks, Wave, NetSuite, and Sage. Online accounting services offer some advantages over conventional in-house accounting installations:

- Lower initial cost because you do not buy the software.
- Rapid installation because the service provider already has the system in place.
- Scalability because you can increase your usage as business growth dictates.
- Technical support that you may not have in-house.
- Greater accessibility, portability, and ease of use.
- Integration with online banking services, payment systems, and payroll reporting with the tax office.
- Automatic software upgrades.
- Automatic daily backups.

BALANCE SHEET

The balance sheet is a report that contains the assets your business owns, the liabilities that your business owes, and what the business is worth to you as the owner. Here is an example of a balance sheet for My Small Business (MSB) at the end of the first year of operation.

MY SMALL BUSINESS
Balance Sheet
End of Year 1

	$	$
Current assets		
Cash	79,800	
Accounts receivable	45,000	
Inventory	95,200	220,000
Non-current assets		
Plant and equipment	100,000	
Accumulated depreciation	(20,000)	80,000
TOTAL ASSETS		300,000
Current liabilities		
Accounts payable	40,200	
Taxes payable	22,000	62,200
Non-current liabilities		
Bank loan	80,000	80,000
TOTAL LIABILITIES		142,200
Owner's equity		
Contributed capital	120,000	
Retained earnings	37,800	157,800
TOTAL LIABILITIES AND OWNER'S EQUITY		300,000

Assets

Assets are what your business owns. They are recorded in descending order of their convertibility into cash. Those that can be converted into cash within a year are called *current assets*. Those that stay in the business over a longer period of time are called *non-current assets*.

In this example, current assets consist of cash, accounts receivable, and inventory.

- *Cash* is money that is immediately available to use without restrictions. It usually consists of your account balance at the bank, cash register money, and petty cash. If you are in overdraft, the cash account will be a negative number.
- *Accounts receivable* are amounts owed to the business by its customers as a result of credit sales.
- *Inventory* may consist of raw materials, goods in the process of manufacture, and finished goods held for sale.

Non-current assets are items owned by a business that have a relatively long life. In our example, they consist of plant and equipment. Most non-current assets are subject to depreciation whereby the cost is apportioned over its useful life. For example, in MSB's balance sheet, plant and equipment was acquired one year ago for $100,000. It has a useful life of five years, so each year 20 percent of its original cost goes into another account called *accumulated depreciation*. After the first year, there is $20,000 in accumulated depreciation. The difference between the original cost and the accumulated depreciation is the remaining *book value* for plant and equipment amounting to $80,000. There are a number of accepted ways in which to calculate how much of an asset's cost can be deducted for depreciation in a given year. Ask your accountant.

Liabilities

Liabilities are debts owed by a business. They are recorded in order of maturity. They are claims against the total assets although they are not usually claims against any specific assets except for mortgages. Liabilities are divided into *current liabilities* and *non-current liabilities*.

Current liabilities consist of those debts that fall due within a year. MSB's balance sheet contains two current liability accounts. *Accounts payable* are amounts owed to vendors and suppliers from whom MSB has bought items on account and for which payment is expected in less than one year. *Taxes payable* is the amount of tax that MSB has yet to pay.

Claims of outsiders that come due in more than a year are called non-current liabilities. In MSB's balance sheet, non-current liabilities consist of a bank loan.

Owner's Equity

Owner's equity consists of the capital contributed by the owner plus any earnings that have been retained in the business. Together, they represent the sum due to the owner if the assets were sold for the amounts appearing on the balance sheet and the liabilities were paid off. Owner's equity is essentially a balancing figure in the sense that the owner gets whatever is left over after the liability claims have been satisfied.

INCOME STATEMENT

The income statement, sometimes called the profit and loss account, is a report that summarises the activities of a business over a period of time. It reports sales revenue together with the expenses incurred in obtaining the revenue, and it shows the profit or loss resulting from these activities.

MY SMALL BUSINESS
Income Statement
for Year 1

	$	$
Sales revenue		1,200,000
Cost of sales		(720,000)
Gross profit		480,000
Operating expenses		
Salaries	84,000	
Casual wages	90,000	
Marketing	150,000	
Occupancy	42,000	
Administration	30,000	
Depreciation	20,000	
Interest	10,000	(426,000)
Net profit before tax		54,000
Provision for income tax		(16,200)
Net profit after tax		37,800

Sales Revenue

The major activity of most businesses is the sale of products and/or services. The figure used is net sales after discounts, allowances, and returned goods have been deducted.

Cost of Sales

An important item in calculating profit or loss is the cost of the goods or services that have been sold. There are several generally accepted ways of calculating the cost of sales. Ask your accountant which one applies in your business.

Gross Profit

The difference between sales and the cost of sales is gross profit. Gross profit as a percentage of sales is significant because it represents the average profit margin on each dollar of sales before operating expenses.

Operating Expenses

The other costs of running your business are operating expenses. The amount of detail that you include in the operating expenses section of your income statement is dictated by the requirements of your business. MSB's income statement contains the following operating expense accounts:

- *Salaries* not only include compensation for permanent staff but also the on-costs such as superannuation contributions, workers compensation insurance, and payroll tax. Do not forget to include your own salary. To exclude your compensation from the operating expenses distorts the profitability of the business.
- *Casual wages* represent compensation for casual and hourly staff including the associated on-costs.
- *Marketing* includes advertising, promotion, commissions, travel, and samples.
- *Occupancy* includes rent, insurance, electricity, repairs, and maintenance.

- *Administration* includes phone, stationery, postage, accounting fees, and legal fees.
- *Depreciation* was first discussed when we described the balance sheet. Although no money changes hands, depreciation is a real expense because it represents an apportionment of the cost of non-current assets.
- *Interest* represents interest payments to lenders but not principal repayments.

Net Profit before Tax

When operating expenses have been subtracted from gross profit, the difference is net profit before tax. If the business receives revenue from non-operating sources such as rents, dividends on shares, or interest on money loaned, it is added to net profit before tax at this point. This is the figure on which income tax is calculated.

Provision for Income Tax

This is the amount of income tax payable on net profit before tax. The amount of taxation, and how it is paid, is affected by whether the business is organised as a proprietorship, a partnership, a trust, or a company. The provision for income tax is also shown as a liability on the balance sheet until it is actually paid.

Net Profit after Tax

After the provision for income tax has been deducted from net profit before tax, the last entry is net profit after tax. It is from this amount that dividends or distributions of profits may be made to the owner(s). Any profits that are not paid out to the owner(s) will be added to retained earnings in the balance sheet.

FINANCIAL RATIOS

The most widely practised method of analysing and interpreting financial reports is to use ratios. Comparisons with past financial ratios tell you whether your results are getting better or worse.

Comparisons with the financial ratios of similar firms or industry averages reveal how well you stack up against the financial performance of others in the same line of business. Comparisons with 'rule of thumb' standards tell you how well you compare with commonly accepted norms. Here are seven financial ratios that are especially useful.

Liquidity

The current ratio reflects the ability of a business to meet its current financial commitments. Inability to satisfy the legitimate demands of creditors is sufficient reason for a business to be wound up irrespective of how profitable it may be. Although it helps to monitor the liquidity of a business, it is not a substitute for cash flow budgeting. The current ratio measures the current assets available to meet current liabilities.

$$\text{Current ratio} = \frac{\text{Current assets}}{\text{Current liabilities}} = \frac{\$220,000}{\$62,200} \approx 3.5$$

MSB has a current ratio of approximately 3.5. This means current assets are 3.5 times greater than current liabilities compared with the generally accepted rule of thumb of 2.0 or better.

Profitability

Profitability ratios consist of two types. First, there are profitability ratios that relate profit to sales. They are used to assess how well each dollar of sales is generating a profit. Second, there are profitability ratios that relate profit to assets. They are used to evaluate how well each dollar invested in assets is working to generate a profit.

Gross profit margin represents the average profit on each dollar of sales before operating expenses. MSB has a gross profit margin of 40 percent.

$$\text{Gross profit margin} = \frac{\text{Gross profit}}{\text{Sales}} = \frac{\$480,000}{\$1,200,000} = 40 \text{ percent}$$

The gross profit margin varies from one type of business to another, so there is no general rule of thumb that can be applied.

It is compared over time to detect trends, and it is compared to industry averages to assess performance relative to similar firms.

Net profit margin represents the profitability of sales after operating expenses have been subtracted from the gross profit. The net profit margin can also vary from one type of business to another. MSB's net profit margin is 4.5 percent.

$$\text{Net profit margin} = \frac{\text{Net profit before tax}}{\text{Sales}} = \frac{\$54,000}{\$1,200,000}$$

$$= 4.5 \text{ percent}$$

Return on assets is used to assess the profit-earning performance of the assets. It relates the net profit before tax in the income statement to total assets in the balance sheet. MSB's return on assets is 18 percent.

$$\text{Return on assets} = \frac{\text{Net profit before tax}}{\text{Total assets}} = \frac{\$54,000}{\$300,000} = 18 \text{ percent}$$

A decline in the return on assets will occur if expenses rise faster than sales. Therefore, this ratio should always be examined in conjunction with the gross and net profit margins. A decline may also occur if assets increase at a faster rate than net profit.

Return on owner's equity is considered one of the best indicators of overall profitability. It reflects the earning power of the owner's investment in the business. If there are no liabilities, the return on owner's equity will be the same as the return on assets. Return on owner's equity, however, is influenced by the extent to which borrowing leverages the owner's equity. Leveraged firms are more profitable when earnings are positive, but they are also exposed to greater losses if earnings become negative. MSB's return on owner's equity is approximately 34.2 percent.

$$\text{Return on owner's equity} = \frac{\text{Net profit before tax}}{\text{Owner's equity}}$$

$$\frac{\$54,000}{\$157,800} \approx 34.2 \text{ percent}$$

Efficiency

If the assets are being used efficiently, then you would expect the return on assets to be maximised. One way of assessing how efficiently assets are being used is to measure their frequency of turnover. This measure relates the investment in assets to the amount of sales they support, or how hard the firm's asset base is working to generate sales. At MSB, asset turnover is four times per year. For each dollar of assets, $4.00 of sales is generated annually.

$$\text{Asset turnover} = \frac{\text{Sales}}{\text{Total assets}} = \frac{\$1,200,000}{\$300,000} = 4 \text{ times}$$

Greater asset turnover indicates more efficient use of assets to generate sales. Lower asset turnover indicates less efficient use of assets to generate sales. Asset turnover varies from one type of business to another.

Financial Structure

Borrowing not only makes it possible to leverage the owner's equity, but it also enables a business to take advantage of opportunities that would otherwise have to be forgone. One way of looking at financial structure is to calculate the proportion of total assets funded by the owner's equity. This is called the *ownership ratio*. MSB's ownership ratio is 52.6 percent.

$$\text{Ownership ratio} = \frac{\text{Owner's equity}}{\text{Total assets}} = \frac{\$157,800}{\$300,000} = 52.6 \text{ percent}$$

The acceptable proportion of debt varies among different types of businesses. Debt finance enables a business to grow and to improve its profitability, but too much debt exposes it to the risk of financial loss and failure. When the ownership ratio is below 50 percent, the creditors actually have a greater financial stake in the business than the owner.

MONITORING PERFORMANCE

There are three ways in which financial information can be used to monitor performance. First, the financial ratios can be linked together to identify problems that need attention. Second, the analysis can be extended to pinpoint which changes will have the greatest impact on profitability. Third, benchmarking your performance against similar firms can provide you with comparative information about your strengths and weaknesses.

Financial Performance Model

The financial performance model is a powerful tool that combines your financial ratios to identify important variables in your business, determine the cause and effect between them, and direct your attention to areas that need improvement.

Return on owner's equity is driven by the return on assets and the ownership ratio. Return on assets is an overall measure of how well your asset base produces a profit. It reflects *operating decisions* over buying, selling, expense control, and asset management and how they have affected the income-producing capacity of the business. The ownership ratio is a measure of the owner's investment in the business. It reflects *financing decisions* over how much money is borrowed and how highly the business is leveraged.

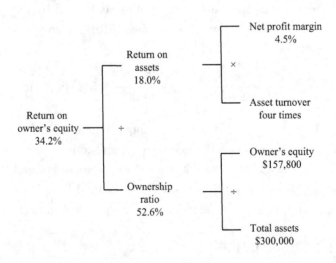

Figure 12.2 Financial Performance Model

The financial performance model is a systematic method for keeping all of the variables in focus to find the best way to maximise the return on your equity. To understand why MSB's return on owner's equity is 34.2 percent and how it might be improved, we can examine the return on assets and the ownership ratio for the factors that influence them.

You can see from the diagram that return on assets is driven by two interdependent factors – net profit margin and asset turnover. MSB's net profit margin, the proportion of net profit to sales, is 4.5 percent. It represents the combined effects of pricing, the effectiveness of the marketing mix in creating sales, and control of the costs incurred in the process of doing business. Since it is the percentage of each dollar of sales going to the owner, we would like to see it as high as possible. MSB's asset turnover is four times. It measures the efficiency of total assets in generating sales. If asset turnover was higher, then the same asset base would be generating greater sales. Therefore, we would also like to see asset turnover as high as possible.

The financial performance model provides a way to look at possible strategies for improving the return on assets. First, you can increase net profit margin in one or more of the following ways:

• Increase the selling price on the same unit sales volume
• Decrease cost of sales by more efficient purchasing
• Decrease operating expenses through leaner operations

Second, you can improve asset turnover in one or more of the following ways:

• Increase the selling price on the same unit sales volume
• Increase unit sales volume at the same selling price
• Reduce current assets
• Reduce fixed assets

Depending on the circumstances, some strategies will produce more effective results than others. For example, the first strategy in each category benefits both net profit margin and asset turnover, while the other strategies benefit only one.

MSB's ownership ratio is 52.6 percent. If MSB's owner had funded the entire asset base, then the ownership ratio would be 100 percent and the return on owner's equity would be the same as the return on assets: 18 percent. The fact that the owner has elected to finance part of the asset base with borrowed funds has increased the return on owner's equity to 34.2 percent.

The optimal ownership ratio is a compromise between the costs, benefits, and risks of borrowing. If the interest cost of borrowing is less than the return on assets, then borrowing is usually a good financing option. Too much debt, however, increases the risk of failure if sales fall unexpectedly.

Sensitivity Analysis

The financial performance model can be extended by comparing the sensitivity of the return on owner's equity to changes in pricing, cost of sales, marketing effort, operating costs, and the investment in assets. The example below illustrates the results from changing each of MSB's variables by 10 percent. Sensitivity analysis puts you in a position to rank each strategy from the most effective to the least effective in maximising your return on owner's equity.

A decrease in the cost of sales is clearly the most effective strategy for maximising return on owner's equity. If customers will pay higher prices, this will be the next best strategy for increasing the return on owner's equity. A reduction in operating costs is also a potent strategy. Marketing strategies designed to increase sales volume are less effective, and reducing total assets produces no change at all.

Benchmarking

Benchmarking is the process of comparing your financial results to an industry standard or best practice. It is another tool that can be used to evaluate your financial reports and improve your business. Ask your accountant if they have access to benchmarking information or inter-firm comparisons for your type of business. Ask your industry association if they survey their members and produce benchmarking

Variable	Change	Net profit before tax	Net profit margin	Asset turnover	ROA	ROE	Change in ROE
Sales price	+10%	$102,000	7.7%	3.1	23.6%	53.3%	+56%
Sales volume	+10%	78,000	5.9%	4.1	24.1%	44.7%	+31%
Cost of sales	−10%	126,000	10.5%	4.0	42.0%	60.5%	+77%
Operating costs	−10%	96,600	8.1%	4.0	32.2%	51.5%	+51%
Total assets	−10%	54,000	4.5%	4.4	20.0%	34.2%	0%

reports or inter-firm comparisons. Free benchmarking information for a variety of businesses is available on the Australian Tax Office website at *ato.gov.au/business/small-business-benchmarks*. A commercial benchmarking website can also be found at *benchmarking.com.au*.

SUMMARY

This chapter describes how to set up an accounting system and how to use the information it provides. Establishing an accounting system begins by creating a paper trail that supports the entries that go into it. There are many small business accounting systems that are designed to simplify and automate the bookkeeping and reporting processes. The one you choose should be tailored to the way you run your business. The main reports produced by an accounting system are the balance sheet and the income statement. The balance sheet tells you about the financial condition of the business and the income statement tells you about its profitability. This information is used to gain insights into the strengths and weaknesses of a business using ratio analysis, the business performance model, sensitivity analysis, and benchmarking.

Thirteen
Managing Liquidity

Liquidity means having enough cash to pay your bills. Managing liquidity consists of controlling the current assets that are used in the day-to-day operation of a business. Small businesses are especially vulnerable to liquidity problems because they often operate with too little working capital and they miss the implications of a cash flow crisis until it is too late. The purpose of this chapter is to explain how to manage liquidity. It describes the nature of the operating cycle, how to control the components of working capital, and how to do a cash flow budget. The chapter concludes with a discussion about how to overcome liquidity problems.

OPERATING CYCLE
The first step in managing liquidity is to become familiar with your operating cycle. It consists of a series of activities that continuously convert the components of working capital from one form to another. It varies from one type of business to another and you need to understand how it works in your business.

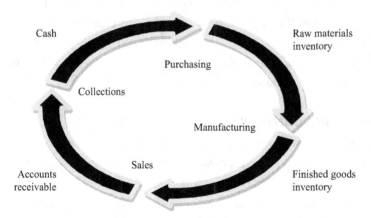

Figure 13.1 Operating Cycle

DOI: 10.4324/9781032676616-23

The diagram illustrates the operating cycle in a manufacturing business. It consists of cash, raw materials inventory, finished goods inventory, and accounts receivable.

- Cash is transformed into raw materials by purchasing.
- Raw materials are transformed into finished goods by manufacturing.
- Finished goods are transformed into accounts receivable by selling on credit.
- Accounts receivable are transformed back into cash when they are collected.

The cycle repeats itself continuously so long as there are no bottlenecks to restrict its flow. When bottlenecks do occur, they cause a stop-start reaction that disrupts the smooth flow of the operating cycle. For example, if collections slow down, accounts receivable will increase and cash will dry up. Without cash, purchases will have to be curtailed. When purchases have been curtailed, finished goods will eventually run out and sales will fall off. The important objective in managing working capital is to keep the operating cycle running smoothly.

A key measure is the average number of days for one revolution of the operating cycle. The shorter this period, the less cash is required to invest in inventory and accounts receivable and the easier it is to maintain cash flow. The longer the period, the more cash is needed to invest in inventory and accounts receivable and the more difficult it is to maintain cash flow. Controlling the length of the operating cycle is an important tool in managing liquidity.

MANAGING ACCOUNTS RECEIVABLE

If you only sell for cash, then you will not have any accounts receivable. If you sell on credit, however, your selling terms define the period of time you agree to defer payment for a customer's purchases. If some customers take longer to pay, then the actual collection period may be longer than your selling terms. Your selling terms and your collection policy are key components in your operating cycle and directly affect your cash flow.

Average Collection Period

The average collection period is the average length of time that sales dollars remain in the form of accounts receivable. The longer it is, the longer the operating cycle becomes. The average collection period is calculated by dividing the accounts receivable balance by average daily credit sales. Credit sales for My Small Business (MSB) are 75 percent of $1,200,000, or $900,000, and the balance sheet shows $45,000 in accounts receivable. Therefore, the average collection period is about 18 days.

$$\text{Average collection period} = \frac{\text{Accounts receivable balance}}{\text{Average daily credit sales}}$$

$$\frac{\$45,000}{\$900,000/365 \text{ days}} \approx 18 \text{ days}$$

Offering customers extended credit terms usually leads to more sales, but longer credit terms also makes the average collection period longer. Similarly, greater credit sales also means more dollars are tied up in accounts receivable. A longer collection period combined with greater credit sales will result in a big increase in accounts receivable.

If MSB's average collection period doubles from 18 days to 36 days, then the investment in accounts receivable will double from $45,000 to $90,000. Similarly, if MSB's credit sales double, then the investment in accounts receivable will double from $45,000 to $90,000. However, if the average collection period doubles *and* the amount of credit sales also doubles, then the cash invested in accounts receivable will need to increase fourfold from $45,000 to $180,000.

Comparing your average collection period with three benchmarks will help to determine if you are over-invested or under-invested in accounts receivable. First, if your average collection period is greater than your selling terms, then it indicates some customers are not complying with your selling terms. Second, comparing your average collection period with previous periods will tell you if it is getting longer or shorter. Third, comparing your average collection period with industry benchmarks will reveal how you measure up compared with other businesses like yours.

Controlling Accounts Receivable

An analysis of the average collection period will identify overall accounts receivable problems. To control accounts receivable, you need to be able to identify individual customers through *ageing analysis*. Ageing analysis divides each customer's account into the amounts that fall into ageing categories such as 0–30 days, 31–60 days, 61–90 days, and over 90 days. Most accounting systems have a module that produces an ageing report for your accounts receivable.

Table 13.1 demonstrates how ageing analysis pinpoints the accounts that are tying up cash flow so that corrective action can be taken. It is clear that Customer F and Customer I are collection problems and action is required to prevent Customer B from becoming one as well. Customer J is no longer an active account and the over-90-days balance could be an unresolved dispute or a bad debt.

The longer an account is past due, the more serious the problem is likely to be. The best time to pursue an overdue account is as soon as the customer exceeds your selling terms. As an account gets further

Table 13.1 Aged Analysis of Accounts Receivable

Customer	Balance	0–30 days	31–60 days	61–90 days	Over 90 days
A	2,500	2,500			
B	5,500	3,000	2,500		
C	2,000	2,000			
D	3,500	3,500			
E	2,250	2,250			
F	10,000	3,000	2,500	2,500	2,000
G	5,000	5,000			
H	4,500	4,500			
I	7,500	2,500	2,500	2,500	
J	2,250				2,250
Total	45,000	28,250	7,500	5,000	4,250
Percent	100	63	17	11	9

behind, the balance may continue to increase while the chances of collection decrease.

Many small business operators are reluctant to enforce strict collections procedures. Some are simply embarrassed to ask for money even though it is a legitimate debt. Others are afraid they will alienate a 'good' customer and lose the account. Still others feel that a rigid collections policy will damage their reputation. These reasons are nonsense. What good is a customer if you are not paid? Wouldn't you be reluctant to accept further orders from a customer with an overdue account anyway? And would you really expect a customer who owes you money to spread this news around? It is your cash flow that is at stake, and you need to protect it.

If you sell relatively expensive goods on credit, you may want to consider putting a condition of sale on the invoice stating that the goods remain your property until the invoice is paid in full. This may enable you to claim ownership and reclaim the goods if your customer becomes insolvent or bankrupt without paying your invoice.

Credit and Debit Cards

Credit and debit cards are an established way of transacting business. When you accept card purchases, you do not need to invest cash in accounts receivable, and the costs and risks of credit and collection are virtually eliminated. Credit and debit card services are available from trading banks and specialist card companies including Mastercard, VISA, and American Express.

Receipts from bank credit and debit card sales are immediately credited to your bank account. The bank assumes all of the credit risks provided you follow their instructions. In return for this service, the bank charges a merchant fee. The amount of the fee is negotiable and you should shop around for the best deal.

Credit and debit card services are particularly important for businesses with a large number of relatively small accounts. They eliminate the paperwork involved in credit approval, invoice preparation, accounts receivable records, and collections. They avoid the need to commit cash to accounts receivable and the risk of uncollectable accounts. And don't forget that the availability of instant credit is an indispensable marketing tool. Although credit and debit cards are most often used for retail customer accounts, they can be used for business accounts as well.

MANAGING INVENTORY

Like accounts receivable, inventory is a key element in the operating cycle and a major influence on your cash flow. How you manage inventory has a tremendous impact on sales. Having the right products in the right quantities is one of the keys to maximising sales. The tradeoff is that the more inventory you carry, the longer the operating cycle will become and the more cash you will tie up in working capital.

One way to evaluate your inventory position is to calculate the number of days' sales that are held in inventory. At MSB, the annual cost of sales is $720,000 and the year-end inventory is $95,200. Therefore, they are holding inventory equal to about 48 days of sales.

$$\text{Days' inventory} = \frac{365 \text{ days}}{\text{Cost of sales} / \text{Inventory balance}}$$

$$\frac{365 \text{ days}}{\$720,000 / \$95,200} \approx 48 \text{ days}$$

When you increase inventory, you lengthen the operating cycle and decrease your cash flow. Investment in inventory is not only dependent on how much inventory you want to carry but also on the level of sales. For example, if MSB wants to double its inventory to have a complete selection of all product lines, *and* at the same time sales volume doubles, then the cash investment in inventory would be likely to blow out from $95,200 to $380,800.

There are a couple of ways to determine if you are over-invested or under-invested in inventory. First, you can compare your days' inventory with similar firms and industry averages. Second, you can track your days' inventory over time to determine if your investment in inventory is increasing or decreasing relative to your sales volume. Both of these comparisons will enable you to monitor your overall investment in inventory.

Knowing your days' inventory helps to evaluate your overall inventory position. Most businesses, however, carry a variety of

Table 13.2 Item Analysis of Inventory

Product	Quantity on hand	Average 60 days' sales	Days' supply on hand	Required action
A	500	150	200	Reduce by 350
B	200	300	40	Increase by 100
C	50	100	30	Increase by 50
D	165	165	60	None
E	600	150	240	Reduce by 450
F	125	100	75	Reduce by 25

products, each of which turns over at a different rate. To control your inventory, you need to analyse each product individually. Most accounting packages have a module that does it for you. Item analysis compares the number of units of each item held in inventory against the amount actually required based on your sales experience. The example in Table 13.2 is an item analysis based on a target of 60 days' supply for all products.

MANAGING ACCOUNTS PAYABLE

An account payable occurs when your supplier gives you time to pay for goods or services after they have been delivered. Essentially, this is an interest-free, short-term loan. Making good use of accounts payable enables you to reduce your net investment in working capital. Take full advantage of your supplier's payment terms. If no discount is offered for early payment and the agreed payment is due 30 days after delivery, then make your payment on the last day. Whenever possible, negotiate extended payment terms with your suppliers. For example, if their regular payment terms are 30 days from the receipt of goods, ask them if they will extend it to 30 days from the end of the month. That amounts to an extra 15 days' credit on average. If you are looking for a significant increase in credit terms, then you need to negotiate with your suppliers.

It is important to monitor your accounts payable to make sure you are keeping your suppliers happy by paying them according to the agreed terms. Most accounting systems have a module that produces

Table 13.3 Aged Analysis of Accounts Payable

Supplier	Balance	0–30 days	31–60 days	61–90 days	Over 90 days
A	5,000	5,000			
B	13,000	7,000	6,000		
C	4,000	4,000			
D	7,000	7,000			
E	3,000		3,000		
F	8,200			3,000	5,200
Total	40,200	23,000	9,000	3,000	5,200

an accounts payable ageing report. It enables you to easily identify the suppliers to whom you owe money and how long their invoices have been outstanding. An example is shown in Table 13.3.

MANAGING CASH FLOW

Maintaining a healthy cash flow is the single most important financial goal in managing working capital. When the cash flowing in exceeds the cash flowing out, you can continue to operate. But if the cash flowing out exceeds the cash flowing in, then your business will eventually run out of money and grind to a halt. Even if you only run out of cash for a short time, it can put you out of business. The purpose of this section is to demonstrate why profits are not cash, describe how to do a cash flow budget, and explain how to use it.

Profits Are Not Cash

First we need to dispel a common myth that if you are making a profit, then the cash flow will take care of itself. Financial accounting systems measure profit by matching *revenues* and *expenses*. Unfortunately, the financial accounting process does not distinguish between financial transactions and cash transactions. To understand how cash flows into and out of your business, you need to be able to match the *receipts* and *disbursements* (sometimes called *payments*). The following example illustrates why profits are not cash.

You have been offered a fantastic new business opportunity. If you give your customers 30 days' credit, sales will be $10,000 in the first month of trading and they will double every month thereafter! Your stock is to be paid for in cash each month and it will cost you 50 percent of the retail price. Your operating expenses will be 10 percent of sales revenue and must also be paid in cash each month. The result is a guaranteed net profit margin of 40 percent, and after four months of trading, your profit will be $60,000.

	Month 1	Month 2	Month 3	Month 4	Total
Revenues	10,000	20,000	40,000	80,000	150,000
Expenses					
Stock	5,000	10,000	20,000	40,000	75,000
Operating	1,000	2,000	4,000	8,000	15,000
Profit	4,000	8,000	16,000	32,000	60,000

Your accountant will be so impressed by your trading results that she will probably double her fees. Your bank manager, however, will not be so impressed. In fact, he will be downright disturbed by what has happened to the balance in your bank account.

Remember, your customers do not have to pay for their purchases for 30 days, but you have to pay your expenses immediately. After the same four months of trading, despite profits of $60,000, you have a $20,000 overdraft!

	Month 1	Month 2	Month 3	Month 4	Total
Receipts	0	10,000	20,000	40,000	70,000
Payments	6,000	12,000	24,000	48,000	90,000
Cash flow	(6,000)	(2,000)	(4,000)	(8,000)	(20,000)

How can a business with $60,000 in profit end up with a $20,000 overdraft? The answer is because $80,000 from Month 4 sales revenue is tied up in accounts receivable. Profits are not cash. Without cash flow planning, this profitable operation could run out of money and go out of business.

Cash Flow Budget

Cash flow budgeting is simple in theory, but it takes a little time and effort. Knowing your way around a computer spreadsheet, such as Excel, will make the job much easier. What follows is a monthly cash flow budget for MSB.

My Small Business
Projected Cash Flow
July–December

	Month before Start-up	July	Aug	Sept	Oct	Nov	Dec
Sales forecast							
Units		2,000	3,000	4,000	5,000	9,000	10,000
Dollars		**40,000**	**60,000**	**80,000**	**100,000**	**180,000**	**200,000**
Receipts from							
Cash sales		10,000	15,000	20,000	25,000	45,000	50,000
Credit sales			30,000	45,000	60,000	75,000	135,000
GST received		1,000	4,500	6,500	8,500	12,000	18,500
Contributed capital	120,000						
Bank loan	100,000						
Total receipts	**220,000**	**11,000**	**49,500**	**71,500**	**93,500**	**132,000**	**203,500**
Disbursements for							
Inventory	25,000	25,000	37,500	50,000	62,500	112,500	125,000
Salary		7,000	7,000	7,000	7,000	7,000	7,000
Casual wages		3,000	4.500	6,000	7,500	13,500	15,000
Marketing		5,000	7,500	10,000	12,500	22,500	25,000
Occupancy		3,500	3,500	3,500	3,500	3,500	3,500
Administration		2,500	2,500	2,500	2,500	2,500	2,500
Equipment	100,000						
GST paid	12,500	3,600	5,100	6,600	8,100	14,100	15,600
Loan payments		2,500	2,500	2,500	2,500	2,500	2,500
Total disbursements	**137,500**	**52,100**	**70,100**	**88,100**	**106,100**	**178,100**	**196,100**
Net cash flow	**82,500**	**–41,100**	**–20,600**	**–16,600**	**–12,600**	**–46,100**	**7,400**
Projected bank balance	**82,500**	**41,400**	**20,800**	**4,200**	**–8,400**	**–54,500**	**–47,100**

My Small Business
Projected Cash Flow
January–June

	Jan	Feb	March	April	May	June	Year Total
Sales forecast							
Units	7,000	5,000	4,000	4,000	4,000	3,000	60,000
Dollars	**140,000**	**100,000**	**80,000**	**80,000**	**80,000**	**60,000**	**1,200,000**
Receipts from							
Cash sales	35,000	25,000	20,000	20,000	20,000	15,000	300,000
Credit sales	150,000	105,000	75,000	60,000	60,000	60,000	855,000
GST received	18,500	13,000	9,500	8,000	8,000	7,500	115,500
Contributed capital							120,000
Bank Loan							100,000
Total receipts	**203,500**	**143,000**	**104,500**	**88,000**	**88,000**	**82,500**	**1,490,500**
Disbursements for							
Inventory	87,500	62,500	50,000	50,000	50,000	37,500	775,000
Salary	7,000	7,000	7,000	7,000	7,000	7,000	84,000
Casual wages	10,500	7,500	6,000	6,000	6,000	4,500	90,000
Marketing	17,500	12,500	10,000	10,000	10,000	7,500	150,000
Occupancy	3,500	3,500	3,500	3,500	3,500	3,500	42,000
Administration	2,500	2,500	2,500	2,500	2,500	2,500	30,000
Equipment							100,000
GST paid	11,100	8,100	6,600	6,600	6,600	5,100	109,700
Loan payments	2,500	2,500	2,500	2,500	2,500	2,500	30,000
Total disburse-ments	**142,100**	**106,100**	**88,100**	**88,100**	**88,100**	**70,100**	**1,410,700**
Net cash flow	**61,400**	**36,900**	**16,400**	**–100**	**–100**	**12,400**	
Projected bank balance	**14,300**	**51,200**	**67,600**	**67,500**	**67,400**	**79,800**	

Establishment Transactions

MSB is a new business. In the month before MSB opens its doors, there will be contributions of capital and the initial setup costs. The funds that are planned to finance the business consist of $120,000 contributed by the owner together with a bank loan of $100,000. These funds will be used to buy equipment costing $100,000 and the initial inventory costing $25,000. The first column in MSB's projected cash flow records these receipts and disbursements during the month before start up leaving $82,500 available to begin operations in July.

Forecasting Sales

Forecasting sales is the first and most important step in cash flow budgeting. Begin by making a physical forecast of sales in terms of the number of units sold, the number of transactions completed, or the number of customers served. Then translate the physical figures into dollar figures according to your pricing schedule.

Actual sales will inevitably differ from the forecast. Nevertheless, an imprecise sales forecast does not make the cash flow budget useless. What you are looking for is a forecast that is within the range of possible outcomes. The more accurately you forecast sales, however, the more accurate will be your cash flow budget.

MSB's sales forecast is based on monthly estimates of unit sales. These are translated into a dollar forecast based on an average price of $20 each. The sales forecast is based on a seasonal pattern that peaks during the Christmas period.

Forecasting Cash Receipts

Cash receipts are divided into two categories: operating and non-operating. Non-operating cash receipts are usually associated with one-off transactions such as new capital contributed by the owner, proceeds of a new loan or selling an asset. In MSB's cash flow budget, the only non-operating cash receipts take place in the month before start up. The remainder of MSB's cash receipts come from operations.

If you only sell for cash, then your forecast for operating cash receipts will be the same as your forecast for sales. If you sell on credit, however, your cash receipts will not only depend on the proportion of your sales that you make on credit but also how long it takes to collect this money from your customers.

MSB's cash flow budget shows forecasted cash receipts based on the sales forecast. Cash sales are estimated to be 25 percent of sales. Credit sales are estimated to be 75 percent of sales and they are expected to be collected in the next month. The GST received is shown separately from the cash receipts from sales. The cash receipts are added together to arrive at a total for each month.

Forecasting Cash Disbursements

Cash disbursements can also be categorised as operating and non-operating. Operating cash disbursements can be further divided into disbursements that vary according to sales and disbursements that are fixed regardless of the level of sales. In MSB's cash flow budget, the main variable cash disbursements consist of inventory purchases, casual wages, and marketing expenses. Fixed operating disbursements consist of salaries, occupancy expenses, administration expenses, and loan payments. GST paid is shown separately from the other cash disbursements. Depreciation is not included in a cash flow budget because it is not a cash disbursement. The cash disbursements are added together to arrive at a total for each month.

Net Cash Flow

Determining net cash flow consists of subtracting the cash disbursements from the cash receipts to reveal the net effect. At this point, MSB can identify the major consequences of its expected cash flow. The cash flow budget forecasts negative net cash flow for the first five months of operations. MSB will need to carefully monitor this cash drain, and they may need to arrange for some short-term financing to make sure they do not run out of cash.

Cash Position

Now MSB is in a position to project their future cash position by adjusting their bank balance up or down according to the net cash flow at the end of each month. The starting capital of $220,000 is not going to be enough to carry MSB through the first half of the year. In fact, their bank balance is projected to go into the red in October. The problem becomes worse in November and persists through December. Without a cash flow budget, MSB may not foresee the cash deficit until it is too late.

The cash drain is very heavy going into the Christmas period, so MSB might want to examine ways to defer some disbursements until February or March. The cash flow budget reveals a maximum cash deficit of $54,500 by November, but there will also be enough cash generated to repay an overdraft by January. This is exactly the information that MSB's bank would like to see when they get a request for an overdraft facility. It tells the bank how much money MSB requires, when it will be needed, and when it will be repaid.

Tracking Your Cash Flow

Doing a cash flow budget is not the end of the story. At the end of each month, you can compare the actual cash flow results with your budget forecasts. You can also revise your sales and disbursements forecasts for the next 11 months based on any new information that has emerged. One more month is added onto the end of the cash flow budget so that you will always have a 12-month rolling forecast of how your cash flow is tracking and what your projected bank balance is likely to be.

OVERCOMING PROBLEMS

One way to monitor your working capital is knowing the number of days that it takes a dollar of working capital to make one revolution of the operating cycle. MSB currently has 18 days of credit sales outstanding in accounts receivable and 48 days of sales in inventory. The result is an average of 66 days for one revolution of the operating cycle. If it increases, then MSB needs to examine the individual components of its working capital to determine why. If it deceases, then they will have less cash tied up in working capital.

If cash flow remains positive, there is usually no need for concern. However, nearly all businesses experience working capital problems at one time or another. If your accounts receivable blows out, your inventory piles up, or your bank balance goes into the red, here are some options you can consider to correct the problem.

Shorten the operating cycle. Essentially, this means increasing the efficiency of the components in the operating cycle and reducing the cash committed to them. This requires more aggressive collection of accounts receivable and tighter control of inventory.

Increase net profit margin. Increasing net profit margin provides a greater number of surplus dollars for the same level of sales. This can be done by increasing price, reducing cost of sales, or reducing operating expenses. Increasing sales volume at the same net profit margin, however, will only make a cash flow problem worse.

Reduce sales volume. Reducing sales volume decreases the investment required in the components that make up the operating cycle. Reducing sales is difficult for most small business operators to contemplate, but holding growth in check is a rational alternative to a cash crisis. One way to slow down sales while increasing both net profit margin and cash flow is to selectively increase prices.

Stretch accounts payable. To slow down your cash disbursements, you may be able to rely more heavily on credit from your suppliers. Ask them to consider extending their credit terms. Look into acquiring inventory on consignment, which means you do not need to pay for it until it is sold. Stretching payments to your suppliers beyond their selling terms may temporarily solve today's cash flow problem, but it may also risk your credit reputation in the future.

Borrow money. Borrowing can be used to solve short-term and long-term cash flow problems. Short-term borrowing is used to finance temporary increases in working capital such as a seasonal buildup of inventory financed by an overdraft. Long-term borrowing can be used for permanent increases in working capital that result from a permanent increase in sales volume.

Look for equity capital. Equity capital consists of putting more of your own money into the business or taking in new owners in the form of partners or shareholders. Equity capital is long-term capital and should only be used for long-term purposes.

Maintain a cash reserve. Cash is an idle asset. It makes no direct contribution to profits. The best cash position is a zero cash balance. However, to ensure that enough cash is on hand to pay the bills as they come due, you should consider some minimum cash reserve. The size of your cash reserve is influenced by the extent to which you can count on collections from your customers, the flexibility of your disbursements, and the availability of outside finance. The more certain your cash flow, the less cash reserves you need.

SUMMARY

This chapter explains how to manage cash flow in the day-to-day operation of a business. It describes the nature of the operating cycle in which cash is used to acquire inventory, inventory is transformed into accounts receivable by selling on credit, and accounts receivable is transformed back into cash when it is collected. A longer (shorter) operating cycle requires more (less) investment in working capital. Accounts receivable is managed by monitoring the average collection period and controlling accounts receivable through ageing analysis and collections. Inventory is managed by monitoring average days' stock and controlling inventory through item analysis and stock adjustments. Cash flow is managed by having a rolling cash flow budget that forecasts receipts, disbursements, and net cash flow. The chapter concludes with a discussion about ways to overcome liquidity problems.

Fourteen
Managing Profitability

A profitable business is the consequence of identifying the key variables that drive profits and how to manage them. It consists of understanding your cost structure, identifying and evaluating your options, and arriving at decisions that you can put into action. The initial purpose of this chapter is to demonstrate how to identify the key variables that drive profits. When this information is applied to your products and services, customers, and market channels, it reveals the options available for managing profitability. The chapter concludes by describing a convenient way to monitor your costs.

COST STRUCTURE

Identifying the dynamics of your cost structure is a powerful tool for managing your profits. The costs listed in your income statement consist of two types. The first is *fixed costs* that remain about the same regardless of the amount of sales. The second is *variable costs* that change in direct proportion to changes in the amount of sales. In practice, some costs are neither totally fixed nor totally variable, but the closer you can identify the fixed and variable cost components, the better you will understand your cost structure. In the example Table 14.1, the fixed and variable costs are applied to My Small Business's (MSB's) income statement from Chapter 12.

Cost of sales represents the cost of the goods and services that have been sold. It has been entered into the variable cost column because it varies in direct proportion to sales activity. Salaries are paid to the permanent staff regardless of the level of sales, so they are a fixed cost. Wages, on the other hand, are paid to the casual and hourly staff, so they are a variable cost. Marketing includes some fixed costs, but since it is predominantly tied to the level of sales activity, it has been entered into

DOI: 10.4324/9781032676616-24

Table 14.1 Analysis of Fixed and Variable Costs

	VARIABLE COSTS $	FIXED COSTS $	$
SALES			12,000,000
COST OF SALES	720,000		
OPERATING EXPENSES			
Salaries		84,000	
Casual wages	90,000		
Marketing	150,000		
Occupancy		42,000	
Administration		30,000	
Depreciation		20,000	
Interest		10,000	
TOTAL COSTS	960,000	186,000	1,146,000
NET PROFIT BEFORE TAX			54,000

the variable cost column. Occupancy, administration, depreciation, and interest expenses will be the same irrespective of sales activity, so they have each been entered into the fixed cost column. Total fixed costs are $186,000. When sales are $1,200,000, the variable costs are $960,000.

CONTRIBUTION MARGIN

The separation of fixed and variable costs enables you to isolate the relationship of costs to sales. MSB has $960,000 in variable costs when sales are $1,200,000. That means the rate of variable cost is 80 percent of sales. The difference between a dollar of sales and the rate of variable cost per dollar of sales is called the *contribution margin*. MSB's contribution margin is 20 percent. It can also be calculated directly.

$$\text{Contribution margin} = \frac{\text{Sales} - \text{Variable cost}}{\text{Sales}}$$

$$\frac{\$1,200,000 - \$960,000}{\$1,200,000} = 20 \text{ percent}$$

The contribution margin is an important piece of information that can be used in a variety of decision-making and planning situations. Here are three examples.

New Investment

MSB wants to invest in new equipment that will add $40,000 in fixed costs per year. MSB's contribution margin is 20 percent. What increase in sales is necessary to cover the extra fixed costs?

$$\text{Sales increase} = \frac{\text{Increase in fixed costs}}{\text{Contribution margin}} = \frac{\$40,000}{20 \text{ percent}} = \$200,000$$

Increasing fixed costs by $40,000 will require extra sales of $200,000. MSB will need to make a judgement about whether the new equipment will generate enough additional sales to cover the higher fixed costs.

Cost Justification

MSB wants to buy magazine advertisements that cost $500 per month. MSB's contribution margin is 20 percent. What increase in sales must the advertisements generate each month to pay for themselves?

$$\text{Sales increase} = \frac{\text{Cost of advertisement}}{\text{Contribution margin}} = \frac{\$500}{20 \text{ percent}} = \$2,500$$

MSB needs to generate additional sales of $2,500 per month to pay for each advertisement. They will need to make a judgement about whether the advertisements will stimulate enough sales to cover the extra cost and generate a profit.

Sales Objectives

MSB wants to increase its net profit before tax from $54,000 to $100,000. The contribution margin is 20 percent and fixed costs are $186,000. What level of sales is necessary to achieve this much profit?

$$\text{Sales objective} = \frac{\text{Fixed costs} + \text{Profit}}{\text{Contribution margin}}$$

$$\frac{\$186,000 + \$100,000}{20 \text{ percent}} = \$1,430,000$$

MSB needs to make a judgement about their ability to increase sales from $1,200,000 to $1,430,000. They should also consider the possibility that such a big increase in sales may force up some of the fixed costs as well.

BREAK-EVEN POINT

Knowing the amount of fixed cost and the rate of variable cost enables you to determine the profit or loss for any level of sales. If there are no sales, then there will be a loss equal to the fixed costs because fixed costs must be met regardless of the level of sales activity. As sales increase, the loss decreases, and at some point MSB will have neither a profit nor a loss because sales revenue will exactly equal total cost. This is called the *break-even point*. The level of sales at which MSB will break even can be calculated by dividing the fixed costs by the contribution margin. MSB will break even when sales are $930,000.

$$\text{Break-even point} = \frac{\text{Fixed costs}}{\text{Contribution margin}} = \frac{\$186{,}000}{20 \text{ percent}} = \$930{,}000$$

A *profit-volume chart* is a picture of the short-run relationship between sales volume and the break-even point. Not only does it provide you with a visual presentation of the break-even point, but it also enables you to anticipate the effect of changes in pricing, sales volume, variable costs, and fixed costs.

MSB's Profit-Volume Chart

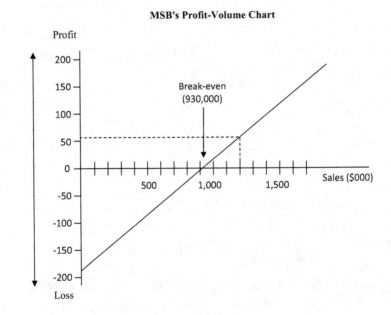

Figure 14.1 MSB's Profit-Volume Chart

The horizontal axis represents sales volume and the vertical axis represents profit or loss. The fixed costs ($186,000) are plotted on the vertical axis as a loss when there are no sales. Net profit before tax ($54,000) and sales ($1,200,000) are the coordinates for a second point. The *profit line* can be drawn between these two points. The break-even point ($930,000) occurs where the profit line crosses the horizontal axis for sales.

Now you can read changes in profit or loss on either side of the break-even point directly from the chart. You are also in a position to anticipate how changes in fixed costs will shift the profit line up or down and how changes in the contribution margin will rotate the profit line to make it steeper or flatter.

Cost Structure and Profitability

We have already demonstrated how the relationship between fixed and variable costs represents your cost structure. It is a key element in decisions that affect profitability. Imagine two firms, A and B, that each have exactly the same break-even point but entirely different cost structures.

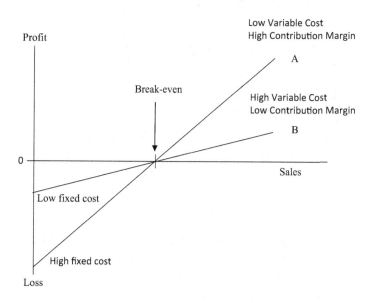

Figure 14.2 Cost Structure

Firm A has high fixed costs and low variable costs. It might be a business that mass produces a manufactured product using expensive equipment. Firm B has low fixed costs and high variable costs. It might be a labour-intensive service business such as a gardening service. Firm A has greater profit potential than Firm B when sales are above break-even. However, with higher fixed costs, it also stands to lose more if sales are below break-even. These differences in cost structure mean that Firm A will have to be especially concerned with achieving its sales targets, whereas Firm B will be more concerned with controlling variable costs. The differences in cost structure not only represent different risk factors but also differences in profitability despite having the same break-even point.

Margin of Safety

The *margin of safety* is the difference between the break-even point and the current level of sales. It indicates the extent to which sales may decline before the firm begins to operate at a loss. It is usually expressed as a percentage of current sales. MSB has a margin of safety of 22.5 percent.

$$\text{Margin of safety} = \frac{\text{Current sales} - \text{Break-even point}}{\text{Current sales}}$$

$$\frac{\$1,200,000 - \$930,000}{\$1,200,000} = 22.5 \text{ percent}$$

A high margin of safety generally indicates a sound sales and cost position. MSB could absorb a 22.5 percent decline in sales before incurring a loss.

Pricing

Suppose MSB is thinking about cutting its average price by 7.5 percent in an effort to boost sales. What level of sales would MSB need to achieve break-even at the lower price? A 7.5 percent cut in the average price would reduce sales from $1,200,000 to

$1,110,000, and the contribution margin would fall from 20 percent to about 13.5 percent.

$$\text{New contribution margin} = \frac{\text{New sales} - \text{Variable costs}}{\text{New sales}}$$

$$\frac{\$1,110,000 - \$960,000}{\$1,110,000} = 13.5 \text{ percent}$$

With a contribution margin of only 13.5 percent, the break-even point blows out from $930,000 to approximately $1,378,000.

$$\text{New break-even point} = \frac{\text{Fixed costs}}{\text{New contribution margin}}$$

$$\frac{\$186,000}{13.5 \text{ percent}} \approx \$1,378,000$$

A price reduction of 7.5 percent raises the break-even point from $930,000 to $1,378,000. This is more than current sales of $1,200,000, and MSB needs to make a serious judgement about whether the price reduction would generate enough additional sales to maintain profitability.

PRODUCT AND SERVICE PROFITABILITY

You can learn a great deal about profitability by analysing the contribution margin and the dollar contribution for each of your products and services. This will tell you which is giving you the greatest *rate* of profit and which is providing the greatest *amount* of profit. It will also tell you which products and services are not paying their way and could be eliminated. As long as a product or service has a positive contribution margin, you can continue to offer it. Your profits will increase if you concentrate on those products and services with the highest contribution margins. See Table 14.2 for an example.

Product A has the greatest contribution margin. Product B has the greatest dollar contribution. Which product is more profitable? Don't be confused between contribution margin and dollar contribution. Product B may have a lower contribution margin, but it clearly has a much higher dollar contribution because of its greater sales volume. Profit is made of dollars, not percentages. Nevertheless, you would be

Table 14.2 Product and Service Analysis

Product/ service	Sales $	Variable cost $	Dollar contribution $	Contribution margin (%)
A	500	200	300	60.0
B	1,500	700	800	53.3
C	600	600	0	0.0
D	400	500	(100)	(25.0)
Overall	3,000	2,000	1,000	33.3

better off if you sold more of Product A than Product B because its greater contribution margin would generate a greater dollar contribution as well.

Product C makes no contribution. Total profit would not change whether you kept Product C or not. Profit would improve, however, if you replaced Product C with one that has a positive contribution margin. Product D is losing money. You would increase total profit if you simply dropped Product D altogether. If Product D is a loss leader, then it should be combined with the product or service it is designed to promote in order to assess their combined contribution.

CUSTOMER PROFITABILITY

Just as products and services are not equally profitable, neither are customers. Some customers are more important to your bottom line than others and knowing who they are helps to:

- Make sure you are looking after them properly.
- Understand what makes them profitable.
- Identify what you want in new customers.
- Increase the number of more profitable customers and reduce the number of less profitable customers.

You can use the same method to analyse which of your customers are responsible for the most sales and contribution to profits. If you only

Table 14.3 Customer Analysis

Customer group	Sales $	Variable cost $	Dollar contribution $	Contribution margin (%)
A	1,000	400	600	60.0
B	1,000	500	500	50.0
C	500	500	0	0.0
D	500	600	(100)	(20.0)
Overall	3,000	2,000	1,000	33.3

have a few customers, then you may want to analyse each one individually. If you have many customers, then you may find it easier to analyse them in groups such as by age, gender, marital status, home ownership, occupation, geographical location, brand loyalty, or some other basis that makes sense in your business. See Table 14.3 for an example.

You may discover that a small group of your customers (such as A and B) are responsible for all of your profits. You may also discover which customers (such as C) contribute little to your bottom line, and you may well find that some customers (such as D) are actually costing you money. This analysis will help you to recognise high contributors, direct your attention towards more profitable types of customers, and provide some clues about how to convert low contributors to become high contributors.

MARKET CHANNEL PROFITABILITY

If you sell products using different channels of distribution, then it may also be worthwhile to analyse your profitability by channels. There is another example in Table 14.4.

In this example, the business does most of its sales over the internet. This channel makes the greatest contribution to profits largely as a result of lower variable costs. Wholesale sales make no contribution to profits and may be worth discontinuing. Retail sales are not as profitable as internet sales, but they do make a positive contribution to

Table 14.4 Channel Analysis

Channel	Sales $	Variable cost $	Dollar contribution $	Contribution margin (%)
Internet	2,000	1,100	900	45.0
Wholesale	500	500	0	0
Retail	500	400	100	20.0
Overall	3,000	2,000	1,000	33.3

profits. Depending on the mix of product lines and customers in each channel, this business might decide to go entirely online and avoid the fixed costs of wholesale and retail operations.

MONITORING COSTS

A useful way to monitor your costs is to compare them over successive periods using a *common size* income statement. This makes it easy to do cost comparisons from one period to the next because each cost category is stated in terms of a percentage of sales. For example, using MSB's income statement from Chapter 12, the percentage for cost of sales is found by dividing the cost of sales by the sales revenue and multiplying by 100.

$$\frac{\text{Cost of sales}}{\text{Sales revenue}} \times 100 = \frac{\$720,000}{\$1,200,000} \times 100 = 60 \text{ percent}$$

The same procedure is used for each cost category to produce a common size income statement like the following example. Now it is easy to regularly compare your costs from one period to the next. You can also compare them with benchmarking information for businesses like yours.

A comparison between Year 1 and Year 2 reveals a 5 percent drop in the cost of sales. However, operating costs have blown out in nearly every category resulting in a 5 percent increase in total operating costs. The result is no change in the 4.5 percent net profit before tax.

MY SMALL BUSINESS
Common Size Income Statements

	Year 1	Year 2	Benchmark
Sales revenue	100.0	100.0	100.0
Cost of sales	**60.0**	**55.0**	**52.0**
Gross profit	40.0	45.0	48.0
Operating expenses			
Salaries	7.0	8.0	7.5
Wages	7.5	9.0	8.5
Marketing	12.5	14.0	15.0
Occupancy	3.5	3.5	3.5
Administration	2.5	3.0	3.0
Depreciation	1.7	2.0	2.0
Interest	0.8	1.0	1.0
Total operating expenses	**35.5**	**40.5**	**40.5**
Net profit before tax	4.5	4.5	7.5

A comparison between Year 2 and the benchmark data reveals that the cost of sales, while greatly improved, is still not equal to the average for similar businesses. Overall operating costs, however, are the same as the benchmark average with small variations in some cost categories. The benchmark has a 7.5 percent net profit before tax compared with only 4.5 percent for MSB.

These comparisons tell MSB that it has achieved progress toward reducing cost of sales. But they need to drive their cost of sales down even further to achieve the same level of profitability enjoyed by other firms in the same industry. Overall, operating costs are in line with the industry, but there is still scope for small improvements in individual cost categories.

SUMMARY

This chapter pinpoints the key variables that drive profits and how to manage them. The costs in the income statement are separated into those that are fixed and those that vary with the volume of sales. The separation of fixed and variable costs makes it possible to calculate the contribution margin. Several examples demonstrate how it is used in a variety of decision-making and planning situations. Knowing the fixed cost and the rate of variable cost makes it possible to determine the profit or loss at any level of sales including the break-even point. Differences in cost structure not only represent different risk factors but also differences in profitability. A great deal of information about improving profitability can be found by analysing the contribution margin based on products, customers, and market channels. A common size income statement is a convenient way to monitor your costs by comparing them with industry benchmarks.

Fifteen
Financing and Taxation

Financing and taxation issues occur less frequently than day-to-day money management, but they are nevertheless important. You may need to seek finance to pay for something like buying a business, the fit-out of business premises, the latest point-of-sale equipment, or to increase your working capital. Depending on the circumstances, you may want to consider borrowing money, leasing, injecting new equity capital, or applying for a government grant. The taxation system impacts just about every phase of business including the GST, income tax, capital gains tax, fringe benefits tax, and the superannuation guarantee. The purpose of this chapter is to explain the major sources of finance and the taxation obligations you will encounter.

BORROWING MONEY

Lenders want to know many things. Are you a good business manager? Are you the sort of person in whom the lender can feel confident? What are you going to do with the money? Will you need the money for a short time or a long time? When do you plan to pay it back? How will you generate the money for repayments? Do you have assets that you can offer as security? What is the outlook for your business? Are you likely to be in business for the duration of the loan?

Lenders want to make loans to businesses that are solvent, profitable, and liquid. Your balance sheet, income statement, and cash flow budget are the lender's tools for determining how well you meet these criteria. The balance sheet is used to assess solvency, the income statement is used to assess profitability, and the cash flow budget is used to evaluate liquidity. Submitting regular financial statements over a period of time is the best way to convince a lender about your financial credentials.

DOI: 10.4324/9781032676616-25

Sometimes your signature is all that a lender requires to give you a loan. This might be the case if the lender knows you and the loan is for a short period. However, most lenders require some form of security, particularly for longer term loans. Whether security is required or not, lenders may want to impose conditions in order to protect themselves against poor business practices. Examples of loan conditions include no further borrowing without the lender's agreement, maintaining working capital at a prescribed level, carrying adequate insurance, and supplying the lender with regular financial statements. Lenders usually try to match the term of a loan with the useful life of the asset it is financing. This distinction between short-term borrowing and long-term borrowing is an important factor in determining the most suitable type of borrowing.

Short-Term Borrowing

Short-term borrowing is used to finance assets that turn over quickly such as accounts receivable and inventory. The main types of short-term borrowing are credit cards, trade credit, overdraft, accounts receivable financing, inventory financing, and bridging finance.

Just as *credit cards* are important for consumer purchases, they are also a source of convenience and credit for a small business. The credit limit on your business credit card is a source of finance, and most banks have card products that are especially tailored to the needs of small businesses including downloading the transactions from your bank statement into your accounting system. Keep in mind, however, that the interest rate on credit card balances is quite high compared to alternative forms of finance.

Trade credit occurs when your supplier gives you time to pay for goods after they have been delivered. Essentially, this is an interest-free, short-term loan. Trade credit is the most easily accessible external source of finance. Unlike other sources of finance, it seldom involves complex and time-consuming negotiations, so take full advantage of available payment terms.

An *overdraft* is an arrangement with your bank in which you borrow through your bank account up to a certain limit. It may be secured or unsecured. Overdrafts are the most flexible form of short-term finance because you only borrow when the need arises and interest is only charged on the daily balance outstanding. An establishment fee is usually charged by the bank plus a periodic administration charge. Together, these extra charges increase the total cost of an overdraft.

A *line of credit* is an arrangement with your bank that you can draw on at any time up to an approved limit. These loans are usually secured by a mortgage over property or a personal guarantee. Interest rates are lower than for overdrafts. An establishment fee and periodic administration charges apply.

Debtor finance or accounts receivable lending consists of cash advances equal to a percentage of your eligible customer invoices. The lender takes a registered security over your accounts receivable and will insist that you have proper accounts receivable collection and control procedures. In some cases, the lender will want to collect directly from your customers. This should be avoided because it sends a message that is similar to a business in administration. The lender will either charge interest or take a percentage of the funds collected. *Factoring* is the cash purchase of your sales invoices at a discount. Generally, you continue to be responsible for any accounts that turn out to be uncollectible.

Inventory finance contributes to your working capital position by enabling you to purchase stock and make repayments that match your cash flow from sales. This is especially helpful for a business with a big seasonal variation in sales. The term *floor plan* is used to describe inventory finance for businesses that carry expensive items such as cars, trucks, boats, and caravans. Funds are advanced so that you can have a suitable range of units on the showroom floor. The inventory is security for the advance and it is repaid when the item is sold.

Bridging finance is money borrowed for a short time until the proceeds from another transaction become available or more permanent financing is arranged. Bridging finance is generally secured and the interest rate varies depending on the lender.

Long-Term Borrowing

Long-term borrowing is used to finance non-current assets such as vehicles, equipment, plant, buildings, and property. When it comes to long-term borrowing, the lender looks for assurances that the business will be able to repay the loan out of earnings over the period of the loan. The main types of long-term borrowing for small businesses are personal loans, hire purchase, term loans, and mortgages.

A *personal loan* is normally used to finance the purchase of consumer goods, but it can also be used to finance a business. For example, a personal loan can be used to pay for a motor vehicle, new shop fixtures, or the initial inventory. Personal loans are repaid in regular instalments including principal and interest.

Hire purchase is an agreement in which the lender buys a vehicle or equipment that you specify and gives you possession of it in return for regular repayments of interest and principal. When you make the final payment, the lender transfers ownership to you. Watch out for low monthly payments with a big 'balloon' payment at the end.

Term loans, sometimes called a *fully drawn advance*, are available for fixed periods of one to ten years. The purposes for which term loans are made include the purchase of a business or investment in fixed assets such as land, buildings, and equipment. They are generally secured and repaid in regular instalments including principal and interest. Sometimes a term loan is *interest only* with the principal repayment in a lump sum at the end of the loan period. The interest rate may be fixed or variable.

A *mortgage* is used to finance the purchase of land and buildings. Mortgage finance is long-term finance and it is secured by the property it is financing. It is generally repaid by regular instalments including principal and interest. The interest rate may be fixed or variable. It is possible to have second and third mortgages on the same property. The *mortgage equity loan* uses the equity in residential property as security.

Shop Around

The major banks dominate small business lending. The ability to mix both business and personal products is an important feature in selecting a lender. Finding the best deal is a matter of shopping around. Look at the eligibility requirements including the minimum amount you need to borrow to qualify as a business customer. Make sure you know about the account fees, transaction limits, and the discounts offered on lending rates. Examine the personal services offered such as financial planning, share trading, home mortgage, insurance, and superannuation. Consider the convenience of having a local branch versus online banking services. However, be aware that some banks don't handle small business loans in the local branches, so you may find yourself having to deal with someone at head office.

LEASING

Despite many claims about the advantages of leases, they are simply an alternative to borrowing. However, leasing can be an attractive alternative if you don't have the cash to buy something outright. It enables you to regulate your cash flow by having predictable, regular monthly lease payments. Leasing may also help to avoid tying up lines of credit that you need to finance other parts of the business.

Leasing is always more expensive than buying if you already have the cash to make the purchase. If the alternative is to borrow the funds to purchase the asset, then the benefit of leasing depends on its after-tax cost compared with the after-tax cost of borrowing. Lease payments are tax deductible as a business expense provided the asset is used to derive taxable income. However, don't be dazzled by the tax deductions if the after-tax cost of leasing is greater than the after-tax cost of borrowing. When a lease runs out, you don't own the asset. *Residual value* is an estimate of the value of the asset at the end of the lease period. You indemnify the lessor for the agreed residual value when they sell the asset. Most lessors, however, will accept an offer to buy the asset for its residual value at the end of the lease.

Leasing arrangements are usually more liberal than loans. Whereas a bank generally requires a longer business history before granting a loan, many leasing companies evaluate your credit history on a shorter period. This can be a significant advantage for a start-up business. There are some things you should be looking for when you negotiate a lease. The term is typically between 24 and 48 months depending on the asset. The shorter the term of a lease or the lower the agreed residual value, the higher will be the monthly lease payments. Make sure you understand the full cost over the entire term of the lease including any initial down payment, monthly lease payments, security deposit, insurance premiums, service or repair costs, and the residual value or 'balloon' payment at the end.

There are other forms of leasing that may be relevant for your business. *Fleet leasing* is a possibility if your business has five or more passenger and light commercial vehicles. The services generally include vehicle sourcing, maintenance, management, and disposal. One fixed monthly rental payment is made for the fleet. *Novated leasing* is designed to finance motor vehicles as part of salary packaging arrangements for your staff. They have the use of the vehicle plus the benefit of paying for it with pretax salary. Your commitment is to make the lease payments which you deduct from the employee's salary package. If they leave your employment, they take the vehicle and the lease with them. An alternative to mortgage finance is the *sale and leaseback* of existing properties. The procedure is to sell a freehold property to a financial institution and then lease it back. You get the use of the property, you have the cash in hand, and the lease payments are tax deductible.

EQUITY CAPITAL

Equity capital is money invested in a business by its owners. You obtain equity capital in the first instance by putting your own money into the business. Later, you can increase the equity capital in the business by investing more of your own money or reinvesting some of the profits. You can also raise additional equity capital by selling part of your business.

Internal Equity Capital

The principal source of internal equity capital for a small business is the owner's money. For some individuals, it will be their life savings. For others, it will be money that has been borrowed on a personal basis to provide equity capital for the business. Another source of internal equity capital is retained profits.

External Equity Capital

Very few small businesses ever seek external equity financing. However, if the need for equity capital exceeds the amounts available from the owner and the retained earnings of the business, then external equity capital may offer the only means by which the firm can expand its financial base. Some small business operators have relatives or acquaintances with spare cash who are willing to invest in the business. There are two sides to making business partners out of those with whom you have a personal relationship. They may be a great source of financial and emotional support, or they may meddle in the business by annoying you with incessant questions or unwanted advice.

Another source of external equity capital is private investors known as *business angels*. These are individuals who are prepared to provide equity capital in the form of share capital or partnership capital for a worthwhile venture. Not only do they provide equity capital, but they can also offer the benefit of their skills, experience, and network contacts. A business angel with experience in your line of business can be a big asset as well as a source of capital. Business angels tend to work informally by seeking investment opportunities through a network of personal contacts. For this reason, they are not always easy to locate. Ask your accountant, solicitor, and Business Enterprise Centre if they can help you locate an equity investor. There are websites that provide matching services such as the Angel Investment Network at ***australianinvestmentnetwork.com***.

GOVERNMENT GRANTS

Commonwealth and state governments offer a number of grant programs designed to help small businesses. In the right circumstances, government grants can be a great way to finance the growth of a business. However, there is a misconception that government grants are an easy source of 'free' money. On the contrary, applying for government funding can be a demanding and time-consuming process with no guarantee of success.

The first step is to find out what is available. The commonwealth government website at ***business.gov.au/grants-and-programs*** lists all government-related grant programs. Industry associations are also an excellent source of information about grants for their industry sector.

If you decide to apply for a government grant, there are a few things you can do to avoid disappointment. First, make sure you are eligible for the grant. Some grant programs restrict what they will fund, so you don't want to go to all the effort of making an application only to be told you are not eligible. Second, give yourself plenty of time. It is not unusual to spend a lot of time preparing an application. It is also not unusual for it to take several months to get an answer. Third, word your application carefully. The people who evaluate grant applications are looking for key words related to eligibility and the way you propose to use the grant. Clues about key words can generally be found in the description of the grant program. Fourth, most grants require you to contribute up to 50 percent of the costs of a project. Make sure you have access to matching funds or another funding source arranged to demonstrate that you can meet your part if a grant is approved. Last, grants come with an obligation to report key milestones and furnish proof about how you used the money. Ensure your record keeping system is up to scratch, and keep copies of all receipts, invoices, and other documentation in case you are audited.

AUSTRALIAN TAXATION SYSTEM

If ever there was a disincentive to operating a small business it is taxation. The problem is not just the amount of tax you have to pay but the mountain of paperwork that it takes to comply with the requirements of the Australian Taxation Office (ATO). The ATO has publications and other information for small businesses available on its website at **ato.gov.au**. The taxation system affects practically every phase of business, and trying to keep up with the ever-changing legislation and legal precedents can be exasperating. To minimise your tax burden and ease the administrative nightmare, you should engage a taxation consultant who is familiar with businesses like yours. In most cases, this will be your accountant.

A tax file number (TFN) is issued by the ATO to identify each taxpayer. If you have decided to operate your business as a sole trader, then you will use your individual TFN for both your personal and business dealings with the ATO. If you have decided to operate your business as a partnership, company, or trust, then you will need to apply for a separate TFN.

Business records are required by law for taxation purposes. They must be kept in the English language and they must be retained for at least five years. Consult your accountant or tax agent about which records you need to keep. They can also give you advice about the most efficient and economical means for complying with the ATO's record keeping requirements.

Pay as You Go (PAYG)

PAYG is a single, integrated system for reporting and paying the GST, withholding obligations, income tax instalments, and Fringe Benefits Tax instalments. If you are registered for the GST, then you report most of your tax entitlements and obligations under the PAYG system on one form called a *Business Activity Statement* (BAS). If you are not registered for the GST, then you lodge an *Instalment Activity Statement*. The ATO sends you an activity statement personalised for your business with some parts already filled in including the tax period it covers and when you need to lodge it.

The BAS asks you to record the total amount of GST that is payable on the goods and services that you sold during the tax period. You also record the total amount of credits for the GST that you paid on the goods and services you bought for use in your business. The difference between your GST payable and your GST credits is the amount you owe or will be refunded.

Withholding obligations are amounts you withhold from payments to others and remit to the ATO as part of your activity statement. The two main withholding obligations are employee deductions and payments to other businesses for which no Australian Business Number is quoted on their invoice. If you employ staff, you are required to deduct income tax from their salary, wages, and other payments. The types and rates of withholding payments are set out in the withholding schedules (tax tables) published on the ATO website. If a business supplies goods or services to you and does not quote an Australian Business Number on their invoice, then you are also required to withhold tax from your payment to the supplier at the top marginal rate and remit it to the ATO as part of your BAS.

PAYG instalments are payable for income tax, GST, and taxes withheld when you lodge your BAS. The final amounts payable to the ATO are reconciled when you lodge your annual returns and claim a credit for your instalments. You generally have a choice at the beginning of each tax year between paying instalment amounts calculated by the ATO or calculating the instalment amounts yourself based on your actual figures.

Goods and Services Tax (GST)

The GST is a broad-based tax of 10 percent on the value of most goods and services sold in Australia. If your annual turnover is $75,000 or more, you are legally required to register for the GST, but there are benefits of registering for the GST even if your turnover is less than $75,000. By registering for the GST, you are entitled to claim input tax credits for the amount of GST included in the things you buy to use in your business. If you are not registered, you cannot claim the input tax credits. You can register for the GST online at the Business Registration Service website. The final purchaser bears the cost of GST, not the business providing the goods and services. Be sure to charge GST each time you make a sale. If you don't add GST to your prices, you will be out of pocket when it comes time to remit your GST to the tax office. Similarly, it is essential to keep track of your purchases to claim the GST credits.

Income Tax

Income tax is imposed by the commonwealth government and collected by the ATO. The *Income Tax Assessment Act* defines the method of assessment of taxable income and the deductions that are allowed. The *Income Tax Act* sets the rates of tax to be levied depending on the legal form of organisation in which you operate. Both acts are amended each year in the commonwealth budget. You are required to furnish an income tax return to the ATO each year.

Individual taxpayers are levied under the PAYG system whereby tax instalments are deducted from salaries and wages as they are received from the employer. However, a taxpayers' final tax liability for the year is not determined until they submit their annual tax return to the ATO and receive an income tax assessment notice. The amount of tax assessed and the amount of tax instalments already paid are reconciled, resulting in either an additional payment or a refund. A sole proprietor includes their business income in their individual tax return.

A partnership information return is filed with the ATO even though no tax is payable on it. Each partner then includes their share of the partnership's taxable income in their individual tax return. A trustee is also required to furnish the ATO with an information return for a trust. Its purpose is to disclose the income of the trust and its distribution among the beneficiaries.

A company pays company tax and is required to lodge a company tax return. Since a company is a separate legal entity, its tax liability is determined separately from the tax liability of its shareholders. The dividend imputation system enables companies to pass on profits to shareholders in the form of franked dividends. A franked dividend means that a shareholder receives a tax credit for tax paid by the company on income from which the dividend was paid. This enables the owners of small companies to achieve the best after-tax balance between salaries, dividends, and retained earnings. This legislation imposes a number of obligations on companies, so get professional advice.

Australia's income tax system works on the basis of self-assessment. This means that the ATO accepts the accuracy of the information you provide and calculates your tax liability accordingly. However, the ATO may ask you to provide the records to substantiate your tax return later. Keep in mind that activity statements are different from income tax returns. Although you report your PAYG income tax instalments during the year, you must also lodge an income tax return at the end of the financial year.

Capital Gains Tax

Gains on the sale of some assets are subject to capital gains tax. You make a capital gain or loss when you sell an asset or your business. Capital gains tax does not generally apply to depreciating assets such as tools or motor vehicles because these are included in your income tax. A gain or loss is essentially equal to the difference between the proceeds of the sale and the cost of the asset. There is rollover relief from capital gains tax for small business owners who sell assets to buy other assets for use in a business or who wish to sell the business to retire.

Fringe Benefits Tax

Fringe benefits tax (FBT) applies to benefits provided to an employee that are not included in the salaries and wages withholding system. FBT is payable by the employer based on the value of the benefit. If you are subject to FBT, then you will need to register with the ATO and lodge an FBT return. The ATO publishes a guide on its website that explains what FBT is, how to calculate it, and detailed information about the different kinds of fringe benefits and how they are treated.

Superannuation Guarantee

When you employ staff, you are required to pay a superannuation contribution for your eligible employees. This also applies to contractors if more than 50 percent of their contract is for labour. This is called the *superannuation guarantee*. Superannuation obligations under an industrial award count toward the minimum level of contributions, but an employee's own contributions do not. Information about the superannuation guarantee is on the ATO website at ***ato.gov.au/super***.

State Taxes

There are taxes and levies imposed by state governments that may apply to your business. The main ones are stamp duty and payroll tax. Refer to your state government website to find information on the taxes in your state. Stamp duty is levied on certain transactions such as leases of commercial premises, mortgages, insurance policies, and transfers of property such as businesses or real estate. It is levied according to the value of the transaction. It is important to consider the impact of stamp duty if you are buying or selling a business. Payroll tax is levied on employers by state governments based on the amount of payroll expenditure. All states have an exemption threshold, but it is different in each state. If your payroll exceeds the threshold, you need to register with your state's revenue office and submit a periodic payroll tax return.

Facing a Tax Audit

If there is anything that can strike terror in the heart of most individuals, it is the thought of a tax audit. To lessen the possibility of an adverse audit, it generally pays to have your tax returns prepared by your accountant. It is up to you, however, to review your tax returns to ensure they are correct. You also need to keep your tax records for at least five years. If you receive a letter from the ATO or your state tax authority asking you to present yourself and your records for an audit, the following tips will help you get through it with a minimum of anxiety.

- Don't ignore it. Whatever you do, don't ignore the letter informing you of an upcoming audit. If they don't hear from you, they assume you are in the wrong and things can quickly escalate.
- Be prepared. The desk audit is the most common form of review. You will be asked to bring records that document the information contained in your tax return. Review your records before the appointment and prepare yourself to answer questions.
- Stay calm. Your meeting with the ATO or state government representative may feel a bit adversarial, but it will not help your case if you become hostile. Remember, they are only doing their job.
- Stick to the point. Answer only the questions asked and don't offer any additional information. This is not the time for a casual chat because anything you say may open up new issues leading to further investigations.

Call in your accountant or tax adviser if you need help. If you are only asked to provide documentary substantiation and you have it, then you can probably handle the audit on your own. If it is something more complex, then ask your accountant or tax adviser to assist you by helping you prepare for the audit and accompanying you to the meeting.

SUMMARY

Financing and taxation issues occur less frequently than day-to-day management, but they are nevertheless important. Lenders want to make loans to businesses that are solvent, profitable, and liquid. Your balance sheet, income statement, and cash flow budget are the lender's tools for determining how well you meet these criteria. Short-term borrowing is generally used to finance current assets such as working capital. Long-term borrowing is generally used to finance non-current assets such as vehicles or property. Leasing is an alternative to borrowing, especially if you prefer regular monthly lease payments compared with a single lump sum purchase. Internal equity capital is money you invest in a business including retaining some of the profits. External equity comes from selling part of your business to another party such as a business angel. Government grants can also be a source of cash for some businesses, but applying for government funding can be a demanding process with no guarantee of success. The Australian taxation system affects practically every phase of business, and keeping up with the ever-changing legislation should be part of your accountant's service. They can help you comply with the pay-as-you-go system, GST, income tax, capital gains tax, fringe benefits tax, and other obligations. They can also help if you are audited by the tax office.

Reflective Exercise: Financial Forecasts

A business idea is not commercially viable unless the numbers make sense. There are only five questions in this exercise. They ask you to forecast how your business idea is likely to perform in its first year of operation.

- What sales can you expect?
- What assets are required and how will you finance them?
- Will the business be profitable?
- What level of sales will it take to break even?
- Will cash flow be positive?

A business idea starts to become exciting when the numbers reveal that the start-up capital is realistic, profits are attractive, the break-even point is low, and cash flow is positive. Answering these questions not only satisfies the need to forecast the financial results, but it also helps you decide if this is a business idea that is worth pursuing.

Sales

A sales forecast builds on your previous responses for anticipated demand, market acceptance, and market strength. It is an important first step in completing the other financial forecasts. If the sales forecast is way off the mark, then it will flow through all the financial forecasts. However, it is not realistic to expect it to be perfectly accurate either. What is your sales forecast for your business idea in its first year? An example of a sales forecast can be found in Chapter 5.

Has a sales forecast for your business idea been completed? If not, has one been started even if it is not finished? Or, you don't know yet what sales for your business idea are likely to be.

DOI: 10.4324/9781032676616-26

Investment

The sales forecast establishes the expected level of activity in the business. You need to identify what physical assets are needed to support that level of activity. Then you are in a position to estimate your investment in assets and how you will finance them. Do this by forecasting a balance sheet at start-up that reflects the investment in assets, the money you intend to put into the business, and any money that may need to be borrowed.

> **Will the required investment in your business idea go mainly into current assets or fixed assets? How much will need to be financed by borrowing?**

Profitability

A projected income statement is used to forecast profitability. You should already have a sales forecast. Subtract the cost of sales from forecasted sales revenue to arrive at gross profit. Identify the operating expenses that will result from running the business at the level of activity in the sales forecast. Subtract the operating expenses from gross profit to arrive at net profit before tax.

> **Will your business idea be likely to make a profit or a loss in the first year?**

Break-even

Break-even analysis is a powerful tool for managing profitability. When the sales forecast exceeds the break-even point, the prospects for a successful business get better. Rearrange your forecasted income statement into fixed and variable costs. Calculate the contribution margin. Find the break-even point by dividing the fixed costs by the contribution margin.

> **Is the sales forecast for your business idea well above the break-even point, about the same as the break-even point, or below the break-even point?**

Cash Flow

If forecasted cash flow is positive, then a business idea begins to look viable. But if forecasted cash flow is negative, then there is a risk that things may end in failure. In this last question, you are asked to do a cash flow budget for the first year and interpret the results. Don't forget to include your start-up cash flows as well as your operating cash flows.

Will the cash flow for your business idea be positive by the end of the first year? Or, you don't know yet what the cash flow for your business idea is likely to be.

Appendix
Assessing Commercial Potential

The purpose of this appendix is to help you form a judgement about whether you want to move to the next stage in developing your business idea. The value you get from it depends on how objectively you apply it. It pulls together the reflective exercises throughout the book. The results provide you with an overall indication of the commercial potential of your business idea. This is a tool that can be repeated as often as you wish to aid you in refining your business idea. It will also help you to decide whether you want to take it further. Use the answer sheet on the next page to circle your response for each of the questions.

ANSWER SHEET

External risks

1. Compliance	a	b	c	d	e
2. Technology	a	b	c	d	e
3. Economic	a	b	c	d	e
4. Political	a	b	c	d	e
5. Dependence	a	b	c	d	e

Internal risks

6. Planning	a	b	c	d	e
7. Marketing	a	b	c	d	e
8. Deliverables	a	b	c	d	e
9. Liquidity	a	b	c	d	e
10. Personal	a	b	c	d	e

Anticipated demand

11. Market size	a	b	c	d	e
12. Market growth	a	b	c	d	e
13. Stability	a	b	c	d	e
14. Life span	a	b	c	d	e
15. Spinoffs	a	b	c	d	e

Market acceptance

16. Need	a	b	c	d	e
17. Recognition	a	b	c	d	e
18. Compatibility	a	b	c	d	e
19. Complexity	a	b	c	d	e
20. Distribution	a	b	c	d	e

Market strength

21. Differentiation	a	b	c	d	e
22. Value	a	b	c	d	e
23. Customers	a	b	c	d	e
24. Suppliers	a	b	c	d	e
25. Competitors	a	b	c	d	e

Expertise

26. Marketing	a	b	c	d	e
27. Technical	a	b	c	d	e
28. Financial	a	b	c	d	e
29. Functional	a	b	c	d	e
30. Managerial	a	b	c	d	e

Resources

31. Financial	a	b	c	d	e
32. Physical	a	b	c	d	e
33. Staff	a	b	c	d	e
34. Information	a	b	c	d	e
35. Help and assistance	a	b	c	d	e

Financial forecast

36. Sales	a	b	c	d	e
37. Investment	a	b	c	d	e
38. Profitability	a	b	c	d	e
39. Break-even	a	b	c	d	e
40. Cash flow	a	b	c	d	e

External Risks

1. **Compliance**—In terms of the relevant laws, standards, and other regulations, will your business idea
   a. meet them without any changes?
   b. require only minor changes?
   c. require moderate changes?
   d. require substantial changes?
   e. possibly not meet them at all.

2. **Technology**—Will the technology on which your business idea is based be
   a. very stable for the foreseeable future?
   b. reasonably stable for the foreseeable future?

    c.   subject to some disruptive developments?

    d.   subject to significant disruptive developments?

    e.   likely to be replaced by new technology relatively soon?

3. **Economic**—Will the near-term outlook for the economy be
   a.   very positive for your business idea?
   b.   reasonably positive for your business idea?
   c.   neutral for your business idea?
   d.   somewhat negative for your business idea?
   e.   very negative for your business idea?

4. **Political**—Will the extent to which your business idea might be
   at risk from current or proposed government policy be
   a.   very low?
   b.   low?
   c.   moderate?
   d.   high?
   e.   very high?

5. **Dependence**—Will the dependence of your business idea
   on another product, process, service, system, person,
   or organisation be
   a.   very low?
   b.   low?
   c.   moderate?
   d.   high?
   e.   very high?

Internal Risks

6. **Planning**—Has a business plan for your business idea been
   a.   completely finished?
   b.   substantially finished?
   c.   started, but there still is much to do?
   d.   put off, but it is intended to do one?
   e.   unnecessary because it is all in your head?

7. **Marketing**—Has the market research for your business idea been
   a. completed and integrated into a marketing strategy?
   b. completed but not yet integrated into a marketing strategy?
   c. under way and it will be finished soon?
   d. put off for now, but it is intended to be done later?
   e. unnecessary because it is all in your head?

8. **Deliverables**—Will you be able to deliver your product or service
   a. consistently at a very high standard?
   b. at a high standard most of the time?
   c. at an acceptable standard most of the time?
   d. at an acceptable standard some of the time?
   e. You are not sure without further investigation.

9. **Liquidity**—Will the money available for starting your business be
   a. more than enough to get started?
   b. just enough to get started?
   c. insufficient requiring minor borrowing?
   d. insufficient requiring major borrowing?
   e. You are not sure without further investigation.

10. **Personal**—Will the personal risks involved in going into this business be
    a. totally within your comfort zone?
    b. reasonably within your comfort zone?
    c. at the limit of your comfort zone?
    d. outside your comfort zone?
    e. well outside your comfort zone?

Anticipated Demand

11. **Market size**—Will the size of the target market for your product or service be
    a. very large—appealing to practically every individual?

b. large—appealing to at least one person in every household or business?

c. medium—appealing to a distinctive group of consumers or businesses?

d. small—appealing to a narrow group of consumers or businesses?

e. very small—appealing to a highly specialised or very limited group of consumers or businesses?

12. **Market growth**—Will the target market for your product or service be likely to
   a. increase rapidly?
   b. increase gradually?
   c. remain constant?
   d. decline gradually?
   e. decline rapidly?

13. **Stability**—Will fluctuations in demand for your product or service be
   a. highly stable—not susceptible to fluctuations?
   b. stable—modest variations that can be accurately foreseen?
   c. predictable—variations that can be reasonably foreseen?
   d. unstable—susceptible to moderately unpredictable fluctuations?
   e. highly unstable—subject to severely unpredictable fluctuations?

14. **Life span**—Will the commercial life span of your product or service be likely to last for a
   a. very long time?
   b. reasonably long time?
   c. moderate period of time?
   d. somewhat limited period of time?
   e. very brief period of time?

15. **Spinoffs**—Will the potential for additional related products or services be
    a. very high—many spinoffs are likely?
    b. high—a few spinoffs are likely?
    c. moderate—a few spinoffs are possible?
    d. limited—minor variations only?
    e. very limited—this is a one-off product or service only?

Market Acceptance

16. **Need**—Will the need fulfilled by your product or service be
    a. very high—an essential need that is highly valued?
    b. high—a nonessential need that is nevertheless highly valued?
    c. moderate—an essential need of average value?
    d. low—a nonessential need of average value?
    e. very low—a superficial need that is relatively unimportant?

17. **Recognition**—Will the features and benefits of your product or service be
    a. very obvious—completely self-evident?
    b. obvious—easy to understand?
    c. noticeable—but requiring some explanation?
    d. obscure—not apparent and requiring substantial explanation?
    e. very obscure—not apparent and complex and/or costly to explain?

18. **Compatibility**—Will the compatibility of your product or service with established customer expectations be
    a. very high—completely consistent with customer expectations?
    b. high—reasonably consistent with customer expectations?
    c. moderate—a slight conflict with customer expectations?
    d. low—considerable conflict with customer expectations?
    e. very low—extreme conflict with customer expectations?

19. **Complexity**—Will the degree of complexity in learning how to use, consume, or purchase your product or service be
    a. very low—no learning is needed?
    b. low—minimal learning is needed?
    c. moderate—normal instruction is enough for most users?
    d. high—detailed instruction is required?
    e. very high—expensive and/or time-consuming instruction is required?

20. **Distribution**—Will the distribution method for your product or service be
    a. very simple and inexpensive?
    b. moderately simple and inexpensive?
    c. about average in effort and cost?
    d. moderately complicated and/or costly?
    e. highly complicated and/or costly?

Market Strength

21. **Differentiation**—Compared with the alternatives, will customers consider the features and benefits of your product or service to be
    a. very superior?
    b. superior?
    c. not noticeably better or worse?
    d. inferior?
    e. very inferior?

22. **Value**—Compared with the alternatives, will customers consider the value of your product or service to be
    a. much better?
    b. better?
    c. about the same?
    d. worse?
    e. much worse?

23. **Customers**—Will the negotiating power of customers be
    a. very low—no alternatives or no incentive to negotiate?
    b. low—limited alternatives or limited incentive to negotiate?
    c. moderate—some alternatives or some incentive to negotiate?
    d. high—many alternatives or strong incentive to negotiate?
    e. very high—variety of alternatives or very strong incentive to negotiate?

24. **Suppliers**—Will the negotiating power of key suppliers be
    a. very low—supply is widely available and pricing is very negotiable?
    b. low—supply is generally available and pricing is usually negotiable?
    c. moderate—supply is sometimes limited and pricing is not always negotiable?
    d. high—supply is frequently limited and pricing is rarely negotiable?
    e. very high—sole source of supply and pricing is never negotiable?

25. **Competitors**—Will competition for your product or service be
    a. very low—no apparent competitors?
    b. low—one or two competitors?
    c. moderate—a few competitors?
    d. high—several competitors?
    e. very high—many competitors?

Expertise

26. **Marketing**—Will the gap between what you have and what you need call for
    a. no additional marketing expertise?
    b. some extra marketing expertise?
    c. a moderate level of marketing expertise?

d. a significant level of marketing expertise?

e. a very high level of marketing expertise?

27. **Technical**—Will the gap between what you have and what you need call for

a. no additional technical expertise?

b. some extra technical expertise?

c. a moderate level of technical expertise?

d. a significant level of technical expertise?

e. a very high level of technical expertise?

28. **Financial**—Will the gap between what you have and what you need call for

a. no additional financial expertise?

b. some extra financial expertise?

c. a moderate level of financial expertise?

d. a significant level of financial expertise?

e. a very high level of financial expertise?

29. **Functional**—Will the gap between what you have and what you need call for

a. no additional functional expertise?

b. some extra functional expertise?

c. a moderate level of functional expertise?

d. a significant level of functional expertise?

e. a very high level of functional expertise?

30. **Managerial**—Will the gap between what you have and what you need call for

a. no additional managerial expertise?

b. some extra managerial expertise?

c. a moderate level of managerial expertise?

d. a significant level of managerial expertise?

e. a very high level of managerial expertise?

Resources

31. **Financial**—Will the gap between what you have and what you need call for
    a. no further financial resources?
    b. modest additional financial resources?
    c. moderate additional financial resources?
    d. significant additional financial resources?
    e. very significant additional financial resources?

32. **Physical**—Will the gap between what you have and what you need call for
    a. no further physical resources?
    b. modest additional physical resources?
    c. moderate additional physical resources?
    d. significant additional physical resources?
    e. very significant additional physical resources?

33. **Staff**—Will the gap between what you have and what you need call for
    a. no extra staff?
    b. one or more casual staff?
    c. one or more full-time staff?
    d. several staff with prior experience?
    e. a highly skilled workforce?

34. **Information system**—Will the gap between what you have and what you need call for
    a. no additions to your existing information system?
    b. a modest investment in information technology?
    c. a moderate investment in information technology?
    d. a significant investment in information technology?
    e. You are not sure what kind of information system will be needed.

35. **Help and assistance**—Will the gap between what you have and what you need call for
    a. no extra help or assistance?
    b. modest help and assistance?
    c. moderate help and assistance?
    d. significant help and assistance?
    e. very significant help and assistance?

Financial Forecast

36. **Sales**—Has a sales forecast for your business idea
    a. been completed?
    b. been completed but subject to some revision?
    c. been started, but it is not finished?
    d. It is unnecessary because it is all in your head.
    e. You don't know what forecasted sales are likely to be.

37. **Investment**—Will the investment in assets for your business idea consist mainly of
    a. current assets financed with owner's equity?
    b. fixed assets financed with owner's equity?
    c. fixed assets financed with borrowing?
    d. current assets financed with borrowing?
    e. You don't know what the investment in assets will be.

38. **Profitability**—In the first year, will your business idea be likely to
    a. earn a good profit?
    b. earn a small profit?
    c. make a small loss?
    d. make a big loss?
    e. You don't know how profitable it is likely to be.

39. **Break-even**—Is the sales forecast for your business idea
    a. well above the break-even point?
    b. moderately above the break-even point?

c. about the same as the break-even point?

d. below the break-even point?

e. You don't know what the break-even point is likely to be.

40. **Cash flow**—Will cash flow for your business idea be positive

a. from the first day?

b. sometime during the first year?

c. by the end of the first year?

d. sometime after the first year?

e. You don't know when cash flow will become positive.

SCORING YOUR ANSWERS

Count the number of a, b, c, d, and e responses in the answer sheet and convert them to numerical scores according to the following scale: a = 5, b = 4, c = 3, d = 2, and e = 1. Sum the total of your scores and divide by 2.

$$
\begin{array}{r}
\underline{\hspace{2em}}\ a's \times 5 = \underline{\hspace{3em}} \\
\underline{\hspace{2em}}\ b's \times 4 = \underline{\hspace{3em}} \\
\underline{\hspace{2em}}\ c's \times 3 = \underline{\hspace{3em}} \\
\underline{\hspace{2em}}\ d's \times 2 = \underline{\hspace{3em}} \\
\underline{\hspace{2em}}\ e's \times 1 = \underline{\hspace{3em}} \\
\text{Total}\ \underline{\hspace{3em}} \\
\text{Divided by}\qquad 2 \\
\text{Commercial potential}\ \underline{\hspace{3em}}
\end{array}
$$

The result will help you form a judgement about the commercial potential of your business idea and whether you think this is a business opportunity that is worth pursuing. It will fall into one of three categories, which are interpreted in terms of a traffic light.

Green Light

If your business idea scored 80 or more, then its commercial potential appears good and further development is likely to be rewarded. A score in the upper half of this range (90 and above) generally represents an acceptable level of risk, excellent market viability, a robust operating strategy, and solid financial projections. A score in the lower half of this range (80–89) generally represents a moderate level of risk, a viable market, a sound operating strategy and realistic financial projections, but it could still have some important concerns that need to be resolved. This does not mean that an idea with a score of 80 or more is automatically ready to go. It means your business idea has passed this reality test and it is likely that you have found a business opportunity that is worth pursuing. The next stage is researching and compiling a complete business plan for putting your business idea into operation.

Yellow Light

If your idea scored between 60 and 79, then its commercial potential appears marginal and you should approach it with caution. A score in this range means further development should be limited to resolving the sources of poor responses. A score in the upper half of this range (70–79) generally represents satisfactory market viability, but there are typically some concerns about risk and/or problems with the operating strategy and the financial projections. A score in this range is likely to have enough potential to warrant further limited and cautious development. A score in the lower half of this range (60–69) generally represents marginal market viability, significant risks, and/ or difficulty with the operating strategy and the financial projections. It is unlikely that it will have enough potential to warrant further development unless major steps can be found to improve its score.

Red Light

If your business idea scored under 60, then its commercial potential appears to be poor and further development is generally not recommended. A score below 60 generally represents unacceptable risks, an inadequate market, or an impractical operating strategy leading to unsatisfactory financial projections. In this situation, abandonment may be the best course of action. Sometimes it is the opportunity itself that is flawed, and sometimes the flaw is in the marketplace. Either way, it is better to reach this conclusion sooner rather than after you have wasted time, money, and effort for no return.

Alternatively, a poor score at this stage may be an indication there has not been enough research to give your business idea an objective evaluation.

Index

Accountant 20–2
accounting system 210–13
accounts payable 233–4
accounts receivable 228–32
advertising 121–7
Advisor Finder 28
Amazon 169
app-based marketing 145–6
assistance 20–31, 147, 172
AusIndustry Outreach Network 28–9
AusTender 29
Australian Border Force 30
Australian Bureau of Statistics (ABS) 30
Australian Business Licence and
    Information Service (ABLIS) 28, 74
Australian Business Number (ABN) 72
Australian Competition and Consumer
    Commission (ACCC) 29
Australian Retailers Association 162
Australian Securities and Investments
    Commission (ASIC) 68, 30
Australian Small Business and Family
    Enterprise Ombudsman 28
Australian Taxation Office (ATO)
    30, 262
Australian Trade Commission 30
award 190–1

balance sheet 214–16
benchmarking 224–6
blog 142
borrowing money 255–9
breakeven 246–9
brochures 120
business card 119–20
Business Enterprise Centre (BEC) 24–5
business incubator 174
business name 72–3
business opportunity 51–6
business plan 79–95
Business Registration Service 72–3
buying a business 56–60

capital gains tax 265–6
cash flow 234–41
commercial assessment 272–85
common size income statement 252–3
commonwealth government 27–30
company 68–70, 73
company director 26, 69–70
competition 161–2
consumer market 6
content marketing 142–3
contribution margin 244–5
cost structure 243–4
customer 105–8, 250–1

digital marketing 134–47
Digital Solutions Program 29
direct mail 120
directory 136–7
display 164–5
distribution 110–11
domain name 71

eBay 169
email marketing 137–40
employees 189–201
enterprise agreement 191
equity finance 260–1
Etsy 169
expertise 202–4

failure 16–18
Fair Work Ombudsman 29
Fair Work System 190
financial forecast 269–71
financial information 209–26
financial performance 222–6
financial plan 85, 207–71
financial ratios 218–22
financing 255–62
flyers 120
franchise 60–4
fringe benefits tax 266

goods and services tax (GST) 73, 264
government grants 29, 261–2

home based business 174–5

income statement 216–18, 252–3
income tax 264–5
information 20–31, 147, 172
in-game marketing 146
insurance 74–8
inventory 232–3
IP Australia 30

layout 173–84
lease 184, 259–60
legal structure 66–70
licences 73–4
liquidity 227–42
local government 183–4
location 173–84
location based marketing 146

management skills 13–15
manufacturing business 10–11, 170–2,
    180–3
margin of safety 248
market channel 110–11, 251–2
market position 108–9
market segmentation 107–8
marketing mix 116–17
marketing plan 82–4, 103–55
marketing strategy 105–18
mentor 23–4
mobile marketing 143–7

name 71–2
networking 26
newsletter 120–1
niche 107–8

occupational health and safety 191–2
online business 8–9, 166–70
operating cycle 227–8
operations plan 84–5, 157–206

paper trail 209
partnership 67–8
Pay-As-You-Go (PAYG) 263–4
permits 73–4
personal characteristics 12–13
personality and self-employment 32–47

point of sale system 165–6
premises 173–84
pricing 114–16, 171–2, 248–9
product 109–10, 249–50
profitability 243–54
profit-volume chart 246–7
promotion 111–14, 140–1
proprietary company 68–70
publicity 128–9

QR code 146–7

recruiting 194–5
resources 204–6
retail business 9–10, 162–6, 175–9
risk 96–101

Safe Work Australia 29
sales forecast 84
search engine 136–7
self-employment decision 5–18
selling 129–32
sensitivity analysis 224–6
service business 7–8, 113–14, 116,
    159–62, 179–80
serviced office 173
shopping centre 177–8
social media 141–3
sole proprietorship 66–7
solicitor 22–3
sponsorship 129
staff 201
state small business agency 27
state taxes 266–7
strategy 92–5
superannuation guarantee 266

target market 149–55
Tax File Number (TFN) 73, 262–3
taxation 262–7
text message marketing 145
trade association 25–6
training programs 31
trust 70

virtual marketplace 168–70

website 135–6, 167–8
workers' compensation 76, 192
Workforce Australia 28

Printed in the United States
by Baker & Taylor Publisher Services